Authors In Depth

. . . .

THE BRITISH TRADITION

PRENTICE HALL
Upper Saddle River, New Jersey
Glenview, Illinois
Needham, Massachusetts

ISBN: 0-13-050405-X

1 2 3 4 5 6 7 8 9 10   03 02 01 00 99

PRENTICE HALL

Acknowledgments

Grateful acknowledgment is made to the following for permission to reprint copyrighted material:

Penguin Books UK
From "The Knight's Tale" and "The Pardoner's Tale" from *The Canterbury Tales* by Geoffrey Chaucer. Copyright © 1977.

Penguin Putnam
"Eveline" from *Dubliners* by James Joyce. Copyright 1916 by B. W. Heubsch. Definitive text Copyright © 1967 by the Estate of James Joyce. From *A Portrait of the Artist as a Young Man* by James Joyce. Copyright 1916 by B. W. Huebsch, Copyright 1944 by Nora Joyce, Copyright © 1964 by the Estate of James Joyce. Used by permission of Viking Penguin, a division of Penguin Putnam Inc.

Simon & Schuster, Inc.
"After Long Silence" by W. B. Yeats. Copyright 1933 by Macmillan Publishing Company; copyright renewed © 1961 by Bertha Georgie Yeats. "Easter, 1916" and "On a Political Prisoner," copyright © 1924 by Macmillan Publishing Company, renewed 1952 by Bertha Georgie Yeats. "The Circus Animals' Desertion," copyright 1940 by Georgie Yeats; copyright renewed © 1968 by Bertha Georgie Yeats, Michael Butler Yeats, and Anne Yeats. All poems reprinted with permission of Simon & Schuster, Inc., from *The Poems of W. B. Yeats: A New Edition*, edited by Richard J. Finneran.

Viking Penguin, a division of Penguin Putnam
Sonnet 73 from *William Shakespeare: The Complete Works*, edited by Alfred Harbage. Copyright © 1969 by Penguin Books, Inc. "O mistress Mine, where are you roaming?," Sonnet 15, Sonnet 30, Sonnet 71, Sonnet 77, and Sonnet 128 from *The Portable Shakespeare*, copyright © 1944 by The Viking Press, Inc. Copyright © renewed The Viking Press, Inc., 1972.

Note: Every effort has been made to locate the copyright owner of material reprinted in this book. Omissions brought to our attention will be corrected in subsequent editions.

Contributing Writer: Carroll Moulton, former English teacher, Stoughton High School, Stoughton, Connecticut

Contents

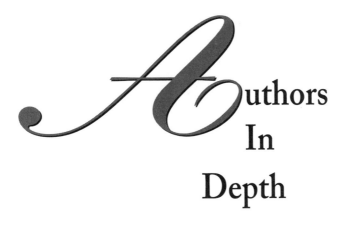

uthors
In
Depth

· · · ·

THE BRITISH TRADITION

Beowulf In Depth

"Courage is the instrument by which the hero realizes himself."
—**E. Talbot Donaldson on** Beowulf

BEOWULF is the earliest long poem in English and one of the great epics of world literature. Although the poem's author and its exact date of composition remain unknown, many experts believe that a Christian poet, perhaps a cleric, shaped the epic as we have it some time during the eighth century A.D. in southern England. Our single manuscript of the poem dates to the early eleventh century. Although it is commonly thought of as English, Beowulf unfolds in southern Scandinavia at least two centuries before the epic reached final form. During the intervening generations, the memory of these events was most probably kept alive through oral tradition.

The Epic Hero Like all great epics, Beowulf is dominated by a larger-than-life hero who embodies the values and ideals of society. Beowulf, whose name may mean "bear," is a superhero of remarkable physical strength who is destined to struggle against three powerful antagonists: the monster Grendel, Grendel's mother, and a fearsome dragon. All three opponents clearly symbolize chaos and savagery. Typically for epic, the hero's glorious victories are also symbolic in that they represent the triumph of good over evil.

Christian and Pagan The Beowulf saga evolved during the formative years of Christianity in Britain, and it is thus not surprising to find Christian and pagan elements side by side in the poem. All the "Christian" references, however, are to the Old Testament: specifically, the Book of Genesis. The values of pagan warrior society—especially prowess in war, courage, and loyalty of warriors to a liege lord—form a strong component of the epic, and these values are sometimes in conflict with the Christian perspective.

The Oral Style Beowulf is almost certainly the product of oral tradition. For centuries, tales of heroic exploits were elaborated and sung by Anglo-Saxon bards, called scops, who accompanied themselves on the harp. Beowulf contains several glimpses of such "singing of tales": for example, King Hrothgar himself is said to "weave stories" to the sound of the harp (lines 364–370), and Beowulf retells his Danish adventures to King Higlac and his assembled warriors at a great feast in Geatland (lines 311–443). The oral roots of Beowulf are also apparent in the poem's style and structure. For example, the poet often uses appositive and adjective phrases to accumulate details. Anglo-Saxon verse employs a strongly rhythmical four-beat line, as well as an intricate pattern of alliteration—sound effects that would be especially striking in oral delivery. Hrothgar's use of the sermon form in his long speech about the dangers of pride (lines 59–134) is another sign of the epic's orally derived character.

The Manuscript Beowulf exists in a single manuscript, dating from about A.D. 1000, which is now in the British Library in London. In the sixteenth century, the manuscript was acquired by the antiquarian and book collector Sir Robert Cotton, but it was damaged during a fire in Cotton's library in 1731. Copies made later in the eighteenth century became the basis for the first published edition of the epic in 1815. The first modern English translation appeared in 1833.

◆ Anglo-Saxon Art and Archaeology

Several passages in *Beowulf* describe skillfully decorated objects, either functional (helmets and swords) or ornamental (rings and necklaces). In 1939, archaeologists made a landmark discovery at Sutton Hoo in southeast England that revealed for the first time the high standard of art and craftsmanship in Anglo-Saxon Britain.

The Sutton Hoo treasure, which was buried in the grave of a king or a prominent noble, included a helmet, sword, and shield of splendid workmanship, as well as golden ornaments inlaid with jewels, silver bowls and spoons with Christian symbols, and various other artifacts. The design of a boar's crest helmet, which was made in eastern Sweden, exactly matches the description in *Beowulf* of a helmet presented by Hrothgar to the hero. The complex interlacings of animal and geometric designs on many of the objects have been compared to the intricate design of the epic's narrative structure, as well as to the sound patterns produced by the strong rhythm and striking alliteration of Old English verse.

Another important find at Sutton Hoo was the remains of a six-stringed harp. Experts have established the instrument's date as not later than A.D. 625. Reconstruction of this harp has led to practical experiments on the relationship of the rhythmic structure of epic verse in *Beowulf* with musical performance.

◆ Literary Works

Anglo-Saxon Poems: *Widsith, The Dream of the Rood, The Battle of Maldon, Judith,* Caedmon's *Hymn*

Heroic Epics in World Literature:

Gilgamesh (ancient Sumeria)

Homer, *Iliad* (ancient Greece)

The Ramayana (ancient India)

The Song of Roland (medieval France)

Sundiata (medieval West Africa)

TIMELINE

Beowulf and Anglo-Saxon Britain		World Events	
410	Romans withdraw from Britain	476	Fall of Roman Empire in West
449	Anglo-Saxon invasions begin	520	King Higlac of Geatland raids the Franks
550	St. David converts Wales		
563	Monastery founded at Iona	c. 550	Toltecs defeat Mayas in Mexico
597	Mission of St. Augustine to Canterbury	552	Buddhism introduced in Japan
		591	Book printing invented in China
664	Synod at Whitby unites English church with Roman Christianity	637	Arab conquest of Jerusalem
		712	Moors conquer Seville in southern Spain
671	Birth of Caedmon		
700–50	Probable date of *Beowulf*	732	Charles Martel defeats Moors at Battle of Poitiers in France
731	Bede, *A History of the English Church and People*	771	Charlemagne becomes king in France
735	Death of Bede		
787	Danish invasions of Britain	800	Charlemagne crowned Holy Roman Emperor
871	Alfred the Great becomes king of Wessex		
		c. 810	Algebra devised in Persia
892	*Anglo-Saxon Chronicle* started	861	Viking discovery of Iceland
899	Death of Alfred the Great	911	Kingdom of Normandy founded in northern France
1000	Probable date of *Beowulf* manuscript		
1066	William the Conqueror leads Norman invasion of England	1053	Norman conquest of Sicily
		1096	First Crusade begins

Beowulf

Translated by Burton Raffel

*Prior to the action in this selection, we are told of
Beowulf, prince of the Geats, and his journey to the
lair of Grendel and Grendel's mother, monsters that
have long terrorized the Danish king Hrothgar and
his people. Once at the lair, Beowulf enters and fights
Grendel's mother with Hrunting, a sword given to him
by the Danish warrior Unferth. The sword fails to
injure the monster, and Beowulf is almost killed.
However, Beowulf finds an old sword in the lair
and slays Grendel's mother by cutting off her head.
He then cuts off the head of Grendel, who is also in the
lair. The blood of the monsters melts the blade so that
only the hilt (the handle of the sword) remains. With
this and the head of Grendel, Beowulf returns to Herot,
the king's banquet hall, to tell Hrothgar of his victory.*

Celebration at Herot

Beowulf spoke:
"Hrothgar! Behold,
Great Healfdane's son, this glorious sign
Of victory, brought you by joyful Geats.
5   My life was almost lost, fighting for it,
Struggling under water: I'd have been dead at once,
And the fight finished, the she-devil victorious,
If our Father in Heaven had not helped me. Hrunting,
Unferth's noble weapon, could do nothing,
10 Nor could I, until the Ruler of the world
Showed me, hanging shining and beautiful
On a wall, a mighty old sword-so God
Gives guidance to those who can find it from no one
Else. I used the weapon He had offered me,
15 Drew it and, when I could, swung it, killed
The monstrous hag in her own home.
Then the ring-marked blade burned away,
As that boiling blood spilled out. I carried
Off all that was left, this hilt.
20 I've avenged their crimes, and the Danes they've killed.
And I promise you that whoever sleeps in Herot

—You, your brave soldiers, anyone
Of all the people in Denmark, old
Or young-they, and you, may now sleep
25 Without fear of either monster, mother—Or son."
           Then he gave the golden sword hilt
To Hrothgar, who held it in his wrinkled hands
And stared at what giants had made, and monsters
30 Owned; it was his, an ancient weapon
Shaped by wonderful smiths, now that Grendel
And his evil mother had been driven from the earth,
God's enemies scattered and dead. That best
Of swords belonged to the best of Denmark's
35 Rulers, the wisest ring-giver Danish
Warriors had ever known. The old king
Bent close to the handle of the ancient relic,
And saw written there the story of ancient wars
Between good and evil, the opening of the waters,
40 The Flood sweeping giants away, how they suffered
And died, that race who hated the Ruler
Of us all and received judgment from His hands,
Surging waves that found them wherever
They fled. And Hrothgar saw runic letters
45 Clearly carved in that shining hilt,
Spelling its original owner's name,
He for whom it was made, with its twisted
Handle and snakelike carvings. Then he spoke,
Healfdane's son[1], and everyone was silent.
50   "What I say, speaking from a full memory
And after a life spent in seeking
What was right for my people, is this: this prince
Of the Geats, Beowulf was born a better
Man! Your fame is everywhere, my friend,
Reaches to the ends of the earth, and you hold it in your
55   heart wisely,
Patient with your strength and our weakness. What I said I
           will do, I will do,
In the name of the friendship we've sworn. Your strength must
           solace your people,
Now, and mine no longer.
                    "Be not
60 As Hermod once was to my people, too proud
To care what their hearts hid, bringing them
Only destruction and slaughter. In his mad

---

1. **Healfdane's son:** Hrothgar.

Rages he killed them himself, comrades
And followers who ate at his table. At the end
65   He was alone, knew none of the joys of life
With other men, a famous ruler

Granted greater strength than anyone
Alive in his day but dark and bloodthirsty
In spirit. He shared out no treasure, showed
70   His soldiers no road to riches and fame.
And then that affliction on his people's face
Suffered horribly for his sins. Be taught
By his lesson, learn what a king must be:
I tell his tale, old as I am,
75   Only for you.
                    "Our eternal Lord
Grants some men wisdom, some wealth, makes others
Great. The world is God's, He allows
A man to grow famous, and his family rich,
80   Gives him land and towns to rule
And delight in, lets his kingdom reach,
As far as the world runs—and who
In human unwisdom, in the middle of such power,
Remembers that it all will end, and too soon?
85   Prosperity, prosperity, prosperity: nothing
Troubles him, no sickness, not passing time,
No sorrows, no sudden war breaking
Out of nowhere, but all the world turns
When he spins it. How can he know when he sins?

90   "And then pride grows in his heart, planted
Quietly but flourishing. And while the keeper of his soul
Sleeps on, while conscience rests and the world
Turns faster a murderer creeps closer, comes carrying
A tight-strung bow with terrible arrows.
95   And those sharp points strike home, are shot
In his breast, under his helmet. He's helpless.
And so the Devil's dark urgings wound him, for he can't
Remember how he clung to the rotting wealth
Of this world, how he clawed to keep it, how he earned
100   No honor, no glory, in giving golden
Rings, how he forgot the future glory
God gave him at his birth, and forgetting did not care.
And finally his body fails him, these bones

And flesh quickened by God fall
105   And die—and some other soul inherits
His place in Heaven, some open-handed
Giver of old treasurers, who takes no delight
In mere gold. Guard against such wickedness,
Beloved Beowulf, best of warriors,
110   And choose, instead, eternal happiness;
Push away pride! Your strength, your power,
Are yours for how many years? Soon
You'll return them where they came from, sickness or a
                        sword's edge
Will end them, or a grasping fire, or the flight
115   Of a spear, or surging waves, or a knife's
Bite, or the terror of old age, or your eyes
Darkening over. It will come, death
Comes faster than you think, no one can flee it.
          "So I have led the Danes for half
120   A hundred years, protected them from all peoples
On this earth, my sword and my spear so ready
That no one anywhere under God's high sun
Was eager to wage war here in Denmark.
And here, here too the change has come,
125   And we wept for our dead when Grendel invaded
Herot, my enemy raided this hall;
My sorrow, my grief, was as great and lasting
As it was helpless. Then thanks be given to God,
Eternal Lord of us all: you came
130   And that endless misery was over and I lived,
Now, to behold this bloody head!
Go in, go in: feast, be as happy
As your fame deserves. When morning shines
We shall each have owned more of my treasures."
135   Beowulf obeyed him, entered Herot
Cheerfully and took his place at the table.
And once again Danes and Geats
Feasted together, a host of famous
Warriors in a single hall.—Then the web
140   Of darkness fell and it was night. They rose;
Hrothgar, the gray-haired old Dane, was heavy
With sleep. And Beowulf was glad that a bed
Was waiting, the bravest of warriors exhausted
With the work he'd done. A Danish servant

145   Showed him the road to that far-off, quiet
        Country where sleep would come and take him
        And his followers; Hrothgar's visitors were well
        Cared for, whatever they needed was theirs.
               Then Beowulf rested; Herot rose high
150   Above him, gleaming in the darkness; the Geats
        Slept till a black-feathered raven sang
        His cheerful song and the shining sun
        Burned away shadows. And those seafarers hurried
        From their beds, anxious to begin the voyage
155   Home, ready to start, their hearts
        Already sailing on a ship's swift back.
        Then Unferth[2] came with Hrunting, his famous
        Sword, and offered it to Beowulf, asked him
        To accept a precious gift. The prince
160   Took it, thanked him, and declared the weapon
        One he was proud to own; his words
        Blamed it for nothing, were spoken like the hero
        He was! The war-gear was ready, the Geats
        Were armored and eager to be gone. Quickly,
165   Beowulf sought Hrothgar's throne, where the king
        Sat waiting for his famous visitor's farewell.

Beowulf Returns Home

        Beowulf spoke:
              "We crossed the sea
        To come here; it is time to return, to go back
170   To our beloved lord, Higlac.[3] Denmark
        Was a gracious host; you welcomed us warmly.
        Anything I can do, here on this earth,
        To earn your love, oh great king, anything
        More than I have done, battles I can fight
175   In your honor, summon me, I will come as I came
        Once before. If I hear, from across the ocean,
        That your neighbors have threatened you with war, or
              oppressed you
        As enemies once oppressed you, here, I will bring
        A thousand warriors, a thousand armed Geats
180   To protect your throne. I trust Higlac:
        Our king is young, but if I need his help
        To better help you, to lend you our strength,
        Our battle-sharp spears, to shield you and honor you

---

2. Unferth: Danish warrior who had questioned Beowulf's bravery.
3. Higlac: Higlac was the King of the Geats and Beowulf's feudal lord and uncle.

As you deserve, I know his words and his deeds
185   Will support me. And someday, if your oldest son,
      Hrethric, comes visiting our court, he will find
      A host of good friends among the Geats:
      No one who goes visiting far-off lands
      Is more welcome than a strong and noble warrior."
190   Hrothgar replied:
                        "All-knowing God
      Must have sent you such words; nothing so wise
      From a warrior so young has ever reached
      These ancient ears. Your hands are strong,
195   Your heart and your lips are knowing! If your lord,
      Hrethel's son,[4] slain by a spear,
      Or falls sick and dies, or is killed by a sword,
      And you have survived whatever battle
      Sweeps him off, I say that the Geats
200   Could do no better, find no man better
      Suited to be king, keeper of warriors
      And their treasure, than you—if you take the throne
      They will surely offer you. Beloved Beowulf,
      You please me more the longer I can keep you
205   Here in Denmark. You've turned Danes
      And Geats into brothers, brought peace where once
      There was war, and sealed friendship with affection.
      This will last as long as I live, and am king here:
      We will share our treasures, greeting travelers
210   From across the sea with outstretched hands;
      Ring-prowed ships will carry our gifts
      And the tokens of our love. Your people live
      By the old ways, their hearts, like ours, are forever
      Open to their friends, but firmly closed
215   Against their enemies."
                        Then he gave the Geats'
      Prince a dozen new gifts, prayed
      For his safety, commanded him to seek his people,
      Yet not to delay too long in visiting
220   Hrothgar once more. The old king kissed him,
      Held that best of all warriors by the shoulder
      And wept, unable to hold back his tears.
      Gray and wise, he knew how slim
      Were his chances of ever greeting Beowulf
225   Again, but seeing his face he was forced
      To hope. His love was too warm to be hidden,

---

4. Hrethel's son: Higlac.

His tears came running too quickly to be checked;
His very blood burned with longing.
And then Beowulf left him, left Herot, walked
230 Across the green in his golden armor,
Exulting in the treasures heaped high in his arms.
His ship was at anchor; he had it ready to sail.
And so Hrothgar's rich treasures would leave him, travel
Far from that perfect king, without fault
235 Or blame until winter had followed winter
And age had stolen his strength, spirited it
Off, as it steals from many men.

Then the band of Geats, young and brave,
Marching in their ring-locked armor, reached
240 The shore. The coast-guard saw them coming
And about to go, as he'd seen them before;
He hurried down the hillside, whipping
His horse, but this time shouted no challenge,
Told them only how the Geats would be watching
245 Too, and would welcome such warriors in shining
Mail. Their broad-beamed ship lay bobbing
At the edge of the sand: they loaded it high
With armor and horses and all the rich treasure
It could hold. The mast stood high and straight
250 Over heaped-up wealth—Hrothgar's, and now theirs.
Beowulf rewarded the boat's watchman,
Who had stayed behind, with a sword that had hammered
Gold wound on its handle: the weapon
Brought him honor. Then the ship left shore, left Denmark,
255 Traveled through deep water. Deck timbers creaked,
And the wind billowing through the sail stretched
From the mast, tied tight with ropes, did not hold them
Back, did not keep the ring-prowed ship
From foaming swiftly through the waves, the sea
260 Currents, across the wide ocean until
They could see familiar headlands, cliffs
That sprang out of Geatish soil. Driven
By the wind the ship rammed high on the shore.
Harbor guards came running to greet them,
265 Men who for days had waited and watched
For their beloved comrades to come crossing the waves;
They anchored the high-bowed ship, moored it
Close to the shore, where the booming sea

Could not pull it loose and lead it away.
270 Then they carried up the golden armor,
The ancient swords, the jewels, brought them
To Higlac's home, their ring-giver's hall
Near the sea, where he lived surrounded
By his followers. . . .
275   Then Beowulf and his men went walking along
The shore, down the broad strip of sand.
The world's bright candle shone, hurrying
Up from the south. It was a short journey
From their ship to Higlac's home, to the hall
280 Where their king, Ongentho's killer,[5] lived
With his warriors and gave treasures away. They walked
Quickly. The young king knew
They were back, Beowulf and his handful of brave
Men, come safely home; he sat,
285 Now, waiting to see them, to greet
His battle-comrades when they arrived at his court.
          They came. And when Beowulf had bowed to his lord,
And standing in front of the throne had solemnly
Spoken loyal words, Higlac
290 Ordered him to sit at his side—he
Who had survived, sailed home victorious, next to
His kinsman and king. Mead cups were filled
And Hareth's daughter took them through the hall,
Carried ale to her husband's comrades.
295 Higlac, unable to stay silent, anxious
To know how Beowulf's adventure had gone,
Began to question him, courteous but eager
To be told everything
          "Beloved Beowulf,
300 Tell us what your trip to far-off places
Brought you, your sudden expedition on the salty
Waves, your search for war in Herot?
Did you end Hrothgar's hopeless misery,
Could you help that glorious king? Grendel's
305 Savagery lay heavy on my heart but I was afraid
To let you go to him; for a long time
I held you here, kept you safe,
Forced you to make the Danes fight
Their own battles. God be praised
310 That my eyes have beheld you once more, unharmed!"

---

5. Ongentho's killer: Ongentho was a Swedish king who was defeated and killed in an attack led by Higlac.

Beowulf spoke, Edgetho's brave son:[6]
"My lord Higlac, my meeting with Grendel
And the nighttime battle we fought are known
To everyone in Denmark, where the monster was once

315 The uncrowned ruler, murdering and eating
Hrothgar's people, forever bringing them
Misery. I ended his reign, avenged
His crimes so completely in the crashing darkness
That not even the oldest of his evil kind

320 Will ever boast, lying in sin
And deceit, that the monster beat me. I sought out
Hrothgar, first, came to him in his hall;
When Healfdane's famous son heard
That I'd come to challenge Grendel, he gave me

325 A seat of honor alongside his son.
His followers were drinking; I joined their feast,
Sat with that band, as bright and loud-tongued
As any I've ever seen. . . .
It was early in the evening, Heaven's

330 jewel had slid to its rest, and the jealous
Monster, planning murder, came seeking us
Out, stalking us as we guarded Hrothgar's
Hall. Hondshew, sleeping in his armor,
Was the first Geat he reached: Grendel

335 Seized him, tore him apart, swallowed him
Down, feet and all, as fate
Had decreed—a glorious young soldier, killed
In his prime. Yet Grendel had only begun
His bloody work, meant to leave us

340 With his belly and his pouch both full, and Herot
Half-empty. Then he tested his strength against mine,
Hand to hand. His pouch hung
At his side, a huge bag sewn
From a dragon's skin, worked with a devil's

345 Skill; it was closed by a marvelous clasp.
The monster intended to take me, put me
Inside, save me for another meal.
He was bold and strong, but once I stood
On my feet his strength was useless, and it failed him.

350 "The whole tale of how I killed him,
Repaid him in kind for all the evil

---

6. **Edgetho's brave son:** Beowulf.

He'd done, would take too long: your people,
My prince, were honored in the doing. He escaped,
Found a few minutes of life, but his hand,
355 His whole right arm, stayed in Herot;
The miserable creature crept away,
Dropped to the bottom of his lake, half dead
As he fell. When the sun had returned, the Danes'
Great king poured out treasure, repaid me
360 In hammered gold for the bloody battle
I'd fought in his name. He ordered a feast;
There were songs, and the telling of tales. One ancient
Dane told of long-dead times,
And sometimes Hrothgar himself, with the harp
365 In his lap, stroked its silvery strings
And told wonderful stories, a brave king
Reciting unhappy truths about good
And evil—and sometimes he wove his stories
On the mournful thread of old age, remembering
370 Buried strength and the battles it had won.
He would weep, the old king, wise with many
Winters, remembering what he'd done, once,
What he'd seen, what he knew. And so we sat
The day away, feasting. Then darkness
375 Fell again, and Grendel's mother
Was waiting, ready for revenge, hating
The Danes for her son's death. The monstrous
Hag succeeded, burst boldly into Herot
And killed Esher, one of the king's oldest
380 And wisest soldiers. But when the sun shone
Once more the death-weary Danes could not build
A pyre and burn his beloved body,
Lay him on flaming logs, return ashes
To dust: she'd carried away his corpse,
385 Brought it to her den deep in the water.
Hrothgar had wept for many of his men,
But this time his heart melted, this
Was the worst. He begged me, in your name, half-weeping
As he spoke, to seek still greater glory
390 Deep in the swirling waves, to win
Still higher fame, and the gifts he would give me.
Down in that surging lake I sought
And found her, the horrible hag, fierce
And wild; we fought, clutching and grasping;
395 The water ran red with blood and at last,

With a mighty sword that had hung on the wall,
I cut off her head. I had barely escaped
With my life, my death was not written. And the Danes'
Protector, Healfdane's great son, heaped tip
400 Treasures and precious jewels to reward me

"He lived his life as a good king must:
I lost nothing, none of the gifts
My strength could have earned me. He opened his store
Of gems and armor, let me choose as I liked,
405 So I could bring his riches to you, my ruler,
And prove his friendship, and my love. Your favor
Still governs my life: I have almost no family,
Higlac, almost no one, now, but you."
         Then Beowulf ordered them to bring in the boar-head
410 Banner, the towering helmet, the ancient,
Silvery armor, and the gold-carved sword:
         "This war-gear was Hrothgar's reward, my gift
From his wise old hands. He wanted me to tell you,
First, whose treasures these were. Hergar
415 Had owned them, his older brother, who was king
Of Denmark until death gave Hrothgar the throne:
But Hergar kept them, would not give them to Herward,
His brave young son, though the boy had proved
His loyalty. These are yours: may they serve you well!"
420   And after the gleaming armor four horses
Were led in, four bays, swift and all
Alike. Beowulf had brought his king
Horses and treasure—as a man must,
Not weaving nets of malice for his comrades,
425 Preparing their death in the dark, with secret,
Cunning tricks. Higlac trusted
His nephew, leaned on his strength, in war,
Each of them intent on the other's joy.
And Beowulf gave Welthow's gift, her wonderful
430 Necklace, to Higd, Higlac's queen,
And gave her, also, three supple, graceful,
Saddle-bright horses; she received his presents,
Then wore that wonderful jewel on her breast . . .
         Then Higlac, protector of his people, brought ill
435 His father's—Beowulf's grandfather's—great sword,
Worked in gold; none of the Geats
Could boast of a better weapon. He laid it
In Beowulf's lap, then gave him seven

Thousand hides of land, houses
440   And ground and all. Geatland was home
For both king and prince; their fathers had left them
Buildings and fields—but Higlac's inheritance
Stretched further, it was he who was king, and was followed.

Beowulf and the Dragon

Afterwards, in the time when Higlac was dead
445   And Herdred, his son, who'd ruled the Geats
After his father, had followed him into darkness
Killed in battle with the Swedes, who smashed
His shield, cut through the soldiers surrounding
Their king—then, when Higad's one son
450   Was gone, Beowulf ruled in Geatland,
Took the throne he'd refused, once,
And held it long and well. He was old
With years and wisdom, fifty winters
A king, when a dragon awoke from its darkness
455   And dreams and brought terror to his people. The beast
Had slept in a huge stone tower, with a hidden
Path beneath; a man stumbled on
The entrance, went in, discovered the ancient
Treasure, the pagan jewels and gold
460   The dragon had been guarding, and dazzled and greedy
Stole a gem-studded cup, and fled.
But now the dragon hid nothing, neither
The theft nor itself; it swept through the darkness,
And all Geatland knew its anger.

465   But the thief had not come to steal; he stole
And roused the dragon, not from desire
But need. He was someone's slave, had been beaten
By his masters, had run from all men's sight,
But with no place to hide; then he found the hidden
470   Path, and used it. And once inside,
Seeing the sleeping beast, staring as it
Yawned and stretched, not wanting to wake it,
Terror-struck, he turned and ran for his life,
Taking the jeweled cup.
475   That tower
Was heaped high with hidden treasure, stored there
Years before by the last survivor
Of a noble race, ancient riches
Left in the darkness as the end of a dynasty

480	Came. Death had taken them, one
	By one, and the warrior who watched over all
	That remained mourned their fate, expecting,
	Soon, the same for himself, knowing
	The gold and jewels he had guarded so long
485	Could not bring him pleasure much longer. He brought
	The precious cups, the armor and the ancient
	Swords, to a stone tower built
	Near the sea, below a cliff, a sealed
	Fortress with no windows, no doors, waves
490	In front of it, rocks behind. Then he spoke:
	"Take these treasures, earth, now that no one
	Living can enjoy them. They were yours, in the beginning;
	Allow them to return. War and terror
	Have swept away my people, shut
495	Their eyes to delight and to living, closed
	The door to all gladness. No one is left
	To lift these swords, polish these jeweled
	Cups: no one leads, no one follows. These hammered
	Helmets, worked with gold, will tarnish
500	And crack; the hands that should clean and polish them
	Are still forever. And these mail shirts, worn
	In battle, once, while swords crashed
	And blades bit into shields and men,
	Will rust away like the warriors who owned them.
505	None of these treasures will travel to distant
	Lands, following their lords. The harp's
	Bright song, the hawk crossing through the hall
	On its swift wings, the stallion tramp—ling
	In the courtyard all gone creatures of every
510	Kind, and their masters, hurled to the gravel!
	And so he spoke, sadly, of those
	Long dead, and lived from day to day,
	Joyless, until, at last, death touched
	His heart and took him too. And a stalker
515	In the night, a flaming dragon, found
	The treasure unguarded; he whom men fear
	Came flying through the darkness, wrapped in fire,
	Seeking caves and stone-split ruins
	But finding gold. Then it stayed, buried
520	Itself with heathen silver and jewels
	It could neither use nor ever abandon.
	So mankind's enemy, the mighty beast,
	Slept in those stone walls for hundreds

Of years; a runaway slave roused it,
525 Stole a jeweled cup and bought
His master's forgiveness, begged for mercy
And was pardoned when his delighted lord took the present
He bore, turned it in his hands and stared
At the ancient carvings. The cup brought peace
530 To a slave, pleased his master, but stirred
A dragon's anger. It turned, hunting
The thief's tracks, and found them, saw
Where its visitor had come and gone. He'd survived,
Had come close enough to touch its scaly
535 Head and yet lived, as it lifted its cavernous
Jaws, through the grace of almighty God
And a pair of quiet, quick-moving feet,
The dragon followed his steps, anxious
To find the man who had robbed it of silver
540 And sleep; it circled around and around
The tower, determined to catch him, but could not,
He had run too fast, the wilderness was empty.
The beast went back to its treasure, planning
A bloody revenge and found what was missing,
545 Saw what thieving hands had stolen.
Then it crouched on the stones, counting off
The hours till the Almighty's candle went out,
And evening came, and wild with anger
It could fly burning across the land, killing
550 And destroying with its breath. Then the sun was gone,
And its heart was glad: glowing with rage
It left the tower, impatient to repay
Its enemies. The people suffered, everyone
Lived in terror, but when Beowulf had learned
555 Of their trouble his fate was worse, and came quickly.

Vomiting fire and smoke, the dragon
Burned down their homes. They watched in horror
As the flames rose up: the angry monster
Meant to leave nothing alive. And the signs
560 Of its anger flickered and glowed in the darkness,
Visible for miles, tokens of its hate
And its cruelty, spread like a warning to the Geats
Who had broken its rest. Then it hurried back
To its tower, to its hidden treasure, before dawn
565 Could come. It had wrapped its flames around
The Geats; now it trusted in stone

Walls, and its strength, to protect it. But they would not.
              Then they came to Beowulf, their king, and announced
That his hall, his throne, the best of buildings,
570   Had melted away in the dragon's burning
Breath. Their words brought misery, Beowulf's
Sorrow beat at his heart: he accused
Himself of breaking God's law, of bringing
The Almighty's anger down on his people.
575   Reproach pounded in his breast, gloomy
And dark, and the world seemed a different place.
But the hall was gone, the dragon's molten
Breath had licked across it, burned it
To ashes, near the shore it had guarded. The Geats
580   Deserved revenge; Beowulf, their leader
And lord, began to plan it, ordered
A battle-shield shaped of iron, knowing that
Wood would be useless, that no linden shield
Could help him, protect him, in the flaming heat
585   Of the beast's breath. That noble prince
Would end his days on earth, soon,
Would leave this brief life, but would take the dragon
With him, tear it from the heaped-up treasure
It had guarded so long. And he'd go to it alone,
590   Scorning to lead soldiers against such
An enemy: he saw nothing to fear, thought nothing
Of the beast's claws, or wings, of flaming
Jaws—he had fought, before, against worse
Odds, had survived, been victorious, in harsher
595   Battles, beginning in Herot, Hrothgar's
Unlucky hall. He'd killed Grendel
And his mother, swept that murdering tribe
Away. And he'd fought in Higlac's war
With the Frisians, fought at his lord's side
600   Till a sword reached out and drank Higlac's
Blood, till a blade swung in the rush
Of battle killed the Geats' great king.
Then Beowulf escaped, broke through Frisian
Shields and swam to freedom, saving
605   Thirty sets of armor from the scavenging
Franks, river people who robbed
The dead as they floated by. Beowulf
Offered them only his sword, ended
So many jackal lives that the few
610   Who were able skulked silently home, glad

To leave him. So Beowulf swam sadly back
To Geatland, almost the only survivor
Of a foolish war. Higlac's widow
Brought him the crown, offered him the kingdom,
615   Not trusting Herdred, her son and Higlac's,
To beat off foreign invaders. But Beowulf
Refused to rule when his lord's own son
Was alive, and the leaderless Geats could choose
A rightful king. He gave Herdred
620   All his support, offering an open
Heart where Higlac's young son could see
Wisdom he still lacked himself: warmth
And good will were what Beowulf brought his new king.
        But Swedish exiles came, seeking
625   Protection; they were rebels against Onela,
Healfdane's son-in-law and the best ring-giver
His people had ever known. And Onela
Came too, a mighty king, marched
On Geatland with a huge army; Herdred
630   Had given his word and now he gave
His life, shielding tile Swedish strangers.
Onela wanted nothing more:
When Herdred had fallen that famous warrior
Went back to Sweden, let Beowulf rule![7]
635   But Beowulf remembered how his king had been killed.
As soon as he could he lent the last
Of the Swedish rebels soldiers and gold,
Helped him to a bitter battle across
The wide sea, where victory, and revenge, and the Swedish
640   Throne were won, and Onela was slain.
        So Edgetho's son survived, no matter
What dangers he met, what battles he fought,
Brave and forever triumphant, till the day
Fate sent him to the dragon and sent him death.

---

7. But Swedish exiles . . . let Beowulf rule: When Onela seized the throne of Sweden, his two nephews sought shelter with the king of the Geats, Herdred. For this act of kindness, Onela attacked Herdred, and Herdred was killed in the battle. After the death of Herdred, Beowulf became the ruler of the kingdom.

☑ Check Your Comprehension

1. What danger does Hrothgar warn Beowulf against in his long speech to the hero?
2. What gift does Unferth present to Beowulf?
3. Why does Hrothgar weep as he bids Beowulf farewell?
4. After Beowulf slew Grendel, what new challenge did the hero confront?
5. (a) What does King Higlac ask Beowulf to tell him? (b) What gifts does Beowulf present to Higlac and Higd?
6. After fifty years of Beowulf's rule, what causes the dragon to awaken and become angry?
7. How does Beowulf react to the dragon's attack?

◆ Critical Thinking

1. How does the description of the decoration of the golden sword hilt (lines 36–48) symbolize the main action of the epic as a whole? **[Interpret]**
2. In the context of the values of Anglo-Saxon warrior society, what is the significance of the numerous exchanges of gifts in the poem? **[Analyze]**
3. Why do you think the poet draws attention to Beowulf's lack of a family at lines 407–408? **[Speculate]**
4. What does Beowulf's reluctance to become king of the Geats show about him? **[Evaluate]**
5. How does the poet foreshadow Beowulf's death? **[Interpret]**

Beowulf
Comparing and Connecting the Epic

◆ Literary Focus: Oral Tradition

Oral tradition is the process of handing down songs, stories, poems, and other features of cultural heritage from generation to generation by word of mouth. Even though it is a long poem whose full text runs to over 3,000 lines, *Beowulf* is most likely the product of oral tradition. The epic was originally composed to be heard in performance, rather than read.

Main Features of Oral Style

- Appositives and adjective phrases; coordinate sentence structure

- Caesura, or strong break in middle of verse line

- Kennings, or two-word metaphors such as "whales' home" for the sea

- Typical scenes, such as feasting, sea-voyaging, and gift-giving

- Extensive use of flashback and fore-shadowing

- Prominence of speeches such as verbal duels, messenger speeches, sermons, and retellings of events

- Emphasis on epic song as the main vehicle for keeping alive the memory of heroic deeds

1. What features of oral tradition can you find at the start of Hrothgar's long speech to Beowulf (lines 50–56)?

2. How does the poem represent both Beowulf and Hrothgar as oral "tellers of tales" at lines 350–373?

3. Identify two examples of kennings in the text.

◆ Drawing Conclusions About *Beowulf*

One way to evaluate *Beowulf* is to respond to critical opinions about the epic. Read the following evaluation by James W. Earl:

It is no accident that Beowulf belongs to a tribe famous for its heroes but equally noteworthy for its complete disappearance from history long before the composition of the poem. This striking fact points to one of the chief themes of the poem, which does not so much describe and praise the heroic world generally as focus on its disappearance in particular. . . . The poem ends with the passing of Beowulf, the passing of his nation, and the passing of the heroic world altogether, and mourns all these losses. It is a poem of mourning, an act of cultural mourning.

Earl's evaluation of Beowulf is largely an appraisal of the epic's tone. The **tone** of a work conveys an attitude toward the audience or the subject. The chart below shows how details, imagery, diction or word choice, and voice or manner of speaking are related to tone.

TONE			
Details	**Images**	**Diction**	**Voice**
(specific choices)	(sensory appeal)	(word connotations)	(manner of speaking)

Do you agree with Earl that the overall tone of *Beowulf* is one of mourning? Write your response in a paragraph or two, giving reasons and examples to support your opinion.

◆ Idea Bank

Writing

1. **Timeline** Create a timeline for these excerpts from *Beowulf,* taking into account the flashbacks you identify in the text.
2. **Dialogue** Write a dialogue in which you dramatize the farewell between Beowulf and Unferth (see lines 157–163). Try to imitate the overall style of the epic in your writing.
3. **Evaluation** Do you think Beowulf's heroic qualities would have wide appeal in today's world? Write an evaluation of *Beowulf* as the basis for a Hollywood film.

Speaking and Listening

4. **Oral Performance** Rehearse and deliver an oral interpretation of one of the long speeches in these excerpts: for example, Hrothgar's sermon to Beowulf (lines 50–134) or Beowulf's retelling of his exploits in Denmark (lines 311–443).
   [Performing Arts Link]
5. **Music Choice** Choose one of the incidents in these excerpts and then select a piece of music that you think expresses the same overall atmosphere or mood as the episode from the epic. Play a recording of your selection to an audience of classmates, and then explain the reasons for your choice. **[Music Link]**

Researching and Representing

6. **Oral Report** With a small group, research the Sutton Hoo ship-burial and its significance for our knowledge about the Anglo-Saxon world of *Beowulf.* Each member of your group should present a brief oral report summarizing some of your results to the class as a whole. **[Group Activity; Art Link]**

◆ Further Reading, Listening, and Viewing

- Joseph Tuso, ed.: *Beowulf* (1975). The Norton Critical Edition contains a prose translation and much useful background and criticism

- James W. Earl: *Thinking About Beowulf* (1994). A largely psychological reading of the epic

- Edward B. Irving, Jr.: *Rereading Beowulf* (1989). A critical study that stresses the importance of oral tradition and oral style in *Beowulf*

- *Beowulf* [unabridged]. Audiocassette with George Guidall narrating the Gummere translation

- J. Campbell: *The Anglo-Saxons* (1991). A survey of Anglo-Saxon art

On the Web:

http://www.phschool.com/atschool/literature
Go to the student edition of *The British Tradition.* Proceed to Unit 1. Then, click Hot Links to find Web sites featuring *Beowulf.*

Geoffrey Chaucer In Depth

> "A keen ironist with a many-sided sense of humor, Chaucer explores the relationship between art and life as has no other poet before or after him."
>
> —*George D. Economou*

GEOFFREY CHAUCER has been called the father of English poetry. His dazzling skill in a broad array of literary forms made him the greatest writer in Middle English, the transitional form of the language that developed after the Norman invasion of England in 1066.

Youth in London The son of a prosperous London wine merchant, Chaucer was born around 1343 and probably attended school in London. At the age of fourteen, he entered the service of Lionel, the Earl of Ulster and the king's second son. Two years later, Chaucer served as a soldier in King Edward III's invasion of France, was taken prisoner, and was ransomed. In 1366, he went on a diplomatic mission to Spain. Also in this year, Chaucer married Philippa, the daughter of a knight.

Early Career Chaucer's marriage brought him even more connections with the English nobility and gentry. He secured a number of positions in the royal service, including that of customs inspector for the Port of London. Philippa's sister became the third wife of the powerful nobleman John of Gaunt, King Edward III's fourth son and the father of the future King Henry IV. John of Gaunt became Chaucer's most influential patron, and it was probably to commemorate the death of John's first wife that Chaucer composed his first major work, *The Book of the Duchess*, around 1369.

In 1372, Chaucer traveled on a diplomatic mission to Italy. This journey marked a turning point in his career as a poet. Not only was Chaucer exposed to the culture of the Italian Renaissance—the "rebirth" of art and literature that was to spread through Europe during the next two centuries—but he also became familiar with the works of three literary giants: Dante Alighieri, Francesco Petrarca (known as Petrarch), and Giovanni Boccaccio. The influence of Boccaccio was especially important. Chaucer used the framing device of Boccaccio's masterpiece, *The Decameron*, for *The Canterbury Tales*, and he based two of his greatest poems, "The Knight's Tale" from *The Canterbury Tales* and *Troilus and Criseyde*, on works by Boccaccio.

Mature Years In the 1380's and 1390's, Chaucer served as a justice of the peace and as a forester for the royal forests. He probably started his masterpiece, *The Canterbury Tales*, in 1386 when he was living in Greenwich, near London. From his house, he may have been able to see the pilgrim road leading from London to Canterbury.

His original plan called for 120 tales, with two stories told by each pilgrim on the journey from London to Canterbury and two more on the way back. In fact, the poet lived to complete only twenty-two tales; two others survive in fragmentary form. The variety of the tales he did finish and the diversity of the storytellers make *The Canterbury Tales* an unforgettably rich portrait of medieval life.

Chaucer died in 1400; he was buried in the Poets' Corner of Westminster Abbey.

◆ Thomas Becket and Canterbury

The pilgrims' destination in *The Canterbury Tales* was a small town about seventy miles southeast of London. In the late fourteenth century, Canterbury had been an international pilgrimage center for two hundred years, since Archbishop Thomas Becket (c.1118–1170) had been murdered in the cathedral by four knights in the service of King Henry II. When the king wanted clergymen accused of wrongdoing to be tried in civil courts, Becket, himself a former chancellor of England, insisted on upholding the jurisdiction of special ecclesiastical courts. He and the king quarreled bitterly.

Becket's violent death shocked Europe, and in 1173 the Pope declared him a saint and a martyr. King Henry was forced to do public penance at Becket's tomb.

In the twentieth century, the conflict between Becket and Henry II served as the basis for several notable plays, including *Murder in the Cathedral* (1936), by T. S. Eliot, and *Becket* (1959), by the French dramatist Jean Anouilh. The latter was made into a popular film. Today, Canterbury is the seat of the Anglican Communion, which includes the Church of England as well as the Episcopal Church in the United States.

◆ Literary Works

None of Chaucer's works can be dated precisely, but the order given in the list below is fairly certain.

The Book of the Duchess A dream-poem probably written in 1369 as an allegorical lament for the death of Blanche of Lancaster, the first wife of Chaucer's patron John of Gaunt.

The House of Fame An unfinished dream-poem in which the speaker experiences a series of visions revealing the illusory nature of fame

The Parliament of Fowls A dream-poem in which the birds meet on Valentine's Day to choose their mates; perhaps written to celebrate the marriage of King Richard II to Anne of Bohemia in 1382

Troilus and Criseyde Chaucer's longest complete poem, telling the story of a pair of lovers from classical mythology

The Canterbury Tales Chaucer's unfinished masterpiece, written from 1386 to 1400

TIMELINE

Chaucer's Life		World Events	
c.1343	Born in London	1337	Hundred Years' War begins
1357	Serves as a page in the household of Lionel, Earl of Ulster	1341	Petrarch crowned poet laureate of Rome
1359	Serves in the army and is taken prisoner by the French and later ransomed	1348	Black Death begins in England
		1350	Edward III begins to rebuild Windsor Castle
1366	Travels to Spain on diplomatic mission; marries Philippa, the daughter of a knight and the future sister-in-law of John of Gaunt	1351	Open-air tennis first played in England
		1352	Corpus Christi College, Oxford, founded
		1354	Mechanical clock at Strasbourg Cathedral
1367	Serves as yeoman in King Edward III's personal household	1362	Piers Plowman, poem by William Langland in Middle English
1368	Travels to France on diplomatic mission; is named a squire, or "gentleman"	1364	Aztecs of Mexico build capital at Tenochtitlán
1369	Probably writes The Book of the Duchess	1367	King addresses Parliament in English (rather than Norman French) for the first time in 300 years
1372	Diplomatic mission to Italy; probably becomes familiar with the works of Dante, Petrarch, and Boccaccio	1374	Death of Petrarch
		1377	Death of Guillaume de Machaut, French composer; papacy returns from Avignon in southern France to Rome; Richard II becomes king of England
1374	Appointed a controller of customs for the Port of London		
1378	Granted a royal pension; second visit to Italy		
1385	Becomes justice of the peace and knight of the shire in Kent	1381	Peasants' Revolt
1386	Probably starts to write The Canterbury Tales	c.1382	Bible translated into English for the first time
1387	Chaucer's wife dies	1387	Birth of Fra Angelico, Italian painter
1391	Becomes deputy forester of royal forest in Somerset	1399	Richard II deposed; Henry IV, son of John of Gaunt, becomes king
1399	Addresses witty verses entitled "Complaint of Chaucer to His Purse" to King Henry IV		
1400	Chaucer dies		

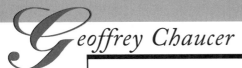

Geoffrey Chaucer

from The Pardoner's Tale

translated by Nevill Coghill

During their journey to Canterbury, each of the pilgrims tells a tale. After the Knight, the Miller, the Reeve, the Nun, and the narrator have finished, the Pardoner entertains the others with a tale that supports his claim that "greed is the root of all evil."

It's of three rioters[1] I have to tell
Who long before the morning service bell[2]
Were sitting in a tavern for a drink.
And as they sat, they heard the hand-bell clink

5   Before a coffin going to the grave;
One of them called the little tavern-knave[3]
And said "Go and find out at once—look spry!—
Whose corpse is in that coffin passing by;
And see you get the name correctly too."

10   "Sir," said the boy, "no need, I promise you;
Two hours before you came here I was told.
He was a friend of yours in days of old,
And suddenly last night, the man was slain,
Upon his bench, face up, dead drunk again.

15   There came a privy[4] thief, they call him Death,
Who kills us all round here, and in a breath
He speared him through the heart, he never stirred.
And then Death went his way without a word.
He's killed a thousand in the present plague,[5]

20   And, sir, it doesn't do to be too vague
If you should meet him; you had best be wary.
Be on your guard with such an adversary,
Be primed to meet him everywhere you go,
That's what my mother said. It's all I know."

25   The publican[6] joined in with, "By St. Mary.
What the child says is right; you'd best be wary,
This very year he killed, in a large village
A mile away, man, woman, serf at tillage,[7]

---

1. rioters (rī′ et ərz) *n.*: Loud, dissolute bullies
2. long before . . . bell: Long before 9:00 A.M.
3. tavern-knave: Serving boy.
4. privy: Secretive.
5. plague: The Black Death, which killed over a third of the population of England in 1348 and 1349.
6. publican: Innkeeper.
7. tillage: Plowing.

	Page in the household, children—all there were.
30	Yes, I imagine that he lives round there.
	It's well to be prepared in these alarms,
	He might do you dishonor." "Huh, God's arms!"
	The rioter said, "Is he so fierce to meet?
	I'll search for him, by Jesus, street by street.
35	God's blessed bones! I'll register a vow!
	Here, chaps! The three of us together now.
	Hold up your hands, like me, and we'll be brothers
	In this affair, and each defend the others,
	And we will kill this traitor Death, I say!
40	Away with him as he has made away
	With all our friends. God's dignity! To-night!"
	They made their bargain, swore with appetite,
	These three, to live and die for one another
	As brother-born might swear to his born brother.
45	And up they started in their drunken rage
	And made towards this village which the page
	And publican had spoken of before.
	Many and grisly were the oaths they swore,
	Tearing Christ's blessed body to a shred;[8]
50	"If we can only catch him, Death is dead!"
	When they had gone not fully half a mile,
	Just as they were about to cross a stile,[9]
	They came upon a very poor old man
	Who humbly greeted them and thus began,
55	"God look to you, my lords, and give you quiet!"
	To which the proudest of these men of riot
	Gave back the answer. "What, old fool? Give place!
	Why are you all wrapped up except your face?
	Why live so long? Isn't it time to die?"
60	The old, old fellow looked him in the eye
	And said, "Because I never yet have found,
	Though I have walked to India, searching round
	Village and city on my pilgrimage,
	One who would change his youth to have my age.
65	And so my age is mine and must be still
	Upon me, for such time as God may will.
	"Not even Death, alas, will take my life;
	So, like a wretched prisoner at strife
	Within himself, I walk alone and wait
70	About the earth, which is my mother's gate,

---

8. Tearing . . . shred: Their oaths included expressions such as "God's arms" (line 32) and "God's blessed bones" (line 35).
9. stile (stīl) *n.*: A step or set of steps used in climbing over a fence or wall.

Knock-knocking with my staff from night to noon
And crying, 'Mother, open to me soon!
Look at me, mother, won't you let me in?
See how I wither, flesh and blood and skin!
75 Alas! When will these bones be laid to rest?
Mother, I would exchange—for that were best—
The wardrobe in my chamber, standing there
So long, for yours! Aye, for a shirt of hair[10]
To wrap me in!' She has refused her grace,
80 Whence comes the pallor[11] of my withered face.
    "But it dishonored you when you began
To speak so roughly, sir, to an old man,
Unless he had injured you in word or deed.
It says in holy writ, as you may read,
85 'Thou shalt rise up before the hoary[12] head
And honor it,' And therefore be it said
'Do no more harm to an old man than you,
Being now young, would have another do
When you are old'—if you should live till then.
90 And so may God be with you, gentlemen,
For I must go whither I have to go."
    "By God," the gambler said, "you shan't do so,
You don't get off so easy, by St. John!
I heard you mention, just a moment gone,
95 A certain traitor Death who singles out
And kills the fine young fellows hereabout.
And you're his spy, by God! You wait a bit.
Say where he is or you shall pay for it,
By God and by the Holy Sacrament!
100 I say you've joined together by consent
To kill us younger folk, you thieving swine!"
    "Well, sirs," he said, "if it be your design
To find out Death, turn up this crooked way
Towards that grove, I left him there today
105 Under a tree, and there you'll find him waiting.
He isn't one to hide for all your prating.[13]
You see that oak? He won't be far to find.
And God protect you that redeemed mankind
Aye, and amend you!" Thus that ancient man.
110 At once the three young rioters began
To run, and reached the tree, and there they found
A pile of golden florins[14] on the ground,

---

10. **shirt of hair:** Here, a shroud.
11. **pallor** (pall ər) *n.*: Unnatural lack of color; paleness.
12. **hoary** (hôr´ ē) *adj.*: White or gray with age.
13. **prating** (prā´ tiŋ) *v.*: Talking much and foolishly.
14: **florins:** Coins.

New-coined, eight bushels of them as they thought.
No longer was it Death those fellows sought.
115   For they were all so thrilled to see the sight,
The florins were so beautiful and bright,
That down they sat beside the precious pile.
The wickedest spoke first after a while.
"Brothers," he said, "you listen to what I say.
120   I'm pretty sharp although I joke away.
It's clear that Fortune has bestowed this treasure
To let us live in jollity and pleasure.
Light come, light go! We'll spend it as we ought.
God's precious dignity! Who would have thought
125   This morning was to be our lucky day?
      "If one could only get the gold away,
Back to my house, or else to yours, perhaps—
For as you know, the gold is ours, chaps—
We'd all be at the top of fortune, hey?
130   But certainly it can't be done by day.
People would call us robbers—a strong gang.
So our own property would make us hang.
No, we must bring this treasure back by night
Some prudent way, and keep it out of sight.
135   And so as a solution I propose
We draw for lots and see the way it goes.
The one who draws the longest, lucky man,
Shall run to town as quickly as he can
To fetch us bread and wine—but keep things dark—
140   While two remain in hiding here to mark
Our heap of treasure. If there's no delay,
When night comes down we'll carry it away,
All three of us, wherever we have planned."
      He gathered lots and hid them in his hand
145   Bidding them draw for where the luck should fall.
It fell upon the youngest of them all,
And off he ran at once towards the town.
      As soon as he had gone, the first sat down
And thus began a parley[15] with the other:
150   "You know that you can trust me as a brother;
Now let me tell you where your profit lies;
You know our friend has gone to get supplies
And here's a lot of gold that is to be
Divided equally amongst us three.
155   Nevertheless, if I could shape things thus
So that we shared it out—the two of us—
Wouldn't you take it as a friendly turn?"

---

15. parley (pär′ lē): Discussion.

"But how!" the other said with some concern,
"Because he knows the gold's with me and you;
160   What can we tell him? What are we to do?'
"Is it a bargain," said the first, "or no?
For I can tell you in a word or so
What's to be done to bring the thing about."
"Trust me." the other said, "you needn't doubt
165   My word. I won't betray you, I'll be true."
"Well," said his friend, "you see that we are two,
And two are twice as powerful as one.
Now look; when he comes back, get up in fun
To have a wrestle; then, as you attack,
170   I'll up and put my dagger through his back
While you and he are struggling, as in game;
Then draw your dagger too and do the same.
Then all this money will be ours to spend,
Divided equally of course, dear friend.
175   Then we can gratify our lusts and fill
The day with dicing at our own sweet will."
Thus these two miscreants[16] agreed to slay
The third and youngest, as you heard me say.
The youngest, as he ran towards the town,
180   Kept turning over, roiling up and down
Within his heart the beauty of those bright
New florins, saying, "Lord, to think I might
Have all that treasure to myself alone!
Could there be anyone beneath the throne
185   Of God so happy as I then should be?"
And so the Fiend,[17] our common enemy,
Was given power to put it in his thought
That there was always poison to be bought,
And that with poison he could kill his friends.
190   To men in such a state the Devil sends
Thoughts of this kind, and has a full permission
To lure them on to sorrow and perdition;[18]
For this young man was utterly content
To kill them both and never to repent.
195   And on he ran, he had no thought to tarry,[19]
Came to the town, found an apothecary[20]
And said, "Sell me some poison if you will,
I have a lot of rats I want to kill
And there's a polecat too about my yard

---

16. **miscreants** (mis´ krē ənts): Villains.
17. **Fiend:** Satan.
18. **perdition:** Damnation.
19. **tarry** (tar´ ē) v.: To delay, linger, be tardy.
20. **apothecary** (ə päth´ ə ker´ ē) n.: Pharmacist or druggist.

200   That takes my chickens and it hits me hard;
             But I'll get even, as is only right,
             With vermin that destroy a man by night."
                The chemist answered, "I've a preparation
             Which you shall have, and by my soul's salvation
205   If any living creature eat or drink
             A mouthful, ere he has the time to think,
             Though he took less than makes a grain of wheat,
             You'll see him fall down dying at your feet;
             Yes, die he must, and in so short a while
210   You'd hardly have the time to walk a mile,
             The poison is so strong, you understand."
                This cursed fellow grabbed into his hand
             The box of poison and away he ran
             Into a neighboring street, and found a man
215   Who lent him three large bottles. He withdrew
             And deftly poured the poison into two.
             He kept the third one clean, as well he might,
             For his own drink, meaning to work all night
             Stacking the gold and carrying it away.
220   And when this rioter, this devil's clay,
             Had filled his bottles up with wine, all three,
             Back to rejoin his comrades sauntered he.
                Why make a sermon of it? Why waste breath?
             Exactly in the way they'd planned his death
225   They fell on him and slew him, two to one.
             Then said the first of them when this was done.
             "'Now for a drink. Sit down and let's be merry,
             For later on there'll be the corpse to bury."
             And, as it happened, reaching for a cup,
230   He took a bottle full of poison up
             And drank; and his companion, nothing loth,
             Drank from it also, and they perished both.
                There is, in Avicenna's long relation[21]
             Concerning poison and its operation.
235   Trust me, no ghastlier section to transcend
             What these two wretches suffered at their end.
             Thus these two murderers received their due,
             So did the treacherous young poisoner too.

---

21. Avicenna's (a´ və sen´ əz) **long relation:** A book of medicines written by Avicenna (980–1037), an Arab physician, which contains a chapter on poisons.

☑ Check Your Comprehension

1. What do the three rioters pledge to do?
2. (a) What does the old man tell the rioters they will find under a tree? (b) What do they actually find there?
3. How do the two older rioters decide to increase their share of the gold? Explain their plan.
4. What does the youngest rioter do when he goes to town for bread and wine?

◆ Critical Thinking

1. In line 39, Death is presented as a traitor. Do you think this description is appropriate? Explain your answer. **[Evaluate]**

2. Do the rioters keep the pledge they made in the tavern? Why or why not? **[Interpret]**

3. How does the youngest rioter's dialogue with the apothecary help to characterize both the rioter and his two companions? **[Analyze]**

4. Does the old man know that in directing the three rioters to the oak tree he is sending them to their deaths? Explain. **[Infer]**

5. (a) What is the moral of this tale? (b) Is this moral still relevant today? **[Apply]**

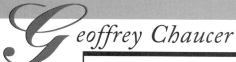

Geoffrey Chaucer

from The Knight's Tale

translated by Nevill Coghill

> *Duke Theseus, ruler of Athens, declares war on the tyrant Creon, lord of Thebes. Theseus and his army attack and defeat the Theban king, who is slain in the battle. Two young Theban knights—Palamon and Arcite—are taken prisoner and locked up in a tower in Athens. This excerpt from Chaucer's* The Knight's Tale *tells of Palamon's and Arcite's imprisonment and their mutual love for Emily, the fair maiden and sister-in-law to Theseus, whom they spy daily from their prison chamber.*

And in a tower, in grief and anguish lay
Arcite and Palamon, beyond all doubt
For ever, for no gold could buy them out.
   Year after year went by, day after day,
5   Until one morning in the month of May
Young Emily, that fairer was of mien[1]
Than is the lily on its stalk of green,
And fresher in her coloring that strove
With early roses in a May-time grove
10   —I know not which was fairer of the two—
Ere[2] it was day, as she was wont[3] to do,
Rose and arrayed her beauty as was right,
For May will have no sluggardry[4] at night,
Season that pricks in every gentle heart,
15   Awaking it from sleep, and bids it start,
Saying, "Arise! Do thine observance due!"
And this made Emily recall anew
The honor due to May and she arose,
Her beauties freshly clad. To speak of those,
20   Her yellow hair was braided in a tress
Behind her back, a yard in length, I guess,
And in the garden at the sun's uprising,
Hither and thither at her own devising,
She wandered gathering flowers, white and red,
25   To make a subtle garland for her head,
And like an angel sang a heavenly song.
   The great, grim tower-keep, so thick and strong,
Principal dungeon at the castle's core
Where the two knights, of whom I spoke before
30   And shall again, were shut, if you recall,
Was close-adjoining to the garden wall

---

1. **mien** (mēn): Appearance.
2. **Ere:** Before.
3. **wont:** Accustomed.
4. **sluggardry** (slug´er drē) *n.*: Laziness; idleness.

Where Emily chose her pleasures and adornings.
Bright was the sun this loveliest of mornings
And the sad prisoner Palamon had risen,
35   With license from the jailer of the prison,
As was his wont, and roamed a chamber high
Above the city, whence he could descry[5]
The noble buildings and the branching green
Where Emily the radiant and serene
40   Went pausing in her walk and roaming on.
      This sorrowful prisoner, this Palamon,
Was pacing round his chamber to and fro
Lamenting to himself in all his woe.
"Alas," he said, "that ever I was born!"
45   And so it happened on this May day morn,
Through a deep window set with many bars
Of mighty iron squared with massive spars,[6]
He chanced on Emily to cast his eye
And, as he did, he blenched[7] and gave a cry
50   As though he had been stabbed, and to the heart.
And, at the cry, Arcita gave a start
And said, "My cousin Palamon, what ails you?
How deadly pale you look! Your color fails you!
Why did you cry? Who can have given offence?
55   For God's love, take things patiently, have sense,
Think! We are prisoners and shall always be.
Fortune has given us this adversity,
Some wicked planetary dispensation.[8]
Some Saturn's trick[9] or evil constellation
60   Has given us this, and Heaven, though we had sworn
The contrary, so stood when we were born.
We must endure it, that's the long and short.
      And Palamon in answer made retort,
"Cousin, believe me, your opinion springs
65   From ignorance and vain imaginings.
Imprisonment was not what made me cry.
I have been hurt this moment through the eye,
Into my heart. It will be death to me.
The fairness of the lady that I see
70   Roaming the garden yonder to and fro
Is all the cause, and I cried out my woe.
Woman or Goddess, which? I cannot say.
I guess she may be Venus[10]—well she may!"
He fell upon his knees before the sill

---

5. descry: Catch sight of.
6. spars: Beams; poles.
7. blenched: Became pale.
8. dispensation (dis′ pən sā′ shən) *n.*: A system by which anything is administered.
9. Saturn's trick: Saturn, the Roman god of agriculture, is associated with noisy merrymaking and riotous celebration.
10. Venus: Roman goddess of love and beauty.

75	And prayed: "O Venus, if it be thy will
	To be transfigured in this garden thus
	Before two wretched prisoners like us,
	O help us to escape, O make us free!
	Yet, if my fate already is shaped for me
80	By some eternal word, and I must pine[11]
	And die in prison, have pity on our line
	And kindred, humbled under tyranny!"
	Now, as he spoke, Arcita chanced to see
	This lady as she roamed there to and fro,
85	And, at the sight, her beauty hurt him so
	That if his cousin had felt the wound before,
	Arcite was hurt as much as he, or more,
	And with a deep and piteous sigh he said:
	"The freshness of her beauty strikes me dead,
90	Hers that I see, roaming in yonder place!
	Unless I gain the mercy of her grace,
	Unless at least I see her day by day,
	I am but dead. There is no more to say."
	On hearing this young Palamon looked grim
95	And in contempt and anger answered him,
	"Do you speak this in earnest or in jest?"
	"No, in good earnest," said Arcite, "the best!
	So help me God, I mean no jesting now."
	Then Palamon began to knit his brow:
100	"It's no great honor then," he said, "to you
	To prove so false, to be a traitor too
	To me, that am your cousin and your brother,
	Both deeply sworn and bound to one another,
	Though we should die in torture for it, never
105	To loose the bond that only death can sever,
	And when in love neither to hinder other,
	Nor in what else soever, dearest brother,
	But truly further me in all I do
	As faithfully as I shall further you.
110	This was our oath and nothing can untie it,
	And well I know you dare not now deny it.
	I trust you with my secrets, make no doubt,
	Yet you would treacherously go about
	To love my lady, whom I love and serve
115	And ever shall, till death cut my heart's nerve.
	No, false Arcite! That you shall never do!
	I loved her first and told my grief to you
	As to the brother and the friend that swore
	To further me, as I have said before,
120	So you are bound in honor as a knight
	To help me, should it lie within your might;
	Else you are false, I say, your honor vain!"

---

11. pine: Waste away through grief.

Arcita proudly answered back again:
"You shall be judged as false," he said, "not me;
125   And false you are, I tell you, utterly!
I loved her as a woman before you.
What can you say? Just now you hardly knew
If she were girl or goddess from above!
Yours is a mystical, a holy love,
130   And mine is love as to a human being,
And so I told you at the moment, seeing
You were my cousin and sworn friend. At worst
What do I care? Suppose you loved her first,
Haven't you heard the old proverbial saw
135   'Who ever bound a lover by a law?'
Love is law unto itself. My hat!
What earthly man can have more law than that?
All man-made law, all positive injunction[12]
Is broken every day without compunction[13]
140   For love. A man must love, for all his wit;
There's no escape though he should die for it,
Be she a maid, a widow or a wife.
    "Yet you are little likely, all your life,
To stand in grace with her; no more shall I.
145   You know yourself, too well, that here we lie
Condemned to prison both of us, no doubt
Perpetually. No ransom buys us out.
We're like two dogs in battle on their own;
They fought all day but neither got the bone,
150   There came a kite above them, nothing loth,
And while they fought he took it from them both.
And so it is in politics, dear brother,
Each for himself alone, there is no other.
Love if you want to; I shall love her too,
155   And that is all there is to say or do.
We're prisoners and must endure it, man,
And each of us must take what chance he can."
    Great was the strife for many a long spell
Between them had I but the time to tell,
160   But to the point. It happened that one day,
To tell it you as briefly as I may,
A certain famous Duke, Perotheus,
Friend and companion of Duke Theseus
Since they were little children, came to spend
165   A holiday in Athens with his friend,
Visiting him for pleasure as of yore,
For there was no one living he loved more.
His feelings were as tenderly returned;

---

12. injunction (in juŋk´ shən) *n.*: Official command or order from a court.
13. compunction (kəm puŋk´ shən) *n.*: Uneasiness brought on by a sense of guilt.

Indeed they were so fond, as I have learned,
170   That when one died (so ancient authors tell)
The other went to seek him down in Hell;
But that's a tale I have no time to treat.
Now this Perotheus knew and loved Arcite
In Theban days of old for many years,
175   And so, at his entreaty, it appears,
Arcita was awarded his release
Without a ransom; he could go in peace
And was left free to wander where he would
On one condition, be it understood,
180   And the condition, to speak plain, went thus,
Agreed between Arcite and Theseus,
That if Arcite were ever to be found
Even for an hour, in any land or ground
Or country of Duke Theseus, day or night,
185   And he were caught, it would to both seem right
That he immediately should lose his head,
No other course or remedy instead.
        Off went Arcite upon the homeward trek.
Let him beware! For he has pawned[14] his neck.
190   What misery it cost him to depart!
He felt the stroke of death upon his heart,
He wept, he wailed. How piteously he cried
And secretly he thought of suicide.
He said, "Alas the day that gave me birth!
195   Worse than my prison is the endless earth,
Now I am doomed eternally to dwell
Not in Purgatory,[15] but in Hell.
Alas that ever I knew Perotheus!
For else I had remained with Theseus.
200   Fettered[16] in prison and without relief
I still had been in bliss and not in grief.
Only to see her whom I love and serve,
Though it were never granted to deserve
Her favor, would have been enough for me.
205   O my dear cousin Palamon," said he,
"Yours is the victory in this adventure.
How blissfully you serve your long indenture
In prison—prison? No, in Paradise!
How happily has Fortune cast her dice
210   For you! You have her presence, I the loss.
For it is possible, since your paths may cross
And you're a knight, a worthy one, and able,
That by some chance—for Fortune is unstable—
You may attain to your desire at last.

---

14. **pawned**: Staked; wagered; risked.
15. **Purgatory**: A state or place of temporary punishment.
16. **Fettered**: Shackled; chained.

215 But I, that am an exile and outcast,
Barren of grace and in such deep despair
That neither earth nor water, fire nor air,
Nor any creature that is made of these
Can ever bring me help, or do me ease,
220 I must despair and die in my distress.
Farewell my life, my joy, my happiness!
    "Alas, why is it people so dispraise
God's providence or Fortune and her ways,
That oft and variously in their scheme
225 Includes far better things than they could dream?
One man desires to have abundant wealth,
Which brings about his murder or ill-health;
Another, freed from prison as he'd willed,
Comes home, his servants catch him, and he's killed.
230 Infinite are the harms that come this way;
We little know the things for which we pray.
Our ways are drunkard ways—drunk as a mouse;
A drunkard knows quite well he has a house,
But how to get there puts him in a dither,[17]
235 And for a drunk the way is slip and slither.
Such is our world indeed, and such are we.
How eagerly we seek felicity,
Yet are so often wrong in what we try!
Yes, we can all say that, and so can I,
240 In whom the foolish notion had arisen
That if I only could escape from prison
I should be well, in pure beatitude,[18]
Whereas I am an exile from my good,
For since I may not see you, Emily,
245 I am but dead and there's no remedy."
    Now, on the other hand, poor Palamon,
When it was told him that Arcite had gone,
Fell in such grief, the tower where he was kept
Resounded to his yowling as he wept.
250 The very fetters on his mighty shins
Shine with his bitter tears as he begins,
"Alas, Arcite, dear cousin! In our dispute
And rivalry God knows you have the fruit.
I see you now in Thebes, our native city,
255 As free as air, with never a thought of pity
For me! You, an astute, determined man
Can soon assemble all our folk and clan
For war on Athens, make a sharp advance,
And by some treaty or perhaps by chance
260 She may become your lady and your wife

---

17. **dither**: A nervously excited or confused state.
18. **beatitude** (bē at´ ə tōōd´) *n.*: Perfect blessedness or happiness.

For whom, needs must, I here shall lose my life.
For, in the way of possibility,
As you're a prisoner no more, but free,
A Prince, you have the advantage to engage
265 In your affair. I perish in a cage,
For I must weep and suffer while I live
In all the anguish that a cell can give
And all the torment of my love, O care
That doubles all my suffering and despair."
270   With that he felt the fire of jealousy start,
Flame in his breast and catch him by the heart
So madly that he seemed to fade and fail,
Cold as dead ashes, or as box-wood pale.
He cried, "O cruel Gods, whose government
275 Binds all the world to your eternal bent,[19]
And writes upon an adamantine[20] table
All that your conclave[21] has decreed as stable,
What more is man to you than to behold
A flock of sheep that cower in the fold?
280 For men are slain as much as other cattle,
Arrested, thrust in prison, killed in battle,
In sickness often and mischance, and fall,
Alas, too often for no guilt at all.
Where is right rule in your foreknowledge, when
285 Such torments fall on innocent, helpless men?
Yet there is more, for added to my load,
I am to pay the duties that are owed
To God, for Him I am to curb[22] my will
In all the lusts that cattle may fulfill.
290 For when a beast is dead, he feels no pain,
But after death a man must weep again
That living has endured uncounted woe;
I have no doubt that it may well be so.
I leave the answer for divines to tell,
295 But that there's pain on earth I know too well.
    "I have seen many a serpent, many a thief
Bring down the innocent of heart to grief,
Yet be at large and take what turn they will.
But I lie languishing in prison still.
300 Juno[23] and Saturn in their jealous rage
Have almost quelled[24] our Theban lineage;
Thebes stands in waste, her walls are broken wide.
And Venus slays me on the other side
With jealous fears of what Arcite is doing.

---

19. bent: Inclination; tendency.
20. adamantine (ad´ ə man´ tin) *adj.*: (1) Unbreakable; (2) Firm; unyielding.
21. conclave: Private or secret meeting.
22. curb: Restrain; check; control.
23. Juno: Roman goddess of marriage.
24. quelled: Crushed; put an end to.

305   Now I will turn a little from pursuing
           Palamon's thoughts, and leave him in his cell,
           For I have something of Arcite to tell.
              The summer passes, and long winter nights
           Double the miseries and appetites
310   Of lover in jail and lover free as air.
           I cannot tell you which had most to bear.
           To put it shortly, Palamon the pale
           Lies there condemned to a perpetual jail,
           Chained up in fetters till his dying breath;
315   Arcita is exiled on pain of death
           For ever from the long-desired shore
           Where lives the lady he will see no more.
              You lovers, here's a question I would offer,
           Arcite or Palamon, which had most to suffer?
320   The one can see his lady day by day,
           But he must dwell in prison, locked away.
           The other's free, the world lies all before,
           But never shall he see his lady more.

☑ Check Your Comprehension

1. Where are Palamon and Emily when he first sees her?
2. Why do Palamon and his friend Arcite quarrel?
3. (a) How is Arcite freed? (b) Why does he now envy Palamon?
4. What question does the knight ask his audience at the end of this tale?

◆ Critical Thinking

1. What arguments does Arcite use to justify himself in lines 124–157? **[Interpret]**
2. In the second half of the tale, what similarities can you identify in the attitudes of Palamon and Arcite toward human destiny? **[Connect]**
3. What do you think the knight's purpose is in telling this tale? **[Speculate]**

COMPARING LITERARY WORKS

4. In what sense, if any, could the stories told by the Pardoner and the Knight be called "realistic"? Explain your answer. **[Connect]**

Geoffrey Chaucer
Comparing and Connecting the Author's Works

◆ Literary Focus: Irony

Irony involves surprising, amusing, or interesting reversals or contradictions of expectation. In **verbal irony,** words are used to suggest the opposite of their usual meaning. In **irony of situation,** an event occurs that directly contradicts expectations. In **dramatic irony,** what a character thinks contradicts what the reader or audience knows to be true.

1. Explain the verbal irony in lines 106–107 and 201–202 of the excerpt from "The Pardoner's Tale."
2. Review lines 227–228 of "The Pardoner's Tale" and lines 252–256 of "The Knight's Tale." Then explain how each passage illustrates dramatic irony.
3. Consider the outcome of both tales and describe how each exemplifies irony of situation.

◆ Drawing Conclusions About Chaucer's Work

Chaucer deliberately sets the stories in *The Canterbury Tales* in an oral framework: the narratives are told by individual storytellers to the group of pilgrims in order to pass away the time during their journey.

In a brief essay, evaluate the effectiveness of these excerpts from "The Pardoner's Tale" and "The Knight's Tale" as oral storytelling. Use criteria such as the following:

- characterization
- dialogue
- humor
- suspense
- surprise
- pace

You may also find it helpful to use the graphic organizer below when you organize main ideas and details for your essay.

Criteria	The Pardoner's Tale	The Knight's Tale
Characterization		
Dialogue		
Humor		
Suspense		
Surprise		
Pace		

◆ Idea Bank

Writing

1. **Summary** Write a prose summary of either "The Pardoner's Tale" or "The Knight's Tale." When you have finished, exchange summaries with a partner and compare your ideas about how to retell the story and what to emphasize.
2. **Analysis** In a brief essay, analyze Chaucer's use of plot, dialogue, moral, symbolism, and figurative language in either "The Pardoner's Tale" or "The Knight's Tale."
3. **A Modern Tale** Tell a pilgrim's tale that uses modern characters in a contemporary setting. Work with a small group and develop your tale to illustrate the moral, "Greed is the root of all evil." When you have finished work, present your story to the class in a Reader's Theater format. **[Group Activity]**

Speaking and Listening

4. Speeches Together with a partner, give an oral presentation of one of the following passages from "The Knight's Tale": (a) the debate between Palamon and Arcite (lines 100–157), or (b) the laments of the two characters (lines 194–245, 252–269, and 274–304). **[Performing Arts Link]**

5. Reading in Middle English Find both a printed edition and an audio recording of *The Canterbury Tales* that use the original Middle English. Listen to the recording while you follow along in the text. Pay attention to the treatment of sounds like *r* and *gh,* to groups of letters not pronounced in modern English, and to vowel sounds. Use your observations to write a report suggesting some rules for pronouncing Middle English. **[Foreign Language Link]**

6. Public Service Announcement Would the two poisoned rioters in "The Pardoner's Tale" be able to save their own lives today? Research the Poison Control Center in your community and learn about the services offered. Then prepare and read a brief public service announcement about the center. **[Health Link; Media Link]**

Researching and Representing

7. Multimedia Report Research medieval Canterbury and prepare a multimedia report on some aspect of the town. For example, you could focus on the architecture of the cathedral, its stained glass windows, or medieval music, or you could concentrate on businesses catering to pilgrims. **[Art Link; Social Studies Link]**

◆ Further Reading, Listening, and Viewing

- D. W. Robertson, Jr.: *A Preface to Chaucer* (1962). A comprehensive survey of the author's work
- R. Hart: *English Life in Chaucer's Day.* A pictorial companion to fourteenth-century England
- J. Singman and W. McLean: *Daily Life in Chaucer's England* (1995).
- Geoffrey Chaucer: *The Canterbury Tales* (1992). Unabridged audio recording
- Nigel Soul, ed.: *The Oxford Illustrated History of Medieval England* (1997).

On the Web:

http://www.phschool.com/atschool/literature
Go to the student edition of *The British Tradition.* Proceed to Unit 1. Then click Hot Links to find Web sites featuring Geoffrey Chaucer.

Edmund Spenser In Depth

"For deeds do die, however nobly done,
And thoughts of men do as themselves decay,
But wise words taught in numbers for to run,
Recorded by the Muses, live for ay."

—Edmund Spenser, **The Ruines of Time**

EDMUND SPENSER was the greatest nondramatic poet of the English Renaissance. One of the first English writers to make a professional career of poetry, Spenser was a bold innovator in his use of meter, language, and verse forms. His superb craftsmanship has earned him the nickname "a poet's poet."

Youth and Education Spenser was born into a working-class London family in 1552. He won a scholarship to attend the Merchant Taylors' School, where he received a thorough grounding in the classics. Spenser then studied at Cambridge University, where he began to form ambitious plans for a career as a professional poet.

After earning his B.A. degree, he served as secretary to the Bishop of Rochester and then to the Earl of Leicester, whose nephew was Sir Philip Sidney. Sidney's broad range of interests and accomplishments won him a reputation during his lifetime as the quintessential Renaissance man: soldier, poet, lover, and patron of the arts. Spenser dedicated his first important work, *The Shepheardes Calender*, to Sidney.

A Poet's Poet In the poems comprising *The Shepheardes Calender*, Spenser used thirteen different meters. Technical boldness characterized much of his other poetry: For example, he developed a distinctive scheme of interlocking rhymes for his sonnets, and he invented a special nine-line stanza for his epic, *The Faerie Queene*. More than two centuries later, during the Romantic period, the poets Keats, Shelley, and Byron all used the "Spenserian stanza" in major works. Spenser also deliberately mingled archaic diction with sixteenth-century language in his poetry to give his verse a distinctive, antique flavor.

The Faerie Queene In 1580, Spenser was appointed secretary to Lord Grey of Wilton and moved with his employer to Ireland. By 1582, the poet was at work on his masterpiece, *The Faerie Queene*. This was to be a national epic honoring Queen Elizabeth and the English nation. Spenser originally planned twelve books but lived to complete only the first six. The poem is an allegorical romance, in which a series of knights strive to attain the virtues of holiness, temperance, chastity, friendship, justice, and courtesy.

Late Years Spenser spent the rest of his life in Ireland. Little is known of his first marriage; in 1592, however, he met Elizabeth Boyle, and he married her two years later. It is usually assumed that Spenser composed his sonnet sequence, entitled *Amoretti*, and his graceful wedding hymn, *Epithalamion*, to commemorate his courtship of Elizabeth and their marriage.

During the late 1590's, Ireland witnessed rebellion and civil war. Spenser's castle was destroyed, and he was forced to return to England, where he died in poverty in early 1599.

◆ The English Renaissance

The word *renaissance*, which means rebirth, designates the remarkable achievements in philosophy, science, and the arts that occurred across Europe during the period 1350–1600. Beginning in Italy, the rediscovery of the languages, literature, and culture of ancient Greece and Rome sparked a great change in many people's world view, which began to focus on human potential rather than on the insignificance of humanity in the eternal scheme.

In England, the humanizing influence of classical Greek and Roman literature was most evident in the work of scholar-statesmen such as Thomas More (1478–1535), the German-born painter Hans Holbein (1497–1543), and the schoolmaster Roger Ascham (1515–1568), who served as tutor to the young Elizabeth. Sir Thomas Wyatt and his contemporary, the Earl of Surrey, courtier poets during the last decade of Henry VIII's reign, introduced the sonnet into English poetry. In 1567, Arthur Golding translated into English the *Metamorphoses* of the Roman poet Ovid, a storehouse of mythological tales that profoundly influenced Elizabethan writers, including Shakespeare. Twelve years later, in 1579, Thomas North translated Plutarch's *Lives of the Noble Greeks and Romans*, which Shakespeare used as a source for several of his history plays.

In the second half of the sixteenth century, manuals of rhetoric and dictionaries began to appear, testifying to a new awareness of the power of language. Before the Renaissance came to an end, a rich variety of literary forms had taken hold in England, including plays, brief lyrics, satires, epics, travel narratives, sermons, and religious meditations.

◆ Literary Works

The Shepheardes Calender (1579), twelve pastoral poems, one for each month of the year, whose idealized rustic setting was inspired by the ancient Roman poet Virgil

Amoretti (Little Loves) (1595), Spenser's major sonnet sequence, consisting of eighty-eight poems recounting his courtship of his second wife, Elizabeth Boyle

Epithalamion (1595), marriage hymn celebrating Spenser's wedding to Elizabeth Boyle

The Faerie Queene (1590–96), the poet's masterpiece; an unfinished allegorical epic celebrating Elizabeth's reign and the perfection of Christian virtues

Prothalamion (1596), hymn celebrating the double wedding of a nobleman's daughters

TIMELINE

Spenser's Life		World Events	
1552	Born in London	1549	Church of England issues *The Book of Common Prayer*
1561	Enters Merchant Taylors' School	1552	Sir Walter Ralegh born
1569	Enters Pembroke Hall, Cambridge	1554	Cellini completes his sculpture *Perseus* in Italy; Sir Philip Sidney born
1573	Receives B.A. degree		
1576	Receives M.A. degree		
1578	Serves as secretary to John Young, Bishop of Rochester; then employed by Robert Dudley, Earl of Leicester; meets Sir Philip Sidney, Dudley's nephew	1556	Mughal emperor Akbar the Great comes to power in India
		1557	Sonnets by Sir Thomas Wyatt and Henry Howard, Earl of Surrey, published in *Tottel's Miscellany*
1579	*The Shepheardes Calender*, dedicated to Sidney, published	1558	Accession of Elizabeth I
1580	Appointed secretary to Lord Grey; moves to Ireland	1560	Composer Thomas Tallis publishes English cathedral music
1582	Known to have started work on *The Faerie Queene*	1561	Sir Francis Bacon born
		1563	Plague in London
1588	Acquires castle of Kilcolman in County Cork, Ireland	1564	Shakespeare and Marlowe born; Galileo born; death of Michelangelo
1589	Sir Walter Ralegh visits Spenser in Ireland; Spenser returns to London for visit	1572	John Donne and Ben Jonson born; St. Bartholomew's Day massacre of Protestant Huguenots in France
1590	First three books of *The Faerie Queene* published	1576	Sir Francis Drake completes his circumnavigation of the globe
1591	Contributes poems to a volume entitled *Complaints,* including *The Ruines of Time* and *Mother Hubberds Tale*	1580	Montaigne's *Essays* published in France
		c.1582	Sidney writes his sonnet sequence, *Astrophil and Stella*
1592	Meets Elizabeth Boyle	1586	Sidney dies
1594	Marries Elizabeth Boyle	1587	Mary, Queen of Scots, executed
1595	Publishes *Amoretti* and *Epithalamion,* as well as the elegy "Astrophel," which commemorates the death of Sir Philip Sidney	1588	England defeats Spanish Armada
		1591	Sidney's sonnets published
		1593	George Herbert born; Marlowe dies
1596	Books 4–6 of *The Faerie Queene* published	1594	Shakespeare writes *Romeo and Juliet*
1598	Tyrone's Rebellion in Ireland; Spenser returns to England	1595	Ralegh explores the Orinoco River in South America
1599	Dies in London	1599	Globe Theater opens in London

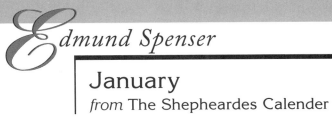

January

from The Shepheardes Calender

One of Spenser's most important early works,
The Shepheardes Calender consists of twelve
eclogues, or short pastoral poems—one written for
each month of the year. The first eclogue, January,
is a complaint by the shepherd Colin Cloute. He
complains of his unfortunate love for the country
lass Rosalind, who thinks little of Colin's affections
and even less of the music he plays to win her heart.

A Shepherd's boy (no better do him call)
When winter's wasteful[1] spite was almost spent,
All in a sunshine day, as did befall,
Led forth his flock, that had been long pent[2]

5   So faint they wax[3] and feeble in the fold,
That now unnethes[4] their feet could them uphold.

All as the Sheep such was the shepherd's look
For pale and wan he was, (alas the while)
May seem he loved, or else some care he took[5]

10   Well could he tune his pipe, and frame his style.
Then to a hill his fainting flock he led,
And thus him 'plained[6] the while his sheep there fed.

"Ye Gods of love, that pity lovers' pain,
(If any gods the pain of lovers pity)

15   Look from above, where you in joy remain,
And bow your ears unto my doleful ditty
And Pan thou shepherd's God[7] that once didst love,
Pity the pains that thou thy self didst prove.[8]

---

1. **wasteful:** Devastating.
2. **pent:** Penned.
3. **wax:** Grew.
4. **unnethes:** Scarcely.
5. **or else some care he took:** Or else he was afflicted by some sorrow.
6. **'plained:** Complained; lamented.
7. **Pan . . . God:** The Greek god of shepherds and huntsmen with the legs, horns, and ears of a goat. Pan pursued the beautiful nymph Syrinx (sir´ iŋks) who, to escape his love, was transformed into a reed.
8. **prove:** Experience.

"Thou barren ground, whom winter's wrath hath wasted,
20   Art made a mirror, to behold my plight:
Whilome⁹ thy fresh spring flowered and after hasted
Thy summer proud with daffodils dight.¹⁰
And now is come thy winter's stormy state,
Thy mantle marred wherein thou maskedst late.

25   "Such rage as winter's, reigneth in my heart,
My life blood freezing with unkindly cold:
Such stormy stoures¹¹ do breed my baleful smart
As if my year were wasted and waxen old.
And yet alas, but now my spring begun,
30   And yet alas, it is already done.

"You naked trees, whose shady leaves are lost,
Wherein the birds were wont to build their bower,
And now are clothed with moss and hoary frost,
Instead of blossoms, wherewith your buds did flower:
35   I see your tears, that from your boughs do rain,
Whose drops in dreary icicles remain.

"All so my lustful leaf is dry and sear,
My timely buds with wailing all are wasted:
The blossom which my branch of youth did bear,
40   With breathèd sighs is blown away, and blasted
And from mine eyes the drizzling tears descend,
As on your boughs the icicles depend.¹²

"Thou feeble flock, whose fleece is rough and rent,
Whose knees are weak through fast and evil fare:
45   Mayst witness well by thy ill government¹³
Thy master's mind is overcome with care.
Thou weak I wan: thou lean, I quite forlorn:
With mourning pine I, you with pining mourn.

---

9. **Whilome:** Formerly.
10. **dight:** Decked.
11. **stoures:** Tumults.
12. **depend:** Hang.
13. **by thy ill government:** By being badly cared for.

"A thousand sithes[14] I curse that careful hour,
50   Wherein I longed the neighbor town to see:
And eke[15] ten thousand sithes I bless the stoure,[16]
Wherein I saw so fair a sight, as she.
Yet all for naught: such sight hath bred my bane.
Ah God, that love should breed both joy and pain.

55   "It is not Hobbinol wherefore I 'plain,
Although my love he seek with daily suit:
His clownish gifts and courtesies I disdain,
His kids, his cracknels[17] and his early fruit.
Ah foolish Hobbinol, thy gifts be vain:
60   Colin them gives to Rosalind again.

"I love this lass (alas why do I love?)
And am forlorn (alas why am I lorn?)
She deigns not[18] my good will, but doth reprove,
And of my rural music holdeth scorn.
65   Shepherd's device she hateth as the snake,
And laughs the songs that Colin Cloute doth make.

"Wherefore my pipe although rude Pan thou please,
Yet for thou pleasest not, where most I would:
And thou unlucky Muse, that wontst to ease
70   My musing mind, yet canst not, when thou should:
Both pipe and Muse, shall sore the while abye"[19]
So broke his oaten pipe, and down did lie.

By that, the welkéd Phoebus gan avail,[20]
His weary wain,[21] and now the frosty night.
75   Her mantle black through heaven gan overhail.[22]
Which seen, the pensive boy half in despite
Arose, and homeward drove his sunnéd sheep
Whose hanging heads did seem his careful case to weep.

---

14. sithes: Times since.
15. eke: Also.
16. stoure: Moment.
17. kids . . . cracknels: The meat of a young goat, and hard crisp biscuits.
18. deigns not: Does not accept.
19. shall sore the while abye: Shall pay the penalty for that time of failure.
20. the welked Phoebus gan avail: The setting sun began to lower.
21. wain: Wagon; cart.
22. gan overhail: Began to draw over.

☑ Check Your Comprehension

1. (a) Who is the main speaker in this poem? (b) How is he described in lines 7–10?

2. In lines 13–18, whom does the speaker address?

3. How would you summarize the speaker's complaint in stanzas 4–7 (lines 19–42) of the poem?

4. In lines 65–66, how is Rosalind said to regard the speaker's songs?

5. (a) In line 72, what does the speaker do with his pipe? (b) What does he do in the poem's last stanza?

◆ Critical Thinking

1. (a) What is the setting for the poem? (b) How does Spenser use specific details of setting to emphasize the speaker's mood or emotional state? **[Interpret]**

2. Describe the stanza form that Spenser uses in "January," and identify the rhythm and rhyme scheme. **[Analyze]**

3. A paradox is an apparently contradictory statement that really expresses a truth. How does Spenser use paradox in lines 49–54? **[Interpret]**

4. Suppose that Spenser had ended the poem at line 72. What effect would the omission of the final stanza have on the overall tone of the poem, in your opinion? **[Modify]**

5. The setting and language in this poem seem very far away from contemporary life. Do you think Spenser's theme remains relevant today? Explain your answer. **[Apply]**

dmund Spenser

Sonnet 9
from Amoretti

Long while I sought to what I might compare
Those powerful eyes, which lighten my dark spright,[1]
Yet I find I naught on earth to which I dare
Resemble[2] the image of their goodly light.

5   Not to the sun: for they do shine by night;
Nor to the moon: for they are changéd never;
Nor to the stars: for they have purer sight;
Nor to the fire: for they consume not ever;
Nor to the lightning: for they still persever;[3]

10 Nor to the diamond: for they are more tender;
Nor unto crystal: for naught may them sever;[4]
Nor unto glass: such baseness might offend her;
Then to the maker self they likest be,
Whose light doth lighten[5] all that here we see.

---

1. **spright:** Spirit.
2. **Resemble:** Liken.
3. **still persever:** Always continue.
4. **sever:** Break.
5. **lighten:** Illuminate.

Edmund Spenser

Sonnet 26

from Amoretti

Sweet is the rose, but grows upon a brere;
Sweet is the juniper, but sharp his bough;
Sweet is the eglantine,[1] but pricketh near;
Sweet is the fir bloom, but his branches rough;
5   Sweet is the cypress, but his rind is tough,
Sweet is the nut, but bitter is his pill;[2]
Sweet is the broom flower, but yet sour enough;
And sweet is moly, but his root is ill.
So every sweet with sour is tempered still,[3]
10 That maketh it be coveted the more:
For easy things that may be got at will,
Most sorts of men do set but little store.
Why then should I account of little pain,
That endless pleasure shall unto me gain.

1. **eglantine:** A European rose with hooked spines.
2. **pill:** Core.
3. **still:** Always.

Sonnet 30

from Amoretti

My love is like to ice, and I to fire;
How comes it then that this her cold so great
Is not dissolved through my so hot desire,
But harder grows the more I her entreat?
5   Or how comes it that my exceeding heat
Is not delayed[1] by her heart frozen cold:
But that I burn much more in boiling sweat,
And feel my flames augmented manifold?
What more miraculous thing may be told,
10   That fire which all thing melts, should harden ice:
And ice which is congealed with senseless cold,
Should kindle fire by wonderful device?
Such is the power of love in gentle mind,
That it can alter all the course of kind.[2]

---

1. **delayed:** Quenched.
2. **kind:** Nature.

Sonnet 34

from Amoretti

Like as a ship that through the ocean wide,
By conduct of some star doth make her way,
When as a storm hath dimmed her trusty guide,
Out of her course doth wander far astray:
5   So I whose star, that wont[1] with her bright ray
Me to direct, with clouds is overcast,
Do wander now in darkness and dismay,
Through hidden perils round about me plast.[2]
Yet hope I well, that when this storm is past
10   My Helice[3] the lodestar[4] of my life
Will shine again, and look on me at last,
With lovely light to clear my cloudy grief.
Till then I wander careful comfortless,
In secret sorrow and sad pensiveness.

1. **wont:** Used to.
2. **plast:** Placed.
3. **Helice:** The name for Ursa Major, a prominent constellation.
4. **lodestar:** A star by which one directs one's course.

Sonnet 37

from Amoretti

What guile is this, that those her golden tresses
She doth attire under a net of gold:
And with sly skill so cunningly them dresses,
That which is gold or hair, may scarce be told?
5   Is it that men's frail eyes, which gaze too bold,
She may entangle in that golden snare:
And being caught may craftily enfold
Their weaker hearts, which are not well aware?
Take heed therefore, mine eyes, how ye do stare
10   Henceforth too rashly on that guileful net,
In which if ever ye entrappéd are,
Out of her bands ye by no means shall get.
Fondness¹ it were for any being free,
To covet fetters, though they golden be.

---

1. **Fondness:** Foolishness

☑ Check Your Comprehension

1. (a) What problem does the speaker confront in Sonnet 9? (b) How does he resolve this problem?
2. According to the speaker in lines 9–10 of Sonnet 26, what is the effect of tempering every "sweet with sour"?
3. What double comparison does the speaker use in line 1 of Sonnet 30?
4. What hope consoles the speaker in Sonnet 34, lines 9–12?
5. What does the speaker warn himself against in Sonnet 37, lines 9–14?

◆ Critical Thinking

1. How does Spenser use parallelism and repetition in Sonnet 9? **[Analyze]**

2. How would you express in today's English what Spenser says in the concluding couplet in Sonnet 26? **[Paraphrase]**

3. What paradox underlies the whole of Sonnet 30? **[Synthesize]**

4. (a) Analyze the rhyme scheme in Sonnet 34. **[Analyze]** (b) The technical term for one feature of this rhyme scheme is interlocking sounds. Can you identify them? **[Define]**

5. Spenser exploits a single metaphor in Sonnet 37. What is compared to what in this metaphor? **[Interpret]**

COMPARING LITERARY WORKS

6. Which is your favorite sonnet in this group, and why? **[Connect]**

# *E*dmund Spenser

The Redcross Knight and the Old Dragon
from The Faerie Queene

The hero of Book I of Spenser's epic, The Faerie Queene, *is the Redcross Knight, who represents the virtue of holiness. The knight has been commissioned by the Queen of the Fairy Land to escort the beautiful damsel Una to the kingdom of her parents and deliver them from the dragon that is terrorizing their land. With strength and courage, and Una's guidance, the knight overcomes the adversity described in the first ten cantos and arrives at the kingdom. In this excerpt, the eleventh canto and climax of Book I, the Redcross Knight engages the dragon in a three-day battle.*

1

High time now gan it wax[1] for Una fair,
To think of those her captive parents dear,
And their forewasted kingdom to repair:[2]
Whereto when as they now approachèd near,
5   With hearty words her knight she gan to cheer,
And in her modest manner thus bespake;
"Dear knight, as dear, as ever knight was dear,
That all these sorrows suffer for my sake,
High heaven behold the tedious toil, ye for me take.

2

10   "Now are we come unto my native soil
And to the place, where all our perils dwell;
Here haunts that friend, and does his daily spoil,
Therefore henceforth be at your keeping well,
And ever ready for your foeman fell.[3]
15   The spark of noble courage now awake,
And strive your excellent self to excel;
That shall ye evermore renownèd make,
Above all knights on earth, that battle undertake."

---

1. **wax:** Grow.
2. **forewasted kingdom to repair:** To restore to health their kingdom, laid waste (by the dragon).
3. **foeman fell:** Fierce enemy or foe.

3

And pointing forth, "lo, yonder is," said she,
20 "The brazen tower in which my parents dear
For dread of that huge fiend imprisoned be,
Whom I from far see on the walls appear,
Whose sight my feeble soul doth greatly cheer:
And on the top of all I do espy
25 The watchman waiting tidings glad to hear,
That O my parents might I happily
Unto you bring, to ease you of your misery."

4

With that they heard a roaring hideous sound,
That all the air with terror fillèd wide,
30 And seemed uneath⁴ to shake the steadfast ground.
Eftsoons,⁵ that dreadful dragon they espied,
Where stretched he lay upon the sunny side
Of a great hill, himself like a great hill.
But all so soon, as he from far descried
35 Those glistering arms, that heaven with light did fill,
He roused himself full blithe, and hastened them until.⁶

8

By this the dreadful beast drew nigh⁷ to hand,
Half flying, and half footing⁸ in his hast,⁹
That with his largeness measurèd much land,
40 And made wide shadow under his huge wast;¹⁰
As mountain doth the valley overcast.
Approching nigh, he rearèd high afore¹¹
His body monstrous, horrible, and vast,
Which to increase his wondrous greatness more,
45 Was swollen with wrath, and poison, and with bloody gore.

9

And over, all with brazen scales was armed,
Like plated coat of steel, so couchèd near,¹²
That naught mote¹³ pierce, might his corpse¹⁴ be harmed nor
With dint of sword, nor push of pointed spear,

---

4. **uneath:** Almost.
5. **Eftsoons:** Soon after.
6. **blithe, and hastened them until:** Joyfully, and moved swiftly toward them.
7. **nigh:** Near; close.
8. **footing:** Walking.
9. **hast:** Haste.
10. **wast:** Waist; girth.
11. **rearèd high afore:** Rose up high in front.
12. **couchèd near:** Closely laid.
13. **naught mote:** Nothing might.
14. **corpse:** A living body.

50   Which as an eagle, seeing prey appear,
          His acry plumes doth rouse, full rudely dight,[15]
          So shakèd he, that horror was to hear,
          For as the clashing of an armor bright,
          Such noise his rousèd scales did send unto the knight.

10

55   His flaggy[16] wings when forth he did display,
          Were like two sails, in which the hollow wind
          Is gathered full, and worketh speedy way:
          And eke the pennes,[17] that did his pinions bind,
          Were like main yards, with flying canvas lined,
60   With which when as him list[18] the air to beat,
          And there by force unwonted passage find,
          The clouds before him fled for terror great,
          And all the heavens stood still amazed with his threat.

11

          His huge long tail wound up in hundred folds,
65   Does overspread his long brass-scaly back,
          Whose wreathed boughts[19] whenever he unfolds,
          And thick entangled knots adown does slack,
          Bespotted as with shields of red and black,
          It sweepeth all the land behind him far,
70   And of three furlongs[20] does but little lack;
          And at the point two stings in fixèd are,
          Both deadly sharp, that sharpest steel exceedeth far.

12

          But stings and sharpest steel did far exceed,[21]
          The sharpness of his cruel rending claws;
75   Dead was it sure, as sure as death in deed,
          Whatever thing does touch his ravenous paws,
          Or what within his reach he ever draws.
          But his most hideous head my tongue to tell
          Does tremble: for his deep devouring jaws
80   Wide gaped, like the grisly mouth of hell,
          Through which into his dark abyss all raven[22] fell.

13

          And what more wondrous was, in either jaw
          Three racks of iron teeth arrangèd were,
          In which yet trickling blood and gobbets raw
85   Of late devourèd bodies did appear,

---

15. rudely dight: Ruggedly arrayed.
16. flaggy: Drooping.
17. eke the pennes: Also the quills, feathers.
18. him list: It pleased him.
19. boughts: Coils.
20. three furlongs: Three eighths of a mile.
21. did far exceed: Were far exceeded by.
22. raven: Prey

That sight thereof bred cold congealèd fear:
Which to increase, and all at once to kill,
A cloud of smothering smoke and sulfur sear[23]
Out of his stinking gorge[24] forth steamèd still,
90   That all the air about with smoke and stench did fill.

14

His blazing eyes, like two bright shining shields,
Did burn with wrath, and sparkled living fire;
As two broad beacons, set in open fields,
Send forth their flames far off to every shire,
95   And warning give, that enemies conspire,
With fire and sword the region to invade;
So flamed his eyes with rage and rancorous ire;
But far within, as in a hollow glade,
Those glaring lamps were set, that made a dreadful shade.

15

100   So dreadfully he towards him did pass,
Forelifting up aloft his speckled breast,
And often bounding on the bruisèd grass,
As for great joyance of his newcome guest.
Eftsoons he gan advance his haughty crest,
105   As chaffed[25] boar his bristles doth uprear,
And shook his scales to battle ready dressed;
That made the Redcross knight nigh quake for fear;
As bidding bold defiance to his foeman near.

16

The knight gan fairly couch[26] his steady spear,
110   And fiercely ran at him with rigorous might:
The pointed steele arriving rudely[27] there,
His harder hide would neither pierce, nor bight,[28]
But glancing by forth passèd forward right;
Yet sore amovèd with so puissant[29] push,
115   The wrathful beast about him turnèd light,[30]
And him so rudely passing by, did brush
With his long tail, that horse and man to ground did rush.

17

Both horse and man up lightly rose again,
And fresh encounter towards him addressed:
120   But the idle stroke yet back recoiled in vain,
And found no place its deadly point to rest.

---

23. **sear:** Burning.
24. **gorge:** Mouth.
25. **chaffed:** Vexed.
26. **couch:** Rest; aim.
27. **rudely:** Roughly.
28. **bight:** Bend.
29. **puissant:** Powerful; strong.
30. **light:** Quickly.

Exceeding rage inflamed the furious beast;
To be avengèd of so great despite
For never felt his impierceable breast
So wondrous force, from hand of living wight;[31]
Yet had he proved[32] the power of many a puissant knight.

125

18

Then with his waving wings displayèd wide,
Himself up high he lifted from the ground,
And with strong flight did forcibly divide
The yielding air, which nigh too feeble found
Her flitting parts, and element unsound,
To bear so great a weight: he cutting way
With his broad sails about him soarèd round:
At last low stooping with unwieldy sway,
Snatched up both horse and man, to bear them quite away.

130

135

19

Long he them bore above the subject plain,[33]
So far as yewen[34] bow a shaft may send,
Till struggling strong did him at last constrain,
To let them down before his flight's end:
As haggard hawk presuming to contend
With hearty fowl above his able might,
His weary pounces[35] all in vain doth spend,
To truss[36] the pray too heavy for his flight;
Which coming down to ground, does free itself by fight.

140

20

He so deseizèd of his gripping gross[37]
The knight his thrillant[38] spear again assayed
In his brass-plated body to emboss,[39]
And three men's strength unto the stroke he laid;
Wherewith the stiff beam quakèd, as afraid,
And glancing from his scaly neck did glide
Close under his left wing, then broad displayed.
The piercing steel there wrought a wound full wide,
That with the uncouth smart the monster loudly cried.

145

150

21

He cried, as raging seas are wont to roar,
When wintry storm his wrathful wreck does threat,
The rolling billows beat the ragged shore,
As they the earth would shoulder from her seat,

155

---

31. **wight:** Being; person.
32. **proved:** Tested.
33. **the subject plain:** The ground below.
34. **yewen:** Of yew, the wood used to make an archer's bow.
35. **pounces:** Claws.
36. **truss:** Seize.
37. **deseizèd of his gripping gross:** Freed from his formidable grip.
38. **thrillant:** Piercing.
39. **emboss:** Plunge.

And greedy gulf[40] does gape, as he would eat
His neighbor element[41] in his revenge:
160   Then gin the blustering brethren[42] boldly threat,
To move the world from off his steadfast henge,[43]
And boisterous battle make, each other to avenge.

22

The steely head stuck fast still in his flesh,
Till with his cruel claws he snatched the wood,
165   And quite asunder broke. Forth flowèd fresh
A gushing river of black gory blood,
That drownèd all the land, whereon he stood;
The stream thereof would drive a water mill.
Trebly augmented was his furious mood
170   With bitter sense of his deep rooted ill,
That flames of fire he threw forth from his large nostril.

23

His hideous tail then hurlèd he about,
And therewith all enwrapped the nimble thighs
Of his froth-foamy steed, whose courage stout
175   Striving to loose the knot, that fast him ties,
Himself in tighter bands too rash implies,[44]
That to the ground he is perforce constrained
To throw his rider: who can[45] quickly rise
From off the earth, with dirty blood bestained,
180   For that reproachful fall right foully he disdained.

24

And fiercely took his trenchant[46] blade in hand,
With which he struck so furious and so fell,
That nothing seemed the puissance could withstand:
Upon his crest the hardened iron fell,
185   But his more hardened crest was armed so well,
That deeper dint[47] therein it would not make;
Yet so extremely did the buff him quell,[48]
That from thenceforth he shunned the like to take,
But when he saw them come, he did them still forsake.

25

190   The knight was wrath to see his stroke beguiled,
And smote again with more outrageous might;
But back again the sparkling steel recoiled,
And left not any mark where it did light;

---

40. **gulf:** The sea.
41. **element:** Land.
42. **gin the blustering brethren:** Begin the winds to.
43. **henge:** Axis.
44. **too rash implies:** Too suddenly entangles.
45. **can:** Began to.
46. **trenchant:** Sharp.
47. **deeper dint:** Deeper gash.
48. **buff him quell:** Blow dismay him.

As if in adamant rock it had been pight.[49]

195   The beast impatient of his smarting wound,
And of so fierce and forcible despite,[50]
Thought with his wings to sty[51] above the ground;
But his late wounded wing unserviceable found.

26

Then full of grief and anguish vehement,
200   He loudly brayed that like was never heard,
And from his wide devouring oven sent
A flake of fire, that flashing in his beard,
Him all amazed and almost made afeared;
The scorching flame sore singèd all his face,
205   And through his armor all his body seared,
That he could not endure so cruel case,
But thought his arms to leave, and helmet to unlace.

27

Not that great champion of the antique world,[52]
Whom famous poets' verse so much doth vaunt,[53]
210   And hath for twelve huge labors high extolled,
So many furies and sharp fits did haunt,
When him the poisoned garment did enchant
With centaur's blood and bloody verses charmed,
As did this knight twelve thousand dolors[54] daunt,
215   Whom fiery steel now burnt, that erst[55] him armed,
That erst him goodly armed, now most of all him harmed.

28

Faint, weary, sore, embroilèd, grievèd, brent[56]
With heat, toil, wounds, arms, smart, and inward fire
That never man such mischiefs did torment;
220   Death better were, death did he oft desire,
But death will never come, when needs require.
Whom so dismayed when that his foe beheld,
He cast to suffer him no more respire,
But gan his sturdy stern about to weld,[57]
225   And him so strongly stuck, that to the ground him felled.

29

It fortunèd (as fair it then befell)
Behind his back unweeting[58] where he stood,
Of ancient time there was a springing well,
From which fast trickled forth a silver flood,

---

49. **pight:** Struck against.
50. **forcible despite:** Powerful injury.
51. **sty:** Climb; rise.
52. **that great . . . world:** Hercules, a mythical hero who performed twelve labors. He
died when he put on the robe of Nessus, soaked in poisoned blood, and by the will of the
gods took his place in the stars.
53. **vaunt:** Boast; brag.
54. **dolors:** Sufferings.
55. **erst:** Before.
56. **brent:** Burnt.
57. **stern about to weld:** Tail about to lash.

230   Full of great virtues, and for medicine good.
         Whylome,[59] before that cursèd dragon got
         That happy land, and all with innocent blood
         Defiled those sacred waves, it rightly hot[60]
         The Well of Life, nor yet its virtues had forgot.

30

235   For unto life the dead it could restore,
         And guilt of sinful crimes clean wash away,
         Those that with sickness were infected sore,
         It could recure, and aged long decay
         Renew, as one were born that very day.
240   Both Silo this, and Jordan did excel,
         And the English Bath, and eke the German Spa,
         Nor can Cephise, nor Hebrus match this well:
         Into the same the knight back overthrown, fell.[61]

31

         Now gan the golden Phoebus[62] for to steep
245   His fiery face in billows of the west,
         And his faint steeds watered in ocean deep,
         Whiles from their journal[63] labors they did rest,
         When that infernal monster, having kest[64]
         His weary foe into that living well,
250   Can high advance his broad discolored breast,
         Above his wonted pitch,[65] with countenance fell,[66]
         And clapped his iron wings, as victor he did dwell.

32

         Which when his pensive lady saw from far,
         Great woe and sorrow did her soul assay,[67]
255   As weening that the sad end of the war,
         And gan to highest God entirely pray,
         That fearèd chance[68] from her to turn away;
         With folded hands and knees full lowly bent
         All night she watched, nor once adown would lay
260   Her dainty limbs in her sad dreariment,
         But praying still did wake, and waking did lament.

---

58. unweeting: Unnoticed.
59. Whylome: Formerly.
60. Hot: Was called,
61. Both Silo . . . overthrown fell: All these waters, either in scripture or in classical accounts, were known for their healing powers.
62. Phoebus: The sun.
63. journal: Daily.
64. kest: Cast.
65. pitch: Height.
66. fell: Sinister.
67. assay: Attack.
68. chance: Fate.

*During the second day of battle, the Redcross
Knight is severely wounded but is still able to inflict
considerable damage to the dragon by severing one of
the beast's claws and a section of its tail. In anger
and pain, the dragon spews out flames and smoke,
the force of which pushes the Redcross Knight back.
He falls into the mire and lands at the foot of
a blessed tree, the Tree of Life. From this tree there
flows a stream of balm in which the wearied knight is
bathed through the night. At dawn, he rises, fully
healed of all his wounds, and rushes into a final con-
frontation with the dragon.*

52

Then freshly up arose the doughty knight,
All healèd of his hurts and wounds wide,
And did himself to battle ready dight;[69]
265 Whose early foe awaiting him beside
To have devoured, so soon as day he spied,
When now he saw himself so freshly rear,
As if late fight had naught him damnified,
He woke dismayed and gan his fate to fear;
270 Nathless[70] with wonted rage he him advanced near.

53

And in his first encounter, gaping wide,
He thought at once him to have swallowed quite,[71]
And rushed upon him with outrageous pride;
Who him reencountring fierce, as hawk in flight,
275 Perforce rebutted back. The weapon bright
Taking advantage of his open jaw,
Ran through his mouth with so importune[72] might,
That deep empierced his darksome hollow maw,
And back retired, his life blood forth with all did draw.

54

280 So down he fell, and forth his life did breathe,
That vanished into smoke and clouds swift;
So down he fell, that the earth him underneath
Did groan, as feeble so great load to lift,
So down he fell, as an huge rocky cliff,
285 Whose false foundation waves have washed away,
With dreadful poise[73] is from the mainland rift[74]
And rolling down great Neptune[75] doth dismay;
So down he fell, and like an heapèd mountain lay.

---

69. **dight:** Prepare.
70. **Nathless:** Nevertheless.
71. **quite:** Entirely
72. **importune:** Violent.
73. **poise:** Falling weight.
74. **rift:** Split.
75. **Neptune:** In Roman mythology, the god of the sea.

55

The knight himself even trembled at his fall,
290   So huge and horrible a mass it seemed;
And his dear Lady, that beheld it all,
Durst not approach for dread, which she misdeemed,
But yet at last, when as the direful fiend
She saw not stir off-shaking vain affright,
295   She nigher drew, and saw that joyous end:
Then God she praised, and thanked her faithful knight,
That had achieved so great a conquest by his might.

☑ Check Your Comprehension

1. At the beginning of this narrative, what does Una ask the Redcross Knight to do?
2. (a) How is the dragon described in lines 37–45? (b) At lines 82–90, what does the dragon have in its jaws?
3. After the Redcross Knight's first two attacks fail, how does the dragon go on the offensive (lines 127–135)?
4. (a) Briefly summarize the action in lines 199–242. (b) How does Una react to these events?
5. How does the Redcross Knight finally defeat the dragon?

◆ Critical Thinking

1. Describe the stanza form that Spenser uses in *The Faerie Queene* by identifying the number of lines in each stanza, the rhythm, and the rhyme scheme. **[Analyze]**

2. Is the description of the dragon realistic or fantastic, in your opinion? Explain your answer. **[Evaluate]**
3. In the simile at lines 154–162, what is being compared to what? **[Interpret]**
4. At lines 208–216, Spenser makes a long allusion to Hercules, the greatest hero of Greek mythology. Reread this passage, as well as the footnote, and then explain how the allusion also involves a paradox, or apparent contradiction. **[Analyze]**
5. (a) How does Spenser use repetition in lines 280–288? **[Analyze]** (b) At line 289, the knight is said to "tremble." What aspect of the dragon's death does this detail emphasize? **[Interpret]**
6. An allegory is a literary work with two or more levels of meaning. In an allegory, the setting, events, and characters stand for ideas or qualities. What clues does Spenser provide hinting that this battle symbolizes a cosmic clash between good and evil? **[Synthesize]**

Edmund Spenser
Comparing and Connecting the Author's Works

◆ Literary Focus: Simile

A **simile** is a figure of speech in which two dissimilar things are compared with the use of a key word such as *like*, *as*, *such*, *than*, or *resembles*. The classical and Renaissance epics that Spenser used as models for *The Faerie Queene* contain many elaborate, extended similes. In Spenser's day, such **epic similes** were considered important hallmarks of the epic. Just like invocations to the poet's Muse, universal themes, an admirable hero, and a lofty style, epic similes were standard features of the genre.

1. What similes does Spenser use to describe the dragon at lines 55–63 of *The Faerie Queene?*
2. (a) What similes does Spenser use at lines 91–99 of *The Faerie Queene?* (b) Some critics have seen an allusion in these lines to the beacons that warned the English of the approach of the Spanish Armada in 1588. How would such an allusion affect Spenser's sixteenth-century readers?
3. Spenser devotes the first eight lines, or octave, of Sonnet 34 to an extended simile. What is being compared to what in these lines?

◆ Drawing Conclusions About Spenser's Work

One way to evaluate *The Faerie Queene* is to respond to critical opinions about it. In the following passage, Elizabeth Heale quotes a phrase from Spenser's introductory letter to Sir Walter Ralegh about his purpose in the epic.

There is . . . a paradox at the heart of Spenser's project. In competition with his desire to educate the virtuous person through the poem is his . . . pessimism about the ultimate fallenness of the human condition and the inevitable failure of human virtue. Even the best-intentioned of Spenser's protagonists need miraculous aid or providential intervention to avert the mortal consequences of their own weakness or error. Even while Spenser sets out to "fashion a gentleman or noble person in vertuous and gentle discipline" . . . success is seen to depend more often on faith and providence than judgment.

Do you agree or disagree with Heale's evaluation? In a brief essay, discuss the theme of human imperfections and limitations in the passage you have read from *The Faerie Queene.* You may find it helpful to use a chart like the one below to organize your main points and supporting details.

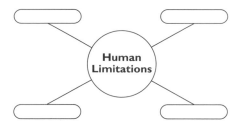

◆ Idea Bank

Writing

1. **Letter** Reread "January" from *The Shepheardes Calender.* Then write a letter that Colin Cloute might have sent Rosalind, or vice versa. You can feel free to invent imaginary incidents in their relationship, but try to make your letter faithful to Spenser's characterization.

2. **Essay** Spenser's sonnets show the speaker experiencing a wide variety of moods. For example, in Sonnet 9 the speaker seems admiring and playful, while in Sonnet 34 he appears puzzled and sorrowful. In a brief essay, compare and contrast at least two of the sonnets you have read, focusing on the speaker's emotional state. Show how imagery, figurative language, and sonnet structure combine to portray the mood of the speaker.

3. **Film Evaluation** Given all the special effects available to filmmakers today, could the battle between the Redcross Knight and the dragon in *The Faerie Queene* be filmed effectively? Write an evaluation of this passage from the epic in which you assess Spenser's "material" as the basis for a film version. **[Media Link]**

Speaking and Listening

4. **Poetry Reading** In a small group, take turns reading these sonnets from Spenser's *Amoretti* aloud, emphasizing complete ideas rather than line breaks. After each reading, invite fellow group members to comment on the oral interpretation. **[Group Activity; Performing Arts Link]**

5. **Dialogue** Using Sonnet 30 as a basis, write a dialogue between a man and a woman in which they discuss their feelings for each other. With a partner, perform your dialogue for the class. **[Performing Arts Link]**

Researching and Representing

6. **Illustration** Together with a small group, develop an illustration for either "January" or a portion of the stanzas from *The Faerie Queene*. When you have finished your work, display your illustration to the class as a whole. **[Group Activity; Art Link]**

◆ Further Reading, Listening, and Viewing

- Paul J. Alpers: *The Poetry of the Faerie Queene* (1967). An important critical study of the epic.

- Elizabeth Heale: *The Faerie Queene: A Reader's Guide* (second edition, 1999). A convenient, helpful guide to Spenser's allegory

- Penguin Audio Verse, Vol. I (the sixteenth century). Audiocassette

- J. S. Morrill: *The Oxford Illustrated History of Tudor and Stuart Britain* (1996). An illustrated companion

On the Web:

http://www.phschool.com/atschool/literature
Go to the student edition of *The British Tradition*. Proceed to Unit 2. Then, click Hot Links to find Web sites featuring Edmund Spenser.

William Shakespeare In Depth

"He was the man who of all modern, and perhaps ancient poets, had the largest and most comprehensive soul."

—John Dryden on Shakespeare

WILLIAM SHAKESPEARE is regarded as the greatest writer in English largely because of his "great-souled" insight into human nature, which John Dryden praised. The power and beauty of Shakespeare's language remain undiminished after four centuries. It might well be said of Shakespeare, as his character Enobarbus says of Cleopatra, that "age cannot wither [him], nor custom stale [his] infinite variety."

Stratford Beginnings Shakespeare was born in 1564, the eldest son of John Shakespeare, a merchant who was active in local politics. The boy probably attended the local grammar school. In 1582, when he was eighteen, he married Anne Hathaway, who was eight years older than he was. Their daughter Susanna was born in 1583, and in early 1585 they became the parents of twins: a son named Hamnet and a daughter, Judith.

Early Poetry and Plays Very little is known of Shakespeare's life during the next few years, but it seems likely that he began his career in the theater in the late 1580's in London. The first printed reference to him, attacking Shakespeare as an "upstart crow," appeared in 1592. By this time Shakespeare had written and produced several early history plays and had possibly written some of his early comedies. In 1593, he published a narrative poem, *Venus and Adonis,* based on classical mythology. This was followed the next year by *The Rape of Lucrece,* another narrative poem that retold an ancient Roman legend.

During the 1590's, Shakespeare probably wrote most of his sonnets, although these were not published until 1609. It was also during this period that Shakespeare became a leading member of the Lord Chamberlain's Men, the acting company that was to occupy the Globe Theater when that playhouse was completed in 1599.

Shakespeare's Middle Period

Although Shakespeare was an actor, producer, and theater shareholder, it is as a playwright that he is most remembered. During his middle period, he wrote many of his best-known tragedies and comedies: for example, *Julius Caesar, Hamlet, King Lear,* and *Macbeth; As You Like It, Much Ado About Nothing,* and *Twelfth Night.* In 1603, with the death of Queen Elizabeth and the accession of King James I, the new monarch became the patron of Shakespeare's company, which changed its name to the King's Men.

Last Plays and Retirement In his final plays, especially *The Winter's Tale* and *The Tempest,* Shakespeare turned to a new form: tragicomic romance. In 1611, having achieved considerable financial success in a demanding and uncertain profession, he was able to retire comfortably to Stratford, the town of his birth. He died five years later, in 1616. In 1623, two members of his company published Shakespeare's collected dramas. It was in this work, known as the First Folio, that Shakespeare's contemporary and rival Ben Jonson praised the playwright as "not of an age, but for all time."

◆ Boy Actors on Shakespeare's Stage

In Shakespeare's time, boy actors between the ages of about ten and eighteen usually played the parts of women on stage. The origins of this custom lay in the medieval roots of English drama. Beginning in the tenth century, Biblical stories were acted out in short plays or "tropes" in such English cathedrals as Winchester. The actors, who were all male, came from the ranks of the clergy.

In the sixteenth century, there were two categories of boy actors: all-boy companies such as the Children of St. Paul's Cathedral and the Children of the Chapel Royal, and young apprentices to individual actors in the adult companies. Apprentices took women's parts for several years and then transferred to men's roles.

The plots of several Shakespearean plays—including *The Merchant of Venice, Twelfth Night,* and *Cymbeline*—involve heroines in male disguise. In such cases, boys played women who disguised themselves in turn as men.

◆ Literary Works

Narrative Poems: *Venus and Adonis* (1593) and *The Rape of Lucrece* (1594)

Sonnets: 154 poems, probably written in the 1590's but not published until 1609

History Plays: *Henry VI* (Parts One, Two, and Three), *Richard III, Richard II, Henry IV* (Parts One and Two), *Henry V, King John*

Comedies: *The Taming of the Shrew, Love's Labour's Lost, The Comedy of Errors, A Midsummer Night's Dream, The Merchant of Venice, As You Like It, Twelfth Night, Measure for Measure, All's Well That Ends Well*

Tragedies: *Romeo and Juliet, Julius Caesar, Hamlet, Troilus and Cressida, Othello, King Lear, Macbeth, Antony and Cleopatra, Coriolanus*

Romances: *Pericles, Cymbeline, The Winter's Tale, The Tempest*

TIMELINE

Shakespeare's Life

1564   Shakespeare born in Stratford-on-Avon

1582   Marries Anne Hathaway in Stratford

1583   Daughter Susanna is born

1585   Twins, Hamnet and Judith, born

1590   Shakespeare probably in London as an actor

1592   First printed allusion to Shakespeare: a theatrical rival calls him "an upstart crow"; *Henry VI* performed

1593   *Venus and Adonis* published

1594   *The Rape of Lucrece* published; Lord Chamberlain's Men re-established as a company

1595   Shakespeare probably writing many of his sonnets

1596   Shakespeare's father granted a coat of arms; death of son Hamnet

1597   Shakespeare purchases New Place, a substantial house in Stratford

1599   Globe Theater completed, with Shakespeare listed as one-tenth owner; *Julius Caesar* produced

1600   Probable date for the composition of *Hamlet*

1602   Death of John Shakespeare, the playwright's father

1603   King James I becomes patron of Shakespeare's company, which changes name to the King's Men

1605   *Macbeth* produced

1607   Daughter Susanna marries a physician

1608   Shakespeare's mother dies; King's Men lease Blackfriars Theater, with Shakespeare listed as a principal shareholder

1609   *Sonnets* published

1611   *The Tempest* produced; Shakespeare retires to Stratford

1616   Death of Shakespeare

World Events

1564   Playwright Christopher Marlowe born

1567   Portuguese found Rio de Janeiro in Brazil; Red Lion playhouse opens in London

c.1572   Birth of John Donne

1576   The Theater playhouse opens in London

1580   Francis Drake completes the circumnavigation of the globe; Montaigne's *Essays* published in France

c.1582   Sir Philip Sidney writes *Astrophel and Stella* (published 1591); Gregorian calendar introduced

1586   Death of Sidney

1588   Defeat of Spanish Armada

1590   Edmund Spenser publishes *The Faerie Queene, Part 1.*

1592   Playwright Thomas Kyd publishes *The Spanish Tragedy*

1593   Death of Marlowe in a tavern brawl

1595   Spenser publishes *Amoretti* and *Epithalamion*

1599   Death of Spenser

1600   East India Company founded

1603   Death of Queen Elizabeth I and accession of King James I

1604   Marlowe's *Dr. Faustus* published

1605   Gunpowder Plot to blow up Parliament is foiled; Cervantes publishes Part 1 of *Don Quixote* in Spain

1606   First open-air opera in Rome

1607   Jamestown colony founded in Virginia

1609   Galileo builds first telescope

1611   King James Bible published

1616   Death of Cervantes; works of Ben Jonson published in the first folio edition of its kind

illiam Shakespeare

from Antony and Cleopatra
from Act II, Scene ii

The triumvirs—Mark Antony, Octavius Caesar, and Lepidus—argue about the state of affairs in Rome and finally reach agreement on their mutual threat, the renegade Roman general, Pompey. Having settled their differences for the time being, the triumvirs exit, leaving behind their officers, Enobarbus, Maecenas, and Agrippa. In the following scene, Enobarbus tells the others about Egypt, describing its luxury, the beauty of its queen, Cleopatra, and the first time Antony met Cleopatra.

MAECENAS. Welcome to Egypt, sir.

ENOBARBUS. Half the heart of Caesar, worthy Maecenas! My honorable friend, Agrippa!

AGRIPPA. Good Enobarbus!

5 **MAECENAS.** We have cause to be glad that matters are so well disgested.[1] You stayed well by it in Egypt.

ENOBARBUS. Ay, sir, we did sleep day out of countenance,[2] and made the night light with drinking.

MAECENAS. Eight wild-boars roasted whole at a break-
10 fast, and but twelve persons there; is this true?

ENOBARBUS. This was but as a fly by an eagle; we had much more monstrous matter of feast, which worthily deserved noting.

MAECENAS. She's a most triumphant[3] lady, if report
15 be square[4] to her.

ENOBARBUS. When she first met Mark Antony, she pursed up[5] his heart upon the river of Cydnus.

AGRIPPA. There she appeared indeed; or my reporter devised well for her.

20 **ENOBARBUS.** I will tell you.
The barge she sat in, like a burnished throne,

---

1. **disgested:** Arranged.
2. **sleep . . . countenance:** Mocked the day by sleeping through it.
3. **triumphant:** Splendid; magnificent.
4. **square:** Just.
5. **pursed up:** Pocketed.

Burnt on the water. The poop[6] was beaten gold,
Purple the sails, and so perfumed that
The winds were lovesick with them; the oars were silver,
25   Which to the tune of flutes kept stroke, and made
The water which they beat to follow faster,
As amorous of their strokes. For her own person,
It beggared all description: she did lie
In her pavilion—cloth of gold, of tissue—
30   O'er-picturing that Venus where we see
The fancy outwork nature.[7] On each side her
Stood pretty dimpled boys, like smiling Cupids,
With diverse-colored fans, whose wind did seem
To [glow] the delicate cheeks which they did cool,
35   And what they undid did.

AGRIPPA.   O, rare for Antony!

ENOBARBUS. Her [gentlewoman], like the Nereides,[8]
So many mermaids, tended her in the eyes,
And made their bends adornings.[9] At the helm
40   A seeming mermaid steers; the silken tackle
Swell with the touches of those flower-soft hands,
That yarely frame[10] the office. From the barge
A strange invisible perfume hits the sense
Of the adjacent wharfs. The city cast
45   Her people out upon her; and Antony
Enthroned in the market-place, did sit alone,
Whistling to the air, which, but for vacancy,[11]
Had gone to gaze on Cleopatra too,
And made a gap in nature.

50   **AGRIPPA.**   Rare Egyptian!

ENOBARBUS. Upon her landing, Antony sent to her,
Invited her to supper. She replied,
It should be better he became her guest;
Which she entreated. Our courteous Antony,
55   Whom ne'er the word of "No" woman heard speak,
Being barbered[12] ten times o'er, goes to the feast;
And for his ordinary[13] pays his heart

---

6. poop: A raised deck at the stern (rear end) of a sailing ship.
7. O'er-picturing . . . nature: Outdoing a famous picture of Venus by the Greek painter Apelles (ə pel´ ēz´) in which art was said to transcend nature.
8. Nereides (nē rē´ ə dēz´): Sea-nymphs, known for their youth and beauty.
9. made . . . adornings: Added to Cleopatra's beauty with their graceful bows.
10. yarely frame: Skillfully performed.
11. but for vacancy: Except that it would have caused a vacuum in nature.
12. barbered: Clean-cut and freshly shaved.
13. ordinary: Meal.

For what his eyes eat only. . . .

                                                I saw her once

60   Hop forty paces through the public street;

And having lost her breath, she spoke, and panted,

That she did make defect perfection,

And breathless, power[14] breathe forth.

MAECENAS.   Now Antony

65   Must leave her utterly.

ENOBARBUS.   Never, he will not:

Age cannot without her, nor custom stale

Her infinite variety. Other women cloy[15]

The appetites they feed, but she makes hungry

70   Where most she satisfies; for vildest[16] things

Become themselves[17] in her, that the holy priests

Bless her when she is riggish.[18]

MAECENAS. If beauty, wisdom, modesty, can settle

The heart of Antony, Octavia is

75   A blessed lottery[19] to him.

AGRIPPA.   Let us go.

Good Enobarbus, make yourself my guest

Whilst you abide here.

ENOBARBUS. Humbly, sir, I thank you.   *Exeunt.*

---

14. power: Charm.

15. cloy (kloĭ) *v.*: Overindulge to the point of displeasure.

16. vildest: Vilest; basest.

17. become themselves: Are becoming; suitable; appropriate.

18. riggish: Undisciplined; unrestrained.

19. lottery: Stroke of fortune.

William Shakespeare

from The Merchant of Venice
Act II, Scene viii

According to her father's will, Portia, the heroine of the play, is to marry the suitor who chooses of three caskets (gold, silver, and lead) the one containing her portrait. In the following scene, one of Portia's suitors, a Moroccan prince, evaluates the caskets, comes to a decision, and discovers his fate.

PORTIA. Go, draw aside the curtains and discover[1]
The several caskets to this noble prince.
Now make your choice.

MOROCCAN PRINCE. This first, of gold, who this
    inscription bears,
5   "Who chooseth me shall gain what many men desire";
The second, silver, which this promise carries,
"Who chooseth me shall get as much as he deserves";
This third, dull lead, with warning all as[2] blunt,
"Who chooseth me must give and hazard all he hath,"
10   How shall I know if I do choose the right?

PORTIA. The one of them contains my picture, Prince:
If you choose that, then I am yours withal.[3]

MOROCCAN PRINCE. Some god direct my judgment! Let
    me see,
I will survey the inscriptions back again.
15   What says this leaden casket?
"Who chooseth me must give and hazard all he hath."
Must give for what? for lead, hazard for lead?
This casket threatens. Men that hazard all
Do it in hope of fair advantages;
20   A golden mind stops not to shows of dross.
I'll then nor give nor hazard aught for lead.
What says the silver with her virgin hue?
"Who chooseth me shall get as much as he deserves."
As much as he deserves! pause there, Morocco,
25   And weigh thy value with an even[4] hand.
If thou beest rated by thy estimation,
Thou dost deserve enough, and yet enough

---

1. **discover:** Reveal.
2. **all as:** Equally.
3. **withal:** Immediately thereafter; thereupon.
4. **even:** Impartial.

May not extend so far as to the lady;
And yet to be afeared of my deserving
30   Were but a weak disabling[5] of myself.
As much as I deserve! why that's the lady.
I do in birth deserve her, and in fortunes,
In graces, and in qualities of breeding;
But more than these, in love I do deserve.
35   What if I strayed no farther, but chose here?
Let's see once more this saying graved in gold:
"Who chooseth me shall gain what many men desire."
Why, that's the lady, all the world desires her.
From the four corners of the earth they come
40   To kiss this shrine,[6] this mortal breathing saint.
The Hyrcanian deserts[7] and the vasty wilds
Of wide Arabia are as throughfares[8] now
For princes to come view fair Portia.
The watery kingdom, whose ambitious head
45   Spits in the face of heaven, is no bar
To stop the foreign spirits, but they come
As o'er a brook to see fair Portia.
One of these three contains her heavenly picture.
Is it like that lead contains her? 'Twere damnation
50   To think so base a thought; it were too gross
To rib[9] her cerecloth[10] in the obscure grave.
Or shall I think in silver she's immured,[11]
Being ten times undervalued to tried gold?[12]
O sinful thought! never so rich a gem
55   Was set in worse than gold. They have in England
A coin that bears the figure of an angel
Stamped in gold, but that's insculped upon;[13]
But here an angel in a golden bed
Lies all within. Deliver me the key.
60   Here do I choose, and thrive I as I may!
PORTIA. There take it, Prince, and if my form lie there,
Then I am yours. *[He unlocks the golden casket.]*
MOROCCAN PRINCE. What have we here?
A carrion Death,[14] within whose empty eye

---

5. **disabling:** Undervaluing.
6. **shrine:** Image.
7. **Hyrcanian** (hər kāʹ nē ənʹ) **deserts:** Referring to the desolate areas on the
south and southest coast of the Caspian Sea.
8. **throughfares:** Thoroughfares, ways or passages through.
9. **rib:** Enclose.
10. **cerecloth** (sirʹ klôthʹ): Shroud, used to wrap the deceased for burial.
11. **immured** (im myo͞ordʹ) *v.*: Shut up within; confined.
12. **Being . . . gold:** Which is worth only one tenth as much as.
13. **insculped upon:** Engraved on the surface.
14. **carrion Death:** A human skull or representation of.

65   There is a written scroll! I'll read the writing.

[Reads.] "All that glisters is not gold,
        Often have you heard that told;
        Many a man his life hath sold
        But my outside to behold.
70   Gilded [tombs] do worms infold.
        Had you been as wise as bold,
        Young in limbs, in judgment old,
        Your answer had not been inscrolled.[15]
        Fare you well, your suit is cold."

75   Cold indeed, and labor lost:
      Then farewell heat, and welcome frost!
      Portia, adieu. I have too grieved a heart
      To take a tedious leave; thus losers part.

                                    Exit [with his train].

PORTIA. A gentle riddance. Draw the curtains, go.
      Let all of his complexion[16] choose me so.

                                                Exeunt.

---

15. **inscrolled:** Set down here; i.e., you would have chosen differently and received a different answer.
16. **complexion:** The qualities of his nature; temperament.

☑ **Check Your Comprehension**

1. According to Enobarbus in *Antony and Cleopatra,* how did the Romans pass their time in Egypt?
2. What is the setting for Enobarbus's lavish description of Cleopatra, the Egyptian queen?
3. (a) In *The Merchant of Venice,* what are the three caskets made of? (b) What does the inscription on each casket promise?
4. Which casket does the Prince of Morocco choose, and what is the result?

◆ **Critical Thinking**

INTERPRET

1. What features of the setting and which qualities of Cleopatra does Enobarbus emphasize in his description of the queen? **[Interpret]**
2. According to Enobarbus (lines 65–70), why will Antony never leave Cleopatra? **[Interpret]**
3. What moral does the casket scene from *The Merchant of Venice* reinforce? **[Synthesize]**

COMPARING LITERARY WORKS

4. If you were a Shakespearean actor, which part would you prefer to play on stage: Enobarbus or the Prince of Morocco? Explain your answer. **[Connect]**

William Shakespeare

Sonnet 15

When I consider every thing that grows
Holds¹ in perfection but a little moment,
That this huge stage presenteth naught but shows
Whereon the stars in secret influence comment;
5   When I perceive that men as plants increase,
Cheered and checked² even by the selfsame sky,
Vaunt³ in their youthful sap, at height decrease,
And wear their brave state out of memory:
Then the conceit⁴ of this inconstant stay
10 Sets you most rich in youth before my sight,
Where wasteful Time debateth with Decay
To change your day of youth to sullied⁵ night
     And, all in war with Time for love of you,
     As he takes from you, I ingraft you new.⁶

---

1. **Holds:** Remains.
2. **Cheered and checked:** Encouraged and restrained.
3. **Vaunt:** Boasting; bragging.
4. **conceit:** Conception; idea.
5. **sullied:** Stained, tarnished.
6. **I ingraft you new:** Restore to beauty by my verse.

Sonnet 30

When to the sessions of sweet silent thought
I summon up remembrance of things past,
I sigh the lack of many a thing I sought
And with old woes new wail¹ my dear time's waste.
5   Then can I drown an eye (unused to flow)
For precious friends hid in death's dateless² night,
And weep afresh love's long since canceled woe,
And moan the expense³ of many a vanished sight.
Then can I grieve at grievances foregone,
10 And heavily from woe to woe tell o'er
The sad account of fore-bemoanèd moan,⁴
Which I new pay as if not paid before.
     But if the while I think on thee, dear friend,
     All losses are restored and sorrows end.

---

1. **wail:** To express grief or pain by long, loud cries.
2. **dateless:** Endless.
3. **expense:** Loss.
4. **fore-bemoanèd moan:** Grieving over past sorrows.

William Shakespeare

Fear No More the Heat o' the Sun

This song, from Cymbeline *(Act IV, Scene ii), is a lament for Imogen, the heroine, who is supposed to be dead.*

Fear no more the heat o' the sun,
    Nor the furious winter's rages;
Thou thy worldly task hast done,
    Home art gone, and ta'en thy wages.
5   Golden lads and girls all must,
As[1] chimney sweepers, come to dust.

Fear no more the frown o' the great;
    Thou art past the tyrant's stroke;
Care no more to clothe and eat;
10   To thee the reed is as the oak:
The scepter, learning, physic[2] must
All follow this, and come to dust.

Fear no more the lightning flash,
    Nor the all-dreaded thunder stone;[3]
15   Fear not slander, censure rash;
    Thou hast finished joy and moan:
All lovers young, all lovers must
Consign to thee, and come to dust.

No exorciser harm thee!
20   Nor no witchcraft charm thee!
Ghost unlaid forbear thee!
Nothing ill come near thee!
Quiet consummation have;
And renownèd be thy grave!

---

1. As: Like.
2. scepter, learning, physic: Kings, scholars, doctors.
3. thunder stone: At the time it was believed that the sound of thunder was caused by falling meteorites.

O Mistress Mine, Where Are You Roaming?

This song is taken from Shakespeare's comedy Twelfth Night (Act II, Scene ii). In this scene, Sir Andrew and Sir Toby request the clown to sing a song. The clown asks them if they would have a "love-song" or a "song of good life." Sir Toby answers a "love-song", and Sir Andrew agrees by saying "I care not for good life." The clown sings the following.

O mistress mine, where are you roaming?
O, stay and hear! your true love's coming,
    That can sing both high and low.
Trip no further, pretty sweeting;
5   Journeys end in lovers meeting,
      Every wise man's son, doth know.

What is love? 'tis not hereafter;
Present mirth hath present laughter;
    What's to come is still unsure:
10   In delay there lies no plenty;
Then come kiss me, sweet and twenty!
      Youth's a stuff will not endure.

☑ Check Your Comprehension

1. (a) In Sonnet 15, who debates with Time? (b) Who goes to war with Time?
2. What consoles the speaker in Sonnet 30?
3. (a) In "Fear No More the Heat of the Sun," what are five aspects of life that the deceased no longer has to worry about? (b) According to lines 17–18, what will inevitably happen to young lovers?
4. In the first stanza of "O Mistress Mine," what does the lover ask his sweetheart to do?

◆ Critical Thinking

1. (a) In Sonnet 15, what is the result of the speaker's realization that life is imperma-nent and fleeting? (b) How does the struc-ture of the sonnet—especially as it is sig-naled at the beginning of lines 1, 5, and 9—reflect the speaker's progression of thought? **[Analyze]**

2. In Sonnet 30, what kinds of disappoint-ments do you think the speaker has expe-rienced in life? **[Draw Conclusions]**

3. In the final stanza of "Fear No More the Heat of the Sun," what do the three con-cerns mentioned have in common? **[Compare and Contrast]**

4. What theme does the speaker drive home in the second stanza of "O Mistress Mine"? **[Interpret]**

William Shakespeare

Sonnet 71

No longer mourn for me when I am dead
Than you shall hear the surly sullen bell[1]
Give warning to the world that I am fled
From this vile world, with vilest worms to dwell.
5   Nay, if you read this line, remember not
The hand that writ it; for I love you so
That I in your sweet thoughts would be forgot
If thinking on me then should make you woe.
O, if, I say, you look upon this verse
10   When I, perhaps, compounded[2] am with clay,
Do not so much as my poor name rehearse,
But let your love even with my life decay,
    Lest the wise world should look into your moan
    And mock you with me after I am gone.

---

1. **surly sullen bell:** The bell tolling at a funeral service.
2. **compounded:** Mixed; combined.

Sonnet 73

That time of year thou mayst in me behold
When yellow leaves, or none, or few, do hang
Upon those boughs which shake against the cold,
Bare ruined choirs where late the sweet birds sang.
5   In me thou see'st the twilight of such day
As after sunset fadeth in the west,
Which by and by black night doth take away,
Death's second self that seals up all in rest.
In me thou see'st the glowing of such fire,
10   That on the ashes of his youth doth lie,
As the deathbed whereon it must expire,
Consumed with that which it was nourished by.[1]
    This thou perceiv'st, which makes thy love more strong.
    To love that well which thou must leave ere long.

---

1. **Consumed . . . by:** Choked by the ashes of that which fueled its flame.

William Shakespeare

Sonnet 77

Thy glass[1] will show thee how thy beauties wear,
Thy dial[2] how thy precious minutes waste.
The vacant leaves thy mind's imprint will bear,[3]
And of this book this learning mayst thou taste.
5   The wrinkles which thy glass will truly show,
Of mouthèd[4] graves will give thee memory.
Thou by thy dial's, shady stealth mayst know
Time's thievish progress to eternity.
Look, what thy memory cannot contain,
10   Commit to these waste blanks, and thou shalt find
Those children[5] nursed, delivered from thy brain,
To take a new acquaintance of thy mind.
    These offices,[6] so oft as thou wilt look,
    Shall profit thee and much enrich thy book.

1. **glass:** Mirror.
2. **dial:** The dial of a watch.
3. **The vacant . . . bear:** The blank pages on which one's thoughts will be written.
4. **mouthèd:** Opened.
5. **Children:** Thoughts.
6. **Offices:** Mirror, watch, and written thoughts.

Sonnet 128

How oft, when thou, my music, music play'st
Upon that blessèd wood[1] whose motion sounds
With thy sweet fingers when thou gently sway'st
The wiry concord that mine ear confounds,[2]
5   Do I envy those jacks[3] that nimble leap
To kiss the tender inward of thy hand,
Whilst my poor lips, which should that harvest reap,
At the wood's boldness by thee blushing stand!
To be so tickled, they would change their state
10   And situation with those dancing chips
O'er whom thy fingers walk with gentle gait,
Making dead wood more blest than living lips.
    Since saucy jacks so happy are in this,
    Give them thy fingers, me thy lips to kiss.

1. **wood:** The keys of the instrument.
2. **confounds:** Bewilders (from the harmony of the strings).
3. **jacks:** Wooden bars that pluck the strings.

☑ Check Your Comprehension

1. (a) In Sonnet 71, what does the speaker
   say should *not* be done after his death?
   (b) What does the speaker fear in lines
   13–14?
2. What comparisons does the speaker use
   for himself in the three quatrains (lines
   1–12) of Sonnet 73?
3. What two objects does the speaker refer
   to in lines 1–2 of Sonnet 77?
4. (a) In what activity is the beloved engaged
   in Sonnet 128? (b) In the concluding couplet, what does the speaker request his
   beloved to do?

◆ Critical Thinking

1. A **paradox** is a statement that seems
   contradictory but that actually presents a
truth. Why might all of Sonnet 71 be considered as an expanded paradox?
[Synthesize]

2. How does the thought in the final couplet
   (lines 13–14) of Sonnet 73 relate to the
   rest of the sonnet? **[Interpret]**
3. Many people regret old age. How do you
   think the speaker in Sonnet 73 feels about
   it? **[Apply]**
4. How are the objects the speaker mentions in the opening lines of Sonnet 77
   linked with the sonnet's overall theme?
   [Interpret]
5. Wordplay is prominent in Sonnet 128.
   Explain how the poet uses individual
   words and grammatical structures
   ingeniously in the sonnet's opening and
   closing lines. **[Analyze]**

William Shakespeare
Comparing and Connecting the Author's Works

◆ Literary Focus: Figurative Language

Writing or speech that is not meant to be interpreted literally is called **figurative language.** Some of the most common types of figurative language are listed and defined below:

- **Simile:** use of a key word such as *like* or *as* to compare two apparently dissimilar things

- **Metaphor:** a direct identification of two dissimilar things by speaking of one thing as if it were something else

- **Personification:** giving human characteristics to a nonhuman subject

- **Paradox:** a statement that seems to be contradictory but that actually presents a truth

- **Oxymoron:** a short phrase that fuses two contradictory or opposing ideas

- **Apostrophe:** direct address to an absent person or to a thing

- **Hyperbole:** deliberate exaggeration or overstatement

Choose three types of figurative language. Identify one example of each type in the selections from Shakespeare you have read. On a separate sheet of paper, copy and label the passages you have chosen.

◆ Drawing Conclusions About Shakespeare's Work

William Wordsworth wrote of Shakespeare's sonnets that "with this key Shakespeare unlocked his heart." The sonnets broke with tradition in at least two ways: Shakespeare addressed many of them to a young man rather than to an idealized lady, and the poems praising

a lady were addressed to a dark, sensuous woman, rather than to a conventionally fair, aloof mistress.

In a brief essay, analyze Shakespeare's treatment of love and friendship in the sonnets you have read in this section. You might find it helpful to use the diagram below in order to organize your main ideas and supporting points.

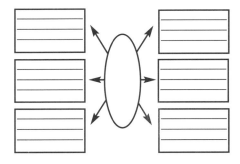

◆ Idea Bank

Writing

1. **Proverb Anthology** Many Shakespearean phrases and lines have become proverbial: for example, "All that glisters is not gold" in the casket scene of *The Merchant of Venice* (line 66). Consult a dictionary of quotations or proverbs and make a list of four Shakespearean sayings that you especially like. Share your list with a small group of classmates.

2. **Plot Summary** Write a plot summary of either *Antony and Cleopatra* or *The Merchant of Venice.* When you have finished, exchange papers with a classmate and review each other's summaries. Which play do you think you would more enjoy reading, and why?

3. **Research Paper** Consult reference works and specialized studies of Shakespeare to investigate the problems and controversies involving Shakespeare's sonnets: for example, their date of composition and the identities of "Mr. W. H.," the "Dark Lady," the young man addressed by Shakespeare in many of the poems, and a rival poet to whom Shakespeare alludes. Sum up your research in a short report.

Speaking and Listening

4. **Oral Interpretation** Rehearse an oral interpretation of *one* of the following: Enobarbus's speeches in praise of Cleopatra, the Prince of Morocco's speech in *The Merchant of Venice,* or your favorite Shakespearean sonnet. When you have polished your interpretation, present it to a small audience of friends, classmates, or family members. **[Performing Arts Link]**

5. **Song Festival** Research three of the more than 100 songs that Shakespeare included in his plays. Try to locate recordings of musical settings for these songs. You might also investigate one musical composition of the Elizabethan composer Thomas Morley (c.1557–1602), who set "O Mistress Mine" and other Shakespearean songs to music and was probably a friend of the playwright. Bring a recording to school and play it for your classmates. **[Music Link]**

Researching and Representing

6. **Illustrated Report** Using Internet and library resources, work with a small group to investigate the reconstruction of the Globe Theatre in London, which opened in 1996. Present the results of your research in an illustrated report to the class. **[Group Activity; Performing Arts Link]**

◆ Further Reading, Listening, and Viewing

- S. Schoenbaum: *William Shakespeare: A Documentary Life* (1975). An authoritative reference work on the many mysteries and puzzles of Shakespeare's life

- Helen Vendler: *The Art of Shakespeare's Sonnets* (1997). Brilliant analyses of all 154 poems

- Andrew Gurr: *Playgoing in Shakespeare's London* (1987). Focuses on theaters and audiences

- Barry Day: *This Wooden "O": Shakespeare's Globe Reborn* (1998)

- William Shakespeare: *The Sonnets* (1990). Readings on audiocassette

- William Shakespeare: *Hamlet* (1997). The Kenneth Branagh production

On the Web:

http://www.phschool.com/atschool/literature
Go to the student edition of *The British Tradition.* Proceed to Unit 2. Then, click Hot Links to find Web sites featuring William Shakespeare.

John Donne In Depth

> "No man is an island, entire of itself; every man is a piece of the continent, a part of the main."
>
> —*John Donne*, Meditation 17

JOHN DONNE was known in his time primarily as a preacher rather than as a poet. Today, however, Donne is considered the most important of the Metaphysical poets and one of the finest writers of the early seventeenth century.

Origins and Education John Donne was born in 1572 into a prosperous London family of Roman Catholics and was educated by tutors at home. Although Donne studied at Oxford, the anti-Catholic feeling of the time prevented him from taking a degree. In the period 1589–91 Donne traveled to continental Europe, and in 1592 he was admitted as a law student in London. In the mid-1590's, Donne joined two expeditions as a gentleman-adventurer: the first to Spain with the Earl of Essex, and the second to the Azores with Sir Walter Ralegh to hunt for Spanish treasure ships.

Gallant, witty, and charming, Donne overcame anti-Catholic prejudice for a while and made important connections at court. In 1597, he secured an appointment as secretary to Sir Thomas Egerton, Lord Keeper of the Great Seal and one of the most powerful courtiers. When Donne fell in love with Egerton's niece Ann More and secretly married her in 1601, however, he was dismissed from his post and briefly imprisoned.

A Troubled Period Donne's secret marriage negatively affected his fortunes for over a decade. Depressed and anxious, he tried to recover from his disgrace. At first, he depended on the charity of friends to support his family but

later he was able to rely on his literary talents. He published several attacks on Catholicism in 1610–11, publicly signaling that he had renounced the Catholic faith. In 1615, when Donne finally agreed to convert to Anglicanism and take orders as a priest, no less a patron than King James I made him a chaplain and forced Cambridge University to grant him a doctoral degree. In 1621, Donne gained the coveted position of Dean of St. Paul's, one of the most important posts in the entire Anglican hierarchy.

Mature Years In his new post, Donne won acclaim as a preacher, addressing large congregations of powerful and wealthy courtiers and merchants. Although his sermons were published, his poems circulated mainly in handwritten copies, since their subject matter might have damaged Donne's reputation as an upright clergyman.

In both his poems and his sermons, Donne used a tight, challenging style that relied on unique rhythms and unusual, sustained metaphors called conceits. Such comparisons are one of the hallmarks of English Metaphysical poetry, a genre that was not formally labeled until the eighteenth century. Besides Donne, the Metaphysical poets included such writers as Richard Crashaw, George Herbert, Andrew Marvell, and Henry Vaughan. The word Metaphysical, which simply means "beyond the physical," refers to the frequent preoccupation in these writers' work with the death of the body and the eternity of the soul. Characteristics of Metaphysical poetry include intellectual playfulness, irony, paradoxes, argument, colloquial speech rhythms, and elaborate and unusual conceits.

Donne died in 1631. Two years later, his son John edited his father's poems and published them in a collected edition. Over the next few decades, three volumes of Donne's collected sermons appeared.

◆ The Expansion of Science in the Early Seventeenth Century

The rapid development of science in the early seventeenth century had an important impact on the Metaphysical poets and their world view. In 1609, the astronomer and mathematician Galileo Galilei (1564–1642) built the first telescope in Italy. Galileo used his invention to discover the four largest moons of Jupiter, as well as the stellar composition of the Milky Way. In 1618, the German astronomer Johannes Kepler (1561–1630) proposed his laws of planetary motion, thus greatly expanding people's knowledge of the solar system.

In England, the philosopher-statesmen Francis Bacon (1561–1626) published his treatise *Novum Organum (New Instrument)* in 1620, outlining his views on scientific inquiry and promoting inductive reasoning as a method of logic. In 1627, Bacon published *The New Atlantis*, an account of an imaginary, utopian island where collective scientific research results in social progress. In 1628, Bacon's younger contemporary William Harvey (1578–1657), changed the course of medicine when he published his explanation of the circulation of the blood.

◆ Literary Works

Poetry Donne's collected poems, edited by his son, were not published until 1633, the year after his death. Much of his poetry, however, is thought to have been circulated in handwritten copies during Donne's lifetime. A brief outline of Donne's verse follows:

Satires and Elegies (1590's)

The Progress of the Soul (1601): a satirical epic

Holy Sonnets (c.1610–11)

Anniversaries (1611–12): poems lamenting the death of Elizabeth Drury, daughter of one of the poet's important patrons

Prose By far the most popular of Donne's works during his lifetime were his sermons. Donne also wrote several religious polemics attacking Catholicism.

Pseudo-Martyr (1610): an attack on Catholics who had died for their faith

Ignatius His Conclave (1611): an attack on the Jesuits

Devotions (1624): meditations by Donne while he was ill from a near-fatal fever

Sermons: three collections were published posthumously, in 1640, 1649, and 1660

TIMELINE

Donne's Life		World Events	
1572	Born in London	1576	The Theater playhouse opens in London
1576	Death of Donne's father		
1584	Enters Hart Hall, Oxford	1580	Francis Drake completes the circumnavigation of the globe; Montaigne's *Essays* published in France
1589	Travels in Europe		
1592	Studies law in London		
1593	Death of brother Henry in Newgate Prison	1582	Gregorian calendar introduced
		1587	Execution of Mary, Queen of Scots
1596–97	Expeditions to Spain and the Azores		
1597	Becomes secretary to Sir Thomas Egerton	1588	Defeat of Spanish Armada
		1599	Globe Theater opens
1601	Secret marriage to Ann More; is dismissed from his post in Egerton's service	1603	Death of Elizabeth I; James I becomes king
		1605	Gunpowder Plot foiled; Shakespeare's *Macbeth* performed
1602	Donne is briefly imprisoned		
1610	Publishes *Pseudo-Martyr*, a religious polemic	1607	Jamestown colony in Virginia
		1608	Birth of John Milton
1611–12	Publishes *Ignatius His Conclave* and *Anniversaries*	1609	Galileo builds first telescope; Shakespeare's sonnets published
1615	Ordination as an Anglican priest	1611	King James Bible
1617	Death of Donne's wife	1616	Death of Shakespeare
1621	Becomes Dean of St. Paul's	1618	Kepler's laws of planetary motion
1622	First sermons published	1620	Francis Bacon's *Novum Organum*; Pilgrims land at Plymouth, Massachusetts
1624	Publishes *Devotions*		
1631	Death of Donne		
1633	First edition of collected poems published	1627	Bacon, *The New Atlantic*
		1628	William Harvey explains the circulation of the blood
1640	Izaak Walton's *Life of Donne* published		

John Donne

A Fever

Oh do not die, for I shall hate
    All women so, when thou art gone,
That thee I shall not celebrate,
    When I remember, thou wast one.

5   But yet thou canst not die, I know,
    To leave this world behind, is death,
But when thou from this world wilt go,
    The whole world vapors[3] with thy breath.

Or if, when thou, the world's soul, go'st
10   It stay, 'tis but thy carcass then,
The fairest woman, but thy ghost,
    But corrupt worms, the worthiest men.

Oh wrangling schools, that search what fire
    Shall burn this world, bad none the wit
15   Unto this knowledge to aspire,
    That this her fever might be it?

And yet she cannot waste by this,
    Nor long bear this torturing wrong,
For much corruption needful is
20   To fuel such a fever long.

These burning fits but meteors be,
    Whose matter in thee is soon spent.
Thy beauty, and all parts, which are thee,
    Are unchangeable firmament.[2]

25   Yet 'twas of my mind, seizing thee,
    Though it in thee cannot perséver.[3]
For I had rather owner be
    Of thee one hour, than all else ever.

---

1. vapors: (1) Evaporates; (2) Becomes worthless.
2. firmament (fʉrm´ ə mənt) *n*.: The sky, viewed poetically as a solid , unchangeable, arched roof.
3. perséver: Persevere.

John Donne

The Bait

*This poem is Donne's response to Christopher
Marlowe's "The Passionate Shepherd to His Love."*

Come live with me, and be my love,
And we will some new pleasures prove[1]
Of golden sands, and crystal brooks,
With silken lines, and silver hooks.

5   There will the river whispering run
Warmed by thy eyes, more than the sun.
And there the enamored fish will stay,
Begging themselves they may betray.

When thou wilt swim in that live bath,
10   Each fish, which every channel hath,
Will amorously[2] to thee swim,
Gladder to catch thee, than thou him.

If thou, to be so seen, be'st loth,
By sun, or moon, thou darkenest both,
15   And if myself have leave to see,
I need not their light, having thee.

Let others freeze with angling reeds,
And cut their legs, with shells and weeds,
Or treacherously poor fish beset,[3]
20   With strangling snare, or windowy net:

Let coarse bold hands, from slimy nest
The bedded fish in banks out-wrest,
Or curious traitors, sleavesilk flies[4]
Bewitch poor fishes' wandering eyes.

25   For thee, thou need'st no such deceit,
For thou thyself art thine own bait,
That fish, that is not catched thereby,
Alas, is wiser far than I.

---

1. **prove:** Try, experiment.
2. **amorously** (am´ ə res´ lē) *adv*.: Lovingly.
3. **beset:** To attack from all sides.
4. **sleavesilk flies:** Artificial flies made out of the threads of unraveled silk.

A Lecture upon the Shadow

Stand still, and I will read to thee
A lecture, love, in love's philosophy.
    These three hours that we have spent,
    Walking here, two shadows went
5   Along with us, which we ourselves produced;
But, now the sun is just above our head,
    We do those shadows tread;
    And to brave clearness all things are reduced.
    So whilst our infant loves did grow,
10   Disguises did, and shadows, flow,
    From us, and our care; but, now 'tis not so.

That love hath not attained the high'st degree,
Which is still diligent lest others see.

Except our loves at this noon stay,
15   We shall new shadows make the other way.
    As the first were made to blind
    Others; these which come behind
Will work upon ourselves, and blind our eyes.
If our loves faint, and westwardly decline;
20   To me thou, falsely, thine,
    And I to thee mine actions shall disguise.[1]
    The morning shadows wear away,
    But these grow longer all the day,
    But oh, love's day is short, if love decay.

25   Love is a growing, or full constant light;
And his first minute, after noon, is night.

---

1. To me thou, falsely thine, / shall disguise: You will falsely disguise your actions from me, and I will falsely disguise my actions from you.

ohn Donne

Holy Sonnet 14

Batter my heart, three-personed God;[1] for You
As yet but knock, breathe, shine, and seek to mend;
That I may rise, and stand, o'erthrow me, and bend
Your force to break, blow, burn and make me new.
5   I, like an usurped town, to another due,
     Labor to admit You, but O, to no end,
Reason Your viceroy[2] in me, me should defend,
But is captived, and proves weak or untrue.
Yet dearly I love You, and would be loved fain,
10   But am betrothed unto Your enemy.
Divorce me, untie, or break that knot again;
Take me to You, imprison me, for I,
Except You enthral[3] me, never shall be free,
Nor ever chaste, except You ravish me.

---

1. **three-personed God:** The Trinity: the Father, the Son, and the Holy Ghost.
2. **viceroy:** Deputy.
3. **enthral:** Enslave.

☑ Check Your Comprehension

1. (a) Who is ill in "A Fever"? (b) In lines 27–28, what does the speaker say he would prefer?
2. What setting does the speaker describe in "The Bait"?
3. In line 25 of "A Lecture upon the Shadow," to what does the speaker compare love?
4. (a) In lines 1–4 of Holy Sonnet 14, what does the speaker want God to do? (b) Why?
5. How is reason characterized in lines 7–8 of the sonnet?

◆ Critical Thinking

1. Explain the speaker's argument in lines 5–8 of "A Fever." What is his claim, and what logic does he use to support it? **[Analyze]**
2. A **conceit** is an unexpected, elaborate metaphor or comparison. What is the central conceit of "The Bait"? **[Interpret]**
3. Is the word *lecture* an appropriate description for Donne's poem on the shadow? Explain why or why not. **[Evaluate]**
4. (a) In Holy Sonnet 14, what simile does the poet use in lines 5–6? (b) How might you link this comparison to the metaphor in line 1? **[Connect]**
5. In Holy Sonnet 14, the speaker wants to be overwhelmed with emotion. What are some of the instances when a person might want to experience a deep emotion? **[Apply]**

The Good Morrow

I wonder by my troth, what thou, and I
    Did, till we loved? were we not weaned till then,
But sucked on country pleasures, childishly?
    Or snorted we in the seven sleepers' den?[1]
5   'Twas so; but this,[2] all pleasures fancies be.
If ever any beauty I did see,
Which I desired, and got, 'twas but a dream of thee.

And now good morrow to our waking souls,
    Which watch not one another out of fear;
10   For love, all love of other sights controls,
    And makes one little room, an everywhere.
Let sea-discoverers to new worlds have gone,
Let maps to others, worlds on worlds have shown,[3]
Let us possess one world, each hath one, and is one.

15   My face in thine eye, thine in mine appears,
    And true plain hearts do in the faces rest,
Where can we find two better hemispheres
    Without sharp north, without declining west?[4]
Whatever dies, was not mixed equally;[5]
20   If our two loves be one, or, thou and I
Love so alike, that none do slacken, none can die.

---

1. seven sleepers' den: The legend in which the seven youths of Ephesus
(ef´ i səs) fleeing from their persecutors, slept in a cave for nearly two centuries.
2. but this: Except for this.
3. Let maps . . . have shown: Maps charting the skies and showing people
new "worlds."
4. Without sharp . . . declining west: Evil and death, respectively.
5. Whatever dies . . . mixed equally: Elements that were mixed imperfectly
were changeable and mortal, but when they were mixed perfectly, they were
unchanging and permanent.

John Donne

The Sun Rising

Busy old fool, unruly sun,
    Why dost thou thus,
Through windows, and through curtains call on us?
Must to thy motions lovers' seasons run?
5   Saucy pedantic wretch, go chide
            Late schoolboys, and sour prentices
        Go tell courthuntsmen, that the King will ride,
        Call country ants to harvest offices;[1]
Love, all alike, no season knows, nor clime,
10   Nor hours, days, months, which are the rags of time.

Thy beams, so reverend, and strong
    Why shouldst thou think?
I could eclipse and cloud them with a wink,
But that I would not lose her sight so long:
15   If her eyes have not blinded thine,
            Look, and tomorrow late, tell me,
        Whether both th' Indias of spice and mine[2]
        Be where thou left'st them, or lie here with me.
Ask for those kings whom thou saw'st yesterday,
20   And thou shalt hear, All here in one bed lay.

She is all states,[3] and all princes, I,
    Nothing else is.
Princes do but play us; compared to this,
All honor's mimic; all wealth alchemy.[4]
25   Thou sun art half as happy as we,
            In that the world's contracted thus;
        Thine age asks ease, and since thy duties be
        To warm the world, that's done in warming us.
Shine here to us, and thou art everywhere;
30   This bed thy center is, these walls, thy sphere[5].

---

1. harvest offices: Autumn chores.
2. both th' . . . and mine: The East and West Indies; one region is famous
for its spice, and the other for gold.
3. all states: All the nations of the world.
4. alchemy (al´ kə mē): The method of seemingly changing one thing into
something better; hence, fraudulent or deceitful.
5. This bed . . . thy sphere: The bed is the earth around which the sun
revolves, and the walls mark the limits of its revolution.

Lovers' Infiniteness

If yet I have not all thy love,
Dear, I shall never have it all,
I cannot breathe one other sigh, to move,
Nor can entreat one other tear to fall.
5   All my treasure, which should purchase thee,
Sighs, tears, and oaths, and letters I have spent,
Yet no more can be due to me,
Than at the bargain made was meant.
If then thy gift of love were partial,
10   That some to me, some should to others fall,
       Dear, I shall never have thee all.

Or if then thou gavest me all,
All was but all, which thou hadst then;
But if in thy heart, since, there be or shall
15   New love created be, by other men,
Which have their stocks[1] entire, and can in tears,
In sighs, in oaths, and letters outbid me,
This new love may beget new fears,
For, this love was not vowed by thee.
20   And yet it was, thy gift being general,
The ground,[2] thy heart is mine; whatever shall
       Grow there, dear, I should have it all.

Yet I would not have all yet,
25   He that hath all can have no more,
And since my love doth every day admit
New growth, thou shouldst have new rewards in store;
Thou canst not every day give me thy heart,
If thou canst give it, then thou never gav'st it;
Love's riddles are, that though thy heart depart,
30   It stays at home, and thou with losing sav'st it:
But we will have a way more liberal,
Than changing hearts, to join them, so we shall
       Be one, and one another's all.

---

1. stocks: Wealth; assets.
2. ground: Legally, in the sale of land, the crops growing on the land belonged to the new owner.

☑ Check Your Comprehension

1. In lines 1–4 of "The Good Morrow," what does the speaker imagine about himself and his beloved in the time before they loved each other?
2. What does the speaker claim about his love in lines 19–21?
3. Why does the speaker scold the sun in the first stanza of "The Sun Rising"?
4. (a) To whom is "Lovers' Infiniteness" addressed? (b) What does the speaker predict in the final three lines of this poem?
5. Identify the unusual stanza form and rhyme scheme in "Lovers' Infiniteness."

◆ Critical Thinking

1. What aspect of love does the speaker stress in the second stanza of "The Good Morrow"? **[Interpret]**

2. Two notable features of Donne's poetry are irregular rhythm and highly compressed phrasing. Identify one or two examples of each of these features in "The Sun Rising," and explain each of your choices. **[Analyze]**

3. **Hyperbole** is deliberate exaggeration or overstatement for effect. How does Donne use hyperbole in the third stanza of "The Sun Rising"? **[Analyze]**

4. A **paradox** is a statement that seems to be contradictory but that actually presents a truth. Explain the paradox in lines 23–26 of "Lovers' Infiniteness." **[Analyze]**

COMPARING LITERARY WORKS

5. These three poems are all about love, but they have quite different tones. Compare and contrast the speakers' tone in these poems. **[Connect]**

John Donne

Song

Go, and catch a falling star,
   Get with child a mandrake root,[1]
Tell me, where all past years are,
   Or who cleft[2] the Devil's foot,
5   Teach me to hear mermaids[3] singing,
   Or to keep off envy's stinging,
     And find
     What wind
Serves to advance an honest mind.

10   If thou be'est born to strange sights,
   Things invisible to see,
Ride ten thousand days and nights,
   Till age snow white hairs on thee,
Thou, when thou return'st, wilt tell me
15   All strange wonders that befell thee,
     And swear
     No where
Lives a woman true, and fair.

If thou find'st one, let me know,
20   Such a pilgrimage were sweet,
Yet do not, I would not go
   Though at next door we might meet,
Though she were true, when you met her,
And last, till you write your letter,
25   Yet she
     Will be
False, ere I come, to two, or three.

---

1. mandrake root: A plant whose forked root is said to have magical qualities because of its resemblance to the human shape.
2. cleft: Split.
3. mermaids: Sea nymphs whose singing lured sailors to crash their ships on rocks.

John Donne

Elegy 10, The Dream

Image of her whom I love, more than she,
    Whose fair impression in my faithful heart,
Makes me her medal,[1] and makes her love me,
    As kings do coins, to which their stamps impart
5   The value: go, and take my heart from hence,
    Which now is grown too great and good for me:
Honors oppress weak spirits, and our sense
    Strong objects dull; the more, the less we see.[2]

When you are gone, and reason gone with you,
10   Then fantasy is queen and soul, and all,
She can present joys meaner[3] than you do;
    Convenient, and more proportional.[4]

So, if I dream I have you, I have you,
    For, all our joys are but fantastical.
15   And so I 'scape the pain, for pain is true;
    And sleep which locks up sense, doth lock out all.
After a such fruition[5] I shall wake,[5]
    And, but the waking, nothing shall repent;
And shall to love more thankful sonnets make,
20   Than if more honor, tears, and pains were spent.

But dearest heart, and dearer image stay;
    Alas, true joys at best are dream enough;
Though you stay here you pass too fast away:
    For even at first life's taper is a snuff.[6]

25   Filled with her love, may I be rather grown
    Mad with much heart, than idiot[7] with none.

---

1. medal: Coin worn as a charm.
2. the more, the less we see: The stronger the impact on our senses, the less we can distinguish an object.
3. meaner: More common.
4. Convenient: More fitting, suitable, appropriate.
5. fruition (frōō ish´ ən) *n.:* Enjoyment.
6. life's taper . . . snuff: Life's candle is a burned wick.
7. Idiot: Without reason.

Meditation 15

Interea insomnes noctes ego duco, Diesque.
(I sleep not day or night.)

Natural men have conceived a twofold use of sleep; that it is a refreshing of the body in this life; that it is a preparing of the soul for the next; that it is a feast, and it is the grace at that feast; that it is our recreation and cheers us, and it is our catechism[1] and instructs us; we lie down in a hope that we shall rise the stronger, and we lie down in a knowledge that we may rise no more. Sleep is an opiate which gives us rest, but such an opiate, as perchance, being under it, we shall wake no more. But though natural men, who have induced secondary and figurative considerations, have found out this second, this emblematical use of sleep, that it should be a representation of death, God, who wrought and perfected his work before nature began (for nature was but his apprentice, to learn in the first seven days, and now is his foreman, and works next under him), God, I say, intended sleep only for the refreshing of man by bodily rest, and not for a figure of death, for he intended not death itself then. But man having induced death upon himself, God hath taken man's creature, death, into his hand, and mended it; and whereas it hath in itself a fearful form and aspect, so that man is afraid of his own creature, God presents it to him in a familiar, in an assiduous,[2] in an agreeable and acceptable form, in sleep; that so when he awakes from sleep, and says to himself, " Shall I be no otherwise when I am dead, than I was even now when I was asleep? " he may be ashamed of his waking dreams, and of his melancholy fancying out a horrid and an affrightful figure of that death which is so like sleep. As then we need sleep to live put our threescore and ten

---

1. catechism (kat´ ə kiz´ əm) n.: A handbook of questions and answers for teaching the principles of a religion.
2. assiduous (ə sij´ o͞o əs) adj.: Done with constant and careful attention.

years,[3] so we need death to live that life which we cannot outlive. And as death being our enemy, God allows us to defend ourselves against it (for we victual[4] ourselves against death twice of every day) often as we eat, so God having so sweetened death unto us as he hath in sleep, we put ourselves into our enemy's hands once every day, so far as sleep is death; and sleep is as much death as meat is life. This then is the misery of my sickness, that death, as it is produced from me and is mine own creature, is now before mine eyes, but in that form in which God hath mollified it to us, and made it acceptable, in sleep I cannot see it. How many prisoners, who have even hollowed themselves their graves upon that earth on which they have lain long under heavy fetters, yet at this hour are asleep, though they be yet working upon their own graves by their own weight? He that hath seen his friend die today, or knows he shall see it tomorrow, yet will sink into a sleep between. I cannot, and oh, if I be entering now into eternity, where there shall be no more distinction of hours, why is it all my business now to tell clocks? Why is none of the heaviness of my heart dispensed into mine eye-lids, that they might fall as my heart doth? And why, since I have lost my delight in all objects, cannot I discontinue the faculty of seeing them by closing mine eyes in sleep? But why rather, being entering into that presence where I shall wake continually and never sleep more, do I not interpret my continual waking here, to be a parasceve[5] and a preparation to that?

---

3. Threescore and ten years: Seventy years.
4. victual (vit´ əl) v.: To eat or feed.
5. parasceve (par´ ə sēv) n.: The day of preparation for an important feast, often religious.

☑ Check Your Comprehension

1. What impossible tasks does the speaker mention in lines 1–4 of "Song"?

2. In the last stanza of "Song," what does the speaker predict about a "true" woman's loyalty?

3. According to the speaker in lines 15–16 of "Elegy 10, The Dream," what benefit does sleep bring?

4. What two uses of sleep are mentioned at the beginning of Meditation 15?

◆ Critical Thinking

1. What seems to be the speaker's attitude toward human relationships in "Song"? **[Synthesize]**

2. Explain the metaphor in lines 1–5 of "Elegy 10, The Dream." **[Analyze]**

3. How do lines 13–14 of "Elegy 10, The Dream" sum up the paradoxical nature of dreaming in the poem as a whole? **[Interpret]**

4. According to "Meditation 15," how has God arranged a beneficial connection between sleep and death for human beings? **[Analyze]**

John Donne
Comparing and Connecting the Author's Works

◆ Literary Focus: Paradox

A *paradox* is a statement that appears to be contradictory but that actually presents a hidden truth. Because a paradox is surprising or even shocking, it draws the reader's attention to what is being said. Paradox is especially common in the poetry of Donne and other English Metaphysical poets of the seventeenth century such as George Herbert, Henry Vaughan, and Andrew Marvell. Their use of this device also influenced Edward Taylor (c.1642–1729), one of the earliest American poets.

Reread the selections and identify one example of paradox from one of the following poems:

"A Fever"
"The Bait"
"A Lecture upon the Shadow"
"The Good Morrow"
"The Sun Rising"

Explain how the paradox in the poem you choose reveals a hidden truth.

◆ Drawing Conclusions About Donne's Work

One way to evaluate literature is to respond to a critical opinion. Read the following appraisal of Donne by the critic Richard Strier:

Perhaps the first thing to say about John Donne is that he was not a professional poet. He was, however, a professional intellectual. Writing poetry, for him, was not merely . . . a gentlemanly accomplishment and recreation. It was a way for Donne to show his wit, his skill, his learning, his rhetorical command. . . . From the beginning of his poetic career, Donne was writing a kind of antipoetry.

Strier explains his description of Donne's work as "antipoetry" by singling

out three of Donne's characteristic techniques:

• bold, colloquial address
• metrical roughness
• striking phrases

In a brief essay, respond to Strier's comments on Donne's poetry. Do you agree or disagree with this critic's assessment of Donne's work? What are the specific reasons for your opinion? You might find it helpful to use the diagram below to organize your main ideas and supporting points.

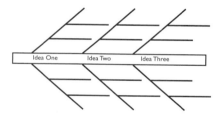

Idea One   Idea Two   Idea Three

◆ Idea Bank

Writing

1. **Paraphrase** A paraphrase is a restatement in your own words of the key ideas in a passage. Choose any of the poems in this group and paraphrase it in prose. When you have finished writing, exchange your paper with a classmate and discuss each other's work.

2. **Diary Entry** Write a diary entry in which you describe and explain the thoughts and feelings that one of Donne's works inspired in you. You might use the form and style of "Meditation 15" as a model for your diary entry.

3. **Poem** Consult a dictionary of quotations or an anthology of proverbs in order to find a paradoxical statement that you think is especially memorable. Then write a free-verse poem in which you expand or elaborate on this paradox. When you have finished work, read your poem aloud to a small audience of classmates, friends, or family members.

Speaking and Listening

4. **Oral Interpretation** Rehearse an oral interpretation of one of the poems in this group. Focus on elements such as pace, volume, pitch, and emphasis. When you have polished your performance, present your interpretation to a small audience. **[Performing Arts Link]**

5. **Oral Report** Research the life and career of one of the scientists mentioned on page 3, or select another seventeenth-century scientist: for example, Robert Boyle, Antony van Leeuwenhoek, or Sir Isaac Newton. Sum up your results in an illustrated oral report to the class as a whole. **[Science Link]**

Researching and Representing

6. **Tourist Brochure** Join with a small group to research and develop a tourist brochure of London. Be sure to include St. Paul's Cathedral, the church where John Donne served as Dean from 1621 until his death ten years later. **[Group Activity; Social Studies Link; Art Link]**

◆ Further Reading, Listening, and Viewing

- John Carey: *John Donne: Life, Mind and Art* (1981). A highly acclaimed biography

- A. J. Smith: *John Donne: The Critical Heritage* (1975). Critical essays

- Vaughan Hart: *St. Paul's Cathedral: London 1675–1710* (1995). A pictorial companion to Christopher Wren's architecture for St. Paul's

On the Web:

http://www.phschool.com/atschool/literature
Go to the student edition of *The British Tradition*. Proceed to Unit 3. Then, click Hot Links to find Web sites featuring John Donne.

Jonathan Swift In Depth

> "Proper words in proper places, make the true definition of a style."
> —*Jonathan Swift*, **Letter to a Young Clergyman**

JONATHAN SWIFT is recognized as the greatest satirist in English. Swift's masterpiece, *Gulliver's Travels,* was an instant bestseller when it first appeared in 1726, and its popularity with adults and children alike has never waned. Swift was also one of the great masters of English prose. He summed up his values of clear, concrete diction and concise expression in a typically epigrammatic (and deceptively simple) definition of style: "proper words in proper places."

Youth and Early Works Swift was born in 1667 to English parents in Dublin, Ireland. He was educated at Kilkenny Grammar School and Trinity College, Dublin. After earning his degree, he was employed in England by a kinsman, Sir William Temple, who was a retired diplomat. At Moor Park, Temple's estate, Swift first met a young servant girl named Esther Johnson, whom he nicknamed "Stella." The exact nature of their relationship is unknown, but it is clear that each had deep feelings for the other.

In 1694, Swift was ordained an Anglican priest. However, his hopes for promotion within the church through Temple's influence were disappointed. During the 1690's, he discovered his genius for satire by writing two works that were not published until 1704: *A Tale of a Tub* and *The Battle of the Books.* These satires poked fun at religious divisions and literary excesses—two themes that remained prominent in Swift's mature works.

Middle Years Church business required Swift to divide his time between Dublin and London for more than a decade. During his London visits, he became acquainted with many leading writers and politicians, including the essayists Joseph Addison and Sir Richard Steele, the poets Alexander Pope and John Gay, the playwright William Congreve, and the Tory leader Robert Harley, the Earl of Oxford. In 1713, Swift was appointed Dean of St. Patrick's Cathedral in Dublin, a post he occupied until shortly before his death.

Triumph and Decline In 1720, Swift published his first important political work on Ireland, whose economic oppression by the English increasingly preoccupied him. Four years later, in 1724, his series of pro-Irish pamphlets, *The Drapier's Letters,* made him a national hero. In 1726, Swift's literary reputation reached its zenith with the publication of his masterpiece, *Gulliver's Travels.* In this work, the bite of Swift's satire was tempered by charming fantasy and descriptions of exotic settings.

In 1727, Swift made his final visit to England. Two years later, he published his pamphlet "A Modest Proposal," which, like the narrative *Gulliver's Travels,* is now regarded as one of the greatest satirical works in English literature. In "A Modest Proposal," Swift uses the metaphorical notion of the English "devouring" the Irish as the basis for a savagely ironic denunciation of economic and political oppression.

Although Swift is often characterized as a misanthrope who hated humanity, he had a gift for friendship and was a generous supporter of charitable causes. His health declined drastically in his final years, and in 1742 he was declared insane—although his symptoms are now thought to have been those of Ménière's disease, a disorder of the inner ear. Swift died in 1745 in Dublin and was buried in St. Patrick's by the side of his beloved Stella.

◆ About *Gulliver's Travels*

Gulliver's Travels is the story of Lemuel Gulliver's four voyages to "remote nations of the world." Gulliver, who narrates the story, is a ship's surgeon; he is portrayed as a well-educated and decent human being. Each of these voyages takes Gulliver to a land of strange wonderment: the miniature kingdoms of Lilliput; Brobdingnag, the land where enlightened giants dwell; the flying island of Laputa, inhabited by overly speculative philosophers and scientists; and the country of the Houyhnhnms—a race of horses who live entirely by reason. *Gulliver's Travels* is regarded as a powerful satire on humanity and its institutions, and as a fascinating tale of voyages to imaginary lands.

◆ Eighteenth-Century Travel Narratives

Swift's full title for *Gulliver's Travels* reads as follows: *Travels into Several Remote Nations of the World. In Four Parts. By Lemuel Gulliver, First a Surgeon, and then a Captain of several Ships.* The title was designed, one assumes, to appeal to readers' growing appetite for accounts of distant, exotic settings and unusual incidents. Swift's work can be seen as an early, rather specialized example of the rise of a new genre in English literature: the travelogue. With their focus on entertainment and escapism, travelogues may be compared

with the more recent literary form of science fiction.

Almost all the leading writers of Swift's age wrote travel books, starting with Daniel Defoe's *Robinson Crusoe* (1719). Defoe based his work, often called the first English novel, on the widely reported adventures of Alexander Selkirk. After running away to sea and quarreling with his captain, Selkirk had been put ashore on an uninhabited island, where he remained for five years.

Other notable travelogues of the century include Samuel Johnson's *Rasselas* (1759), which contains some notable parallels to Voltaire's *Candide* (1759); Oliver Goldsmith's poem *The Traveller* (1764); Tobias Smollett's *Travels Through France and Italy* (1766); and James Boswell's *Journal of a Tour to the Hebrides* (1785). In the hands of eighteenth-century writers such as Swift and Samuel Johnson, travel literature often included elements of philosophy, satire, and fantasy.

◆ Literary Works

A Tale of a Tub (1704), a satire on religious divisions

The Battle of the Books (1704), a literary satire on the conflict between the "ancients" and the "moderns"

Argument Against Abolishing Christianity (1707), an ironic religious tract

The Bickerstaff Papers (1711), satirical articles lampooning a would-be astrologer

A Proposal for the Universal Use of Irish Manufacture (1720), Swift's first important work on Ireland

The Drapier's Letters (1724), a series of articles attacking English rule in Ireland

Gulliver's Travels (1726)

A Modest Proposal (1729), a savage attack on English exploitation of Ireland

Verses on the Death of Dr. Swift (1731)

TIMELINE

Swift's Life		World Events	
1667	Born in Dublin, Ireland, to English parents	1666	Great Fire of London
1673	Enters Kilkenny Grammar School	1667	John Milton's *Paradise Lost* published
1682	Enters Trinity College, Dublin	1668	John Dryden's *An Essay of Dramatic Poesy* published
1686	Receives B.A. degree		
1688	Departs for England	1670	Covent Garden market opens.
1689	Becomes secretary to Sir William Temple; meets Esther Johnson ("Stella")	1673	French comic playwright Molière dies
1690	Visits Ireland	1678	John Dryden writes *All for Love*
1692	Receives M.A. degree from Oxford	1685	Accession of James I
1694	Ordained priest in Ireland	1687	Isaac Newton's *Principia Mathematica* published
1696	Returns to Temple's estate at Moor Park in England; begins to write *A Tale of a Tub*	1689	Accession of William and Mary
		1690	John Locke's *Treatises of Government* published
1699	Death of Sir William Temple; Swift serves as chaplain to Lord Berkeley in Dublin	1702	Accession of Queen Anne
		1706	Benjamin Franklin born in Boston
1702	Receives Doctor of Divinity degree from Trinity College, Dublin	1707	Act of Union unites Scotland with England, Ireland, and Wales
1704	*A Tale of a Tub* and *The Battle of the Books* published	1711	Joseph Addison and Sir Richard Steele start publishing *The Spectator;* philosopher David Hume born
1707	Visits London on mission for the Irish church		
1710–14	Long sojourn in England; writes letters to Esther Johnson, later published as *Journal to Stella;* meets Robert Harley, Earl of Oxford, and joins Tories; is named editor of *The Examiner*	1712	Alexander Pope's *The Rape of the Lock* published
		1714	Accession of George I
		1719	Defoe's *Robinson Crusoe* published
		1721	J. S. Bach writes *Brandenburg Concertos*
1714	Helps to found Scriblerus Club in London; named Dean of St. Patrick's Cathedral, Dublin	1727	Accession of George II
		1732	George Washington born in Virginia; John Gay dies
1720	Begins work on *Gulliver's Travels*	1735	William Hogarth paints *The Rake's Progress*
1724	*The Drapier's Letters* published		
1726	*Gulliver's Travels* published	1740–41	Samuel Richardson's *Pamela* published
1727	Last visit to England		
1729	"A Modest Proposal" published	1742	Henry Fielding's *Joseph Andrews* published; Handel's oratorio, *Messiah,* first performed
1742	Health in decline; found to be of unsound mind		
		1744	Alexander Pope dies
1745	Dies in Dublin	1745	Last Jacobite rebellion in Scotland

Jonathan Swift

from A Voyage to Lillliput
from Gulliver's Travels

Chapter 1

*Gulliver gives a short account of his history, including his edu-
cation in "navigation, and other parts of the mathematics, useful
to those who intend to travel." He becomes a ship's surgeon and
for ten years makes several voyages through various parts of the
world. After becoming weary of the sea, Gulliver returns home to
his family, but three years later accepts an offer for another voyage. The ship on this voyage encounters violent winds and storms
and is wrecked. Gulliver concludes that his companions were lost
in the shipwreck and he alone has survived.*

For my own part, I swam as fortune directed me, and was
pushed forward by wind and tide. I often let my legs drop, and
could feel no bottom; but when I was almost gone, and able to
struggle no longer, I found myself within my depth; and by this
time the storm was much abated. The declivity was so small,
that I walked near a mile before I got to the shore, which I conjectured was about eight o'clock in the evening. I then advanced
forward near half a mile, but could not discover any sign of
houses or inhabitants; at least I was in so weak a condition,
that I did not observe them. I was extremely tired, and with
that, and the heat of the weather, I found myself much inclined
to sleep. I lay down on the grass, which was very short and soft,
where I slept sounder than ever I remember to have done in my
life, and as I reckoned, above nine hours; for when I awaked, it
was just daylight. I attempted to rise, but was not able to stir:
for as I happened to lie on my back, I found my arms and legs
were strongly fastened on each side to the ground; and my hair,
which was long and thick, tied down in the same manner. I likewise felt several slender ligatures across my body, my armpits to
my thighs. I could only look upwards; the sun began to grow
hot, and the light offended my eyes. I heard a confused noise
about me, but in the posture I lay, could see nothing except the
sky. In a little time I felt something alive moving on my left leg,
which advancing gently forward over my breast, came almost up
to my chin; when bending my eyes downwards as much as I
could, I perceived it to be a human creature not six inches
high,[1] with a bow and arrow in his hands, and a quiver at his
back. In the meantime, I felt at least forty more of the same
kind (as I conjectured) following the first. I was in the utmost

---

1. **human creature . . . inches high:** Lilliput is scaled roughly at one-twelfth the
size of Gulliver's world.

astonishment, and roared so loud, that they all ran back in a fright; and some of them, as I was afterwards told, were hurt with the falls they got by leaping from my sides upon the ground. However, they soon returned; and one of them, who ventured so far as to get a full sight of my face, lifting till his hands and eyes by way of admiration, cried out in a shrill, but distinct voice, *Hekinah Degul:* the others repeated the same words several times, but I then knew not what they meant. I lay all this while, as the reader may believe, in great uneasiness; at length, struggling to get loose, I had the fortune to break the strings, and wrench out the pegs that fastened my left arm to the ground; for, by lifting it up to my face, I discovered the methods they had taken to bind me; and, at the same time, with a violent pull, which gave me excessive pain, I a little loosened the strings that tied down my hair on the left side; so that I was just able to turn my head about two inches. But the creatures ran off a second time, before I could seize them; whereupon there was a great shout in a very shrill accent; and after it ceased, I heard one of them cry aloud, *Tolgo phonae;* when in an instant I felt above a hundred arrows discharged on my left hand, which pricked like so many needles; and besides they shot another flight into the air, whereof many, I suppose, fell on my body (though I felt them not) and some on my face, which I immediately covered with my left hand. When this shower of arrows was over, I fell a groaning with grief and pain; and then striving again to get loose, they discharged another volley larger than the first, and some of them attempted with spears to stick me in the sides; but, by good luck, I had on me a buff jerkin,[2] which they could not pierce. I thought it the most prudent method to lie still; and my design was to continue so till night, when, my left hand being already loose, I could easily free myself: and as for the inhabitants, I had reason to believe I might be a match for the greatest armies they could bring against me, if they were all of the same size with him that I saw. But fortune disposed otherwise of me. When the people observed I was quiet, they discharged no more arrows: but by the noise increasing, I knew their numbers were greater; and about four yards from me, over against my right ear, I heard a knocking for above an hour, like people at work; when turning my head that way, as well as the pegs and strings would permit me, I saw a stage erected about a foot and a half from the ground, capable of holding four of the inhabitants, with two or three ladders to mount it: from whence one of them, who seemed

---

2. jerkin: Leather jacket.

to be a person of quality, made me a long speech, whereof I understood not one syllable. But I should have mentioned, that before the principal person began his oration, he cried out three times, *Langro Dehul san:* (these words and the former were afterwards repeated and explained to me). Whereupon immediately about fifty of the inhabitants came, and cut the strings that fastened the left side of my head, which gave me the liberty of turning it to the right, and of observing the person and gesture of him who was to speak. He appeared to be of a middle age, and taller than any of the other three who attended him; whereof one was a page who held up his train, and seemed to be somewhat longer than my middle finger; the other two stood one on each side to support him. He acted every part of an orator, and I could observe many periods[3] of threatenings, and others of promises, pity and kindness. I answered in a few words, but in the most submissive manner, lifting up my left hand and both my eyes to the sun, as calling him for a witness; and being almost famished with hunger, having not eaten a morsel for some hours before I left the ship, I found the demands of nature so strong upon me, that I could not forbear showing my impatience (perhaps against the strict rules of decency) by putting my finger frequently on my mouth, to signify that I wanted food. The Hurgo (for so they call a great lord, as I afterwards learned) understood me very well. He descended from the stage, and commanded that several ladders should be applied to my sides, on which above a hundred of the inhabitants mounted, and walked towards my mouth, laden with baskets full of meat, which had been provided and sent thither by the King's orders upon the first intelligence he received of me. I observed there was the flesh of several animals, but could not distinguish them) by the taste. There were shoulders, legs, and loins shaped like those of mutton, and very well dressed, but smaller than the wings of a lark. I ate them by two or three at a mouthful, and took three loaves at a time, about the bigness of musket bullets. They supplied me as fast as they could, showing a thousand marks of wonder and astonishment at my bulk and appetite. I then made another sign that I wanted drink. They found by my eating that a small quantity would not suffice me; and being a lost ingenious people, they slung up with great dexterity one of their largest hogsheads;[4] then rolled it towards my hand, and beat out the top; I drank it off at a draught,[5] which I might well do, for it hardly held half a pint, and tasted like a small wine of Burgundy, but much more

---

3. **periods:** In rhetoric, well-constructed sentences.
4. **hogsheads:** Large barrels holding liquid.
5. **draught:** British spelling of draft, the amount taken at one drink.

delicious. They brought me a second hogshead which I drank in the same manner, and made signs for more, but they had none to give me. When I had performed these wonders, they shouted for joy and danced upon my breast, repeating several times as they did at first, *Hekinah Degul.* They made me a sign that I should throw down the two hogsheads but first warned the people below to stand out of the way, crying aloud, *Borach Mivola,* and when they saw the vessels in the air, there was an universal shout of *Hekinah Degul.* I confess I was often tempted, while they were passing backwards and forwards on my body, to seize forty or fifty of the first that came in my reach, and dash them against the ground. But the remembrance of what I had felt, which probably might not be the worst they could do; and the promise of honor I made them, for so I interpreted my submissive behavior, soon drove out those imaginations. Besides, I now considered myself as bound by the laws of hospitality to a people who had treated me with so much expense and magnificence. However, in my thoughts I could not sufficiently wonder at the intrepidity of these diminutive mortals, who durst venture to mount and walk on my body, while one of my hands was at liberty, without trembling at the very sight of so prodigious a creature as I must appear to them. After some time, when they observed that I made no more demands for meat, there appeared before me a person of high rank from his Imperial Majesty. His Excellency having mounted on the small of my right leg, advanced forwards up to my face, with about a dozen of his retinue. And producing his credentials under the Signet Royal, which he applied[6] close to my eyes, spoke about ten minutes, without any signs of anger, but with a kind of determinate resolution: often pointing forwards, which, as I afterwards found, was towards the capital city, about half a mile distant, whither it was agreed by his Majesty in council that I must be conveyed. I answered in a few words, but to no purpose, and made a sign with my hand that was loose, putting it to the other (but over his Excellency's head, for fear of hurting him or his train) and then to my own head and body, to signify that I desired my liberty. It appeared that he understood me well enough; for he shook his head by way of disapprobation, and held his hand in a posture to show that I must be carried as a prisoner. However, he made other signs to let me understand that I should have meat and drink enough, and very good treatment. Whereupon I once more thought of attempting to break my bonds; but again, when I felt the smart of their arrows upon my face and hands, which were all in blisters, and many of the darts still sticking in them; and observing likewise

---

6. **applied:** Brought.

that the number of my enemies increased; I gave tokens to let them know that they might do with me what they pleased. Upon this the *Hurgo* and his train withdrew, with much civility and cheerful countenances. . . . But before this, they had daubed my face and both my hands with a sort of ointment very pleasant to the smell, which in a few minutes removed all the smart of their arrows. These circumstances, added to the refreshment I had received by their victuals and drink, which were very nourishing, disposed me to sleep. I slept about eight hours, as I was afterwards assured; and it was no wonder; for the physicians, by the Emperor's order, had mingled a sleeping potion in the hogsheads of wine.

It seems that upon the first moment I was discovered sleeping on the ground after my landing, the Emperor had early notice of it by an express; and determined in council that I should be tied in the manner I have related (which was done in the night while I slept), that plenty of meat and drink should be sent me, and a machine prepared to carry me to the capital city.

This resolution perhaps may appear very bold and dangerous, and I am confident would not be imitated by any prince in Europe on the like occasion; however, in my opinion it was extremely prudent as well as generous. For supposing these people had endeavored to kill me with their spears and arrows while I was asleep; I should certainly have awaked with the first sense of smart, which might so far have roused my rage and strength, as to enable me to break the strings wherewith I was tied; after which, as they were not able to make resistance, so they could expect no mercy.

These people are most excellent mathematicians, and arrived to a great perfection in mechanics by the countenance and encouragement of the Emperor, who is a renowned patron of learning. This prince hath several machines fixed on wheels, for the carriage of trees and other great weights. He often builds his largest men of war, whereof some are nine foot long, in the woods where the timber grows, and has them carried on these engines[7] three or four hundred yards to the sea. Five hundred carpenters and engineers were immediately set at work to prepare the greatest engine they had. It was a frame of wood raised three inches from the ground, about seven foot long and four wide, moving upon twenty-two wheels. The shout I heard was upon the arrival of this engine, which it seems set out in four hours after my landing. It was brought parallel to me as I lay. But the principal difficulty was to raise and place me in this vehicle. Eighty poles, each of one foot high, were erected for this

---

7. **engines:** Manufactured devices or structures.

purpose, and very strong cords of the bigness of packthread were fastened by hooks to many bandages, which the workmen had girt round my neck, my hands, my body, and my legs. Nine hundred of the strongest men were employed to draw up these cords by many pulleys fastened on the poles; and thus, in less than three hours, I was raised and slung into the engine, and there tied fast. All this I was told, for while the whole operation was performing, I lay in a profound sleep, by the force of that soporiferous[8] medicine infused into my liquor, Fifteen hundred of the Emperor's largest horses, each about four inches and a half high, were employed to draw me towards the metropolis, which, as I said, was half a mile distant.

About four hours after we began our journey, I awaked by a very ridiculous accident; for, the carriage being stopped a while to adjust something that was out of order, two or three of the young natives had the curiosity to see how I looked when I was asleep; they climbed up into the engine, and advancing very softly to my face, one of them, an officer in the guards, put the sharp end of his half-pike a good way up into my left nostril, which tickled my nose like a straw, and made me sneeze violently: whereupon they stole off unperceived, and it was three weeks before I knew the cause of my awaking so suddenly. We made a long march the remaining part of the day, and rested at night with five hundred guards on each side of me half with torches, and half with bows and arrows, ready to shoot me if I should offer to stir. The next morning at sunrise we continued our march, and arrived within two hundred yards of the city gates about noon. The Emperor and all his court came out to meet us, but his great officers would by no means suffer his Majesty to endanger his person by mounting on my body.

At the place where the carriage stopped, there stood an ancient temple, esteemed to be the largest in the whole kingdom, which having been polluted some years before by an unnatural murder, was, according to the zeal of those people, looked on as profane, and therefore had been applied to common use, and all the ornaments and furniture carried away. In this edifice it was determined I should lodge. The great gate fronting to the north was about four foot high, and almost two foot wide, through which I could easily creep. On each side of the gate was a small window not above six inches from the ground: into that on the left side, the King's smiths conveyed fourscore[9] and eleven chains, like those that hang to a lady's watch in Europe, and almost as large, which were locked to my left leg with six and thirty padlocks. Over against this temple on the other side of the

---

8. soporiferous (săp ə rif ər əs): Causing or inducing sleep.
9. fourscore: Eighty.

great highway, at twenty foot distance, there was a turret at least five foot high. Here the Emperor ascended with many principal lords of his court, to have an opportunity of viewing me, as I was told, for I could not see them. It was reckoned that above a hundred thousand inhabitants came out of the town upon the same errand; and in spite of my guards, I believe there could not be fewer than ten thousand, at several times, who mounted upon my body by the help of ladders. But a proclamation was soon issued to forbid it upon pain of death. When the workmen found it was impossible for me to break loose, they cut all the strings that bound me; whereupon I rose up with as melancholy a disposition as ever I had in my life. But the noise and astonishment of the people at seeing me rise and walk are not to be expressed. The chains that held my left leg were about two yards long, and gave me not only the liberty of walking backwards and forwards in a semicircle: but, being fixed within four inches of the gate, allowed me to creep in, and lie at my full length in the temple.

☑ Check Your Comprehension

1. (a) When Gulliver awakens from his first night's sleep in Lilliput, what does he discover? (b) What is his immediate reaction?

2. How big are the Lilliputians, compared to ordinary human beings?

3. (a) Why does Gulliver refrain from seizing the Lilliputians and dashing them to the ground? (b) Why does he admire them as intrepid and courageous?

4. How does Gulliver communicate with the Lilliputian officials?

5. (a) According to Gulliver, at what do the Lilliputians excel? (b) How is Gulliver taken to the capital?

◆ Critical Thinking

1. Think about the character traits that Gulliver's actions, reactions, and thoughts reveal. How would you describe his personality? **[Infer]**

2. (a) Which details stand out as realistic in this narrative? (b) Which details are fantastic? **[Distinguish]**

3. (a) Why do you think that Swift goes to some lengths to invent a language for the Lilliputians? (b) Considering the context for each expression, what do you suppose the phrases *Hekinah Degul, Langro Dehul san,* and *Peplom Selan* might mean? **[Speculate]**

4. At the end of Chapter 1, Gulliver has been brought to the capital. How do you think the narrative may unfold from this point on? **[Predict]**

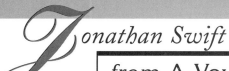

Jonathan Swift

from A Voyage to Lilliput
from Gulliver's Travels

Chapter 2

When I found myself on my feet, I looked about me, and must confess I never beheld a more entertaining prospect. The country round appeared like a continued garden, and the inclosed fields, which were generally forty foot square, resembled so many beds of flowers. These fields were intermingled with woods of half a stang, and the tallest trees, as I could judge, appeared to be seven foot high. I viewed the town on my left hand, which looked like the painted scene of a city in a theater. . . .

The Emperor was already descended from the tower, and advancing on horseback towards me, which had like to have cost him dear; for the beast, although very well trained, yet wholly unused to such a sight, which appeared as if a mountain moved before him, reared up on his hinder feet: but that prince, who is an excellent horseman, kept his seat, until his attendants ran in, and held the bridle, while his Majesty had time to dismount. When he alighted, he surveyed me round with great admiration, but kept beyond the length of my chains. He ordered his cooks and butlers, who were already prepared, to give me victuals and drink, which they pushed forward in a sort of vehicles upon wheels until I could reach them. I took these vehicles, and soon emptied them all; twenty of them were filled with meat, and ten with liquor; each of the former afforded me two or three good mouthfuls, and I emptied the liquor of ten vessels, which was contained in earthen vials, into one vehicle, drinking it off at a draught; and so I did with the rest. The Empress, and young princes of the blood, of both sexes, attended by many ladies, sat at some distance in their chairs; but upon the accident that happened to the Emperor's horse, they alighted, and came near his person; which I am now going to describe. He is taller, by almost the breadth of my nail, than any of his court, which alone is enough to strike an awe into the beholders. His features are strong and masculine, with an Austrian lip, and arched nose, his complexion olive, his countenance erect, his body and limbs well proportioned, all his motions graceful, and his deportment majestic. He was then past his prime, being twenty-eight years and three quarters old, of which he had reigned about seven, in great felicity, and generally victorious. For the better convenience of beholding him, I lay on my side, so that my face was parallel to his, and he stood but three yards off: however, I have had him since many times in my hand, and therefore cannot be deceived in the description. His dress was very plain and simple, the fashion of it between the Asiatic and the European; but he had on his head a light helmet of gold, adorned with jewels, and a plume on the crest. He held his sword drawn in his hand, to defend himself, if I should happen to break loose; it was almost three inches long, the hilt and scabbard were gold enriched with diamonds. His voice was shrill, but very clear and articulate, and I could distinctly hear it when I stood up. The ladies and courtiers were all most magnificently clad, so that the spot they stood upon seemed to resemble a petticoat spread on the ground, embroidered with figures of gold and silver. His Imperial Majesty spoke often to me, and I returned answers, but neither of us could understand a syllable. There were several of his priests and lawyers present (as I conjectured by their habits) who were commanded to address themselves to me, and I spoke to them in as many languages as I had the least smattering of, which were High and Low Dutch, Latin, French, Spanish, Italian, and Lingua Franca,[10] but all to no purpose. After about two hours the court retired, and I was left with a strong guard, to prevent the impertinence, and probably the malice of the rabble, who were very impatient to crowd about me as near as they durst, and some of them had the impudence to shoot their arrows at me as I sat on the ground by the door of my house, whereof one very narrowly missed my left eye. But the Colonel ordered six of the ringleaders to be seized, and thought no punishment so proper as to deliver them bound into my hands, which some of his soldiers accordingly did, pushing them forwards with the butt-ends of their pikes into my reach; I took them all in my right hand, put five of them into my coat pocket; and as to the sixth, I made a countenance as if I would eat him alive. The poor man squalled terribly, and the colonel and his officer were in much pain, especially when they saw me take out my penknife: but I soon put them out of fear; for, looking mildly, and immediately cutting the strings he was bound with, I set him gently on the ground, and away he ran. I treated the rest in the same manner, taking them one by one out of my pocket, and I observed both the soldiers and people were highly obliged at this mark of my clemency, which was represented very much to my advantage at court.

Towards night I got with some difficulty into my house, where I lay on the ground, and continued to do so about a fortnight; during which time the Emperor gave orders to have a bed prepared for me. Six hundred beds of the common measure were brought in carriages, and worked up in my house; a hundred and fifty of their beds sewn together made up the breadth and length, and these were four double, which however kept me but very indifferently from

10. **Lingua Franca:** Language, based on Italian, used by traders.

the hardness of the floor, that was of smooth stone. By the same computation they provided me with sheets, blankets, and coverlets, tolerable enough for one who had been so long enured to hardships as I.

As the news of my arrival spread through the kingdom, it brought prodigious numbers of rich, idle, and curious people to see me; so that the villages were almost emptied, and great neglect of tillage and household affairs must have ensued, if his Imperial Majesty had not provided by several proclamations and orders of state against this inconveniency. He directed that those who had already beheld me should return home, and not presume to come within fifty yards of my house without license from court; whereby the secretaries of state got considerable fees.

In the mean time, the Emperor held frequent councils to debate what course should be taken with me; and I was afterwards assured by a particular friend, a person of great quality, who was as much in the secret as any, that the court was under many difficulties concerning me. They apprehended[11] my breaking loose, that my diet would be very expensive, and might cause a famine. Sometimes they determined to starve me, or at least to shoot me in the face and hands with poisoned arrows, which would soon dispatch me: but again they considered, that the stench of so large a carcass might produce a plague in the metropolis and probably spread through the whole kingdom. In the midst of these consultations, several officers of the army went to the door of the great council chamber; and two of them being admitted, gave an account of my behavior to the six criminals above-mentioned; which made so favorable an impression in the breast of his Majesty, and the whole board, in my behalf, that an imperial commission was issued out, obliging all the villages nine hundred yards round the city to deliver in every morning six beeves, forty sheep, and other victuals for my sustenance; together with a proportionable quantity of bread and wine, and other liquors: for the due payment of which his Majesty gave assignments[12] upon his treasury. For this prince lives chiefly upon his own demesnes;[13] seldom except upon great occasions raising any subsidies upon his subjects, who are bound to attend him in his wars at their own expense. An establishment was also made of six hundred persons to be my domestics, who had board-wages allowed for their maintenance, and tents built for them very conveniently on each side of my door. It was likewise ordered, that three hundred tailors should make me a suit of clothes after the fashion of the country: that six of his Majesty's greatest scholars should be employed to instruct me

---

11. apprehended: Anticipated with fear.
12. assignments: A transfer of a claim, right, or property.
13. demesnes (di māns'): Lands of an estate.

in their language: and, lastly, that the Emperor's horses, and those of the nobility, and troops of guards, should be exercised in my sight, to accustom themselves to me. All these orders were duly put in execution; and in about three weeks I made a great progress in learning their language; during which time the Emperor frequently honored me with his visits, and was pleased to assist my masters in teaching me. We began already to converse together in some sort; and the first words I learned, were to express my desire that he would please to give me my liberty; which I every day repeated on my knees. His answer, as I could apprehend, was, that this must be a work of time, not to be thought on without the advice of his council; and that first I must *Lumos kelmin pesso desmar lon emposo;* that is, swear a peace with him and his kingdom. However, that I should be used with all kindness; and he advised me to acquire by my patience and discreet behavior, the good opinion of himself and his subjects. He desired I would not take it ill, if he gave orders to certain proper officers to search me; for probably I might carry about me several weapons which must needs be dangerous things, if they answered the bulk of so prodigious a person. I said, his Majesty should be satisfied, for I was ready to strip myself, and turn up my pockets before him. This I delivered part in words, and part in signs. He replied, that by the laws of the kingdom, I must be searched by two of his officers; that he knew this could not be done without my consent and assistance; that he had so good an opinion of my generosity and justice, as to trust their persons in my hands; that whatever they took from me should be returned when I left the country, or paid for at the rate which I would set upon them. I took up the two officers in my hands, put them first into my coat-pockets, and then into every other pocket about me, except my two fobs, and another secret pocket which I had no mind should be searched, wherein I had some little necessaries of no consequence to any but myself. In one of my fobs there was a silver watch, and in the other a small quantity of gold in a purse. These gentlemen, having pen, ink, and paper about them, made an exact inventory of everything they saw; and when they had done, desired I would set them down, that they might deliver it to the Emperor. This inventory I afterwards translated into English, and is word for word as follows.

Imprimis,[14] in the right coat-pocket of the Great Man-Mountain (for so I interpret the words *Quinbus Flestrin*) after the strictest search, we found only one great piece of coarse cloth, large enough to be a foot-cloth for your Majesty's chief room of state. In the left pocket, we saw a huge silver

14. **Imprimis** (im prē′ mis): In the first place.

chest, with a cover of the same metal, which we the searchers were not able to lift. We desired it should be opened; and one of us, stepping into it, found himself up to the mid leg in a sort of dust, some part whereof flying up to our faces, set us both a sneezing for several times together. In his right waist-coat-pocket, we found a prodigious bundle of white thin substances, folded one over another, about the bigness of three men, tied with a strong cable, and marked with black figures; which we humbly conceive to be writings; every letter almost half as large as the palm of our hands. In the left there was a sort of engine, from the back of which were extended twenty long poles, resembling the palisados[15] before your Majesty's court; wherewith we conjecture the Man-Mountain combs his head, for we did not always trouble him with questions, because we found it a great difficulty to make him understand us. In the large pocket on the right side of his middle cover (so I translate the word *ranfu-lo* by which they meant my breeches) we saw a hollow pillar of iron, about the length of a man, fastened to a strong piece of timber, larger than the pillar, and upon one side of the pillar were huge pieces of iron sticking out, cut into strange figures; which we know not what to make of. In the left pocket, another engine of the same kind. In the smaller pocket on the right side, were several round flat pieces of white and red metal, of different bulk; some of the white, which seemed to be silver, were so large and heavy that my comrade and I could hardly lift them. In the left pocket were two black pillars irregularly shaped: we could not, without difficulty reach the top of them as we stood at the bottom of his pocket. One of them was covered, and seemed all of a piece; but at the upper end of the other, there appeared a white round substance, about twice the bigness of our heads. Within each of these was inclosed a prodigious plate of steel; which, by our orders, we obliged him to show us, because we apprehended they might be dangerous engines. He took them out of their cases, and told us, that in his own country his practice was to shave his beard with one of these, and to cut his meat with the other. There were two pockets which we could not enter: these he called his fobs; they were two large slits cut into the top of his middle cover, but squeezed close by the pressure of his belly. Out of the right fob hung a great silver chain, with a wonderful kind of engine at the bottom. We directed him to draw out whatever was at the end of the chain, which appeared to be a globe, half silver, and half of some transparent metal: for on the transparent side we saw

---

15. palisados: Fences of stakes used for defense.

certain strange figures circularly drawn, and thought we
could touch them, until we found our fingers stopped with
that lucid substance. He put this engine to our ears, which
made an incessant noise like that of a watermill. And we conjecture it is either some unknown animal, or the god that he
worships: but we are more inclined to the latter opinion,
because he assured us (if we understood him right, for he
expressed himself very imperfectly), that he seldom did any
thing without consulting it. He called it his oracle, and said it
pointed out the time for every action of his life. From the left
fob he took out a net almost large enough for a fisherman,
but contrived to open and shut like a purse, and served him
for the same use: we found therein several massy pieces of
yellow metal, which if they be of real gold, must be of
immense value.

Having thus, in obedience to your Majesty's commands,
diligently searched all his pockets, we observed a girdle[16]
about his waist made of the hide of some prodigious animal;
from which, on the left side, hung a sword of the length of five
men; and on the right, a bag or pouch divided into cells; each
cell capable of holding three of your Majesty's subjects. In one
of these cells were several globes or balls of a most ponderous
metal, about the bigness of our heads, and required a strong
hand to lift them: the other cell contained a heap of certain
black grains, but of no great bulk or weight, for we could hold
above fifty of them in the palms of our hands.

This is an exact inventory of what we found about the body
of the Man-Mountain; who used us with great civility, and due
respect to your Majesty's commission. Signed and sealed on
the fourth day of the eighty-ninth moon of your Majesty's aus-
picious reign.

CLEFREN FRELOCK, MARSI FRELOCK.

When this inventory was read over to the Emperor, he directed
me to deliver up the several particulars. He first called for my scimitar, which I took out, scabbard and all. In the meantime he ordered
three thousand of his choicest troops (who then attended him) to
surround me at a distance, with their bows and arrows just ready to
discharge: but I did not observe it; for my eyes were wholly fixed
upon his Majesty. He then desired me to draw my scimitar, which,
although it had got some rust by the sea water, was in most parts
exceeding bright. I did so, and immediately all the troops gave a
shout between terror and surprise; for the sun shone clear, and the
reflection dazzled their eyes, as I waved the scimitar to and fro in

---

16. **girdle:** Belt.

my hand. His Majesty, who is a most magnanimous prince, was less daunted than I could expect; he ordered me to return it into the scabbard, and cast it on the ground as gently as I could, about six foot from the end of my chain. The next thing he demanded was one of the hollow iron pillars, by which he meant my pocket-pistols. I drew it out, and at his desire, as well as I could, expressed to him the use of it, and charging it only with powder, which by the closeness of my pouch happened to escape wetting in the sea (an inconvenience that all prudent mariners take special care to provide against), I first cautioned the Emperor not to be afraid; and then I let it off in the air. The astonishment here was much greater than at the sight of my scimitar. Hundreds fell down as if they had been struck dead; and even the Emperor, although he stood his ground, could not recover himself in some time. I delivered up both my pistols in the same manner as I had done my scimitar, and then my pouch of powder and bullets; begging him that the former might be kept from fire; for it would kindle with the smallest spark, and blow up his imperial palace into the air. I likewise delivered up my watch, which the Emperor was very curious to see; and commanded two of his tallest yeomen[17] of the guards to bear it on a pole upon their shoulders, as draymen in England do a barrel of ale. He was amazed at the continual noise it made, and the motion of the minute-hand, which he could easily discern; for their sight is much more acute than ours: he asked the opinions of his learned men about him, which were various and remote, as the reader may well imagine without my repeating; although indeed I could not very perfectly understand them. I then gave up my silver and copper money, my purse with nine large pieces of gold, and some smaller ones; my knife and razor, my comb and silver snuffbox, my handkerchief and journal book. My scimitar, pistols, and pouch, were conveyed in carriages to his Majesty's stores; but the rest of my goods were returned me.

I had, as I before observed, one private pocket which escaped their search, wherein there was a pair of spectacles (which I sometimes use for the weakness of my eyes), a pocket perspective,[18] and several other little conveniences; which being of no consequence to the Emperor, I did not think myself bound in honor to discover, and I apprehended they might be lost or spoiled if I ventured them out of my possession.

---

17. **yeomen** (yō′ mən): Servants in a royal household.
18. **perspective:** Telescope.

☑ Check Your Comprehension

1. When the emperor arrives, what does he order his servants to do?
2. How does Gulliver punish the Lilliputians who maliciously shoot arrows at him?
3. What are some of the Lilliputians' fears concerning Gulliver?
4. (a) Gulliver claims to have translated an inventory listing the items the Lilliputians found in his pockets. Identify at least five of these items. (b) What are two personal possessions that escape the notice of the Lilliputians who search Gulliver?

◆ Critical Thinking

1. What details in this passage indicate that the Lilliputians are prudent and cautious by nature? **[Analyze]**
2. Humor often derives from an emphasis on incongruity or inconsistency. How does Swift include touches of humor in (a) Gulliver's description of his communication with the emperor, and (b) the comments about Gulliver's watch in the inventory? **[Analyze]**
3. How might the emperor's policy regarding the curiosity-seekers who flock to gawk at Gulliver have relevance today? **[Apply]**

Jonathan Swift

Comparing and Connecting the Author's Works

◆ Literary Focus: Fantasy

As a literary genre or mode, **fantasy** is a work or style that features imaginary characters with no counterparts in the real world. Fantasy typically involves a striking reversal of the ground rules operating in the real world. At the same time, most successful fantasies include realistic elements—especially psychological detail—in order to establish credibility.

For centuries, many types of literature have included elements of fantasy: for example, the descriptions of the supernatural in epics such as *Beowulf;* the imaginary elves, dragons, and ghosts of medieval romance; classic novels such as Lewis Carroll's *Alice's Adventures in Wonderland* (1865) and George Orwell's *Animal Farm* (1945); the far-off worlds and exotic characters of modern science fiction; and the whimsical distortions explored in the magic-realist style of contemporary Latin American writers such as Julio Cortázar and Gabriel García Márquez. Swift's unique combination of satire and fantasy in *Gulliver's Travels* is one of the chief reasons for the book's enduring, nearly universal appeal.

1. What are some of the specific details that Swift uses in these chapters to increase Gulliver's credibility as he describes the strange world of the Lilliputians?
2. In the inventory of Gulliver's possessions in Chapter 2, how does Swift manipulate point of view or perspective?

◆ Drawing Conclusions About Swift's Work

You can often deepen and refine your own assessment of a literary work by considering the evaluations of other readers. In his introduction to an edition of *Gulliver's Travels,* literary critic Paul Turner cites the twentieth-century novelist and essayist George Orwell (1903–1950) on the merits of Swift's masterpiece:

> Gulliver's Travels . . . *was a bestseller when it first came out in 1726, and people have been rereading it for pleasure, not merely for profit, ever since. George Orwell read it first just before he was eight, re-read it at least half a dozen times during his short life, and found it "impossible to grow tired of." "If I were to make a list," he wrote, "of six books which were to be preserved when all others were destroyed, I would certainly put* Gulliver's Travels *among them."*

Orwell's response to *Gulliver's Travels* suggests an essay topic:

What would be your own choice of six books to preserve above all others? Would *Gulliver's Travels* be on the list? In a brief essay, identify and explain your choices. Use a chart such as the following to organize your thoughts.

Book Title	Reason for Choice
Book 1	
Book 2	
Book 3	
Book 4	
Book 5	
Book 6	

◆ Idea Bank

Writing

1. **Imaginary Language** One strategy that Swift uses to persuade readers to believe in the reality of Lilliput is his invention of an imaginary language. Invent a few more words and phrases for the Lilliputians that would be appropriate for various passages in these chapters. Then copy the passages you have chosen, inserting your new phrases where they would be useful in telling Gulliver's story. Provide footnotes that "translate" the phrases into English.

2. **Updated Inventory** Imagine that you are Gulliver and that you have been captured by the modern-day descendants of the Lilliputians. What would your captors find in your pockets? Write an updated inventory, modeling your approach on Swift's humorous manipulation of perspective in Chapter 2 of "A Voyage to Lilliput." When you have finished work, share your writing with a small group of classmates or friends, and ask for their comments and suggestions.

3. **Satirical Column** One of Swift's major purposes in *Gulliver's Travels* is to ridicule human vices and follies. Choose a modern trend or attitude that you think is ripe for satirical attack in a newspaper column. Consider how you can exaggerate or describe your target so that it will seem even more foolish than it really is. Then write a column in which you mock a foolish behavior or trend in today's world.

Speaking and Listening

4. **Film Conference** With a small group, plan the special effects for a filmed version of these excerpts from "A Voyage to Lilliput." Discuss where in the story you will use the special effects and how you will carry them out. **[Group Activity; Media Link]**

5. **Oral Report** Lilliput is scaled at approximately one-twelfth the size of the normal human world. Examine four details from these passages dealing with measurements and quantities. Are they consistently scaled? Does Swift make any mistakes? Then present an oral report on Swift's manipulation of proportion. **[Math Link]**

Researching and Representing

6. **A New Adventure** Together with a small group, write and illustrate a story in which Gulliver visits another exotic land. Describe the inhabitants, their customs, and their relations with Gulliver. When you have finished work, share your illustrated narrative with the class as a whole. **[Group Activity; Art Link]**

◆ Further Reading, Listening, and Viewing

- Victoria Glendinning: *Jonathan Swift: A Portrait* (1999). A recent, well reviewed biography
- Harold Bloom, ed.: *Jonathan Swift's Gulliver's Travels* (1986). A collection of critical essays
- *Gulliver's Travels,* read by Robert Halvorson (Books on Tape, Newport Beach, Calif., 1985). Audiocassettes
- *Gulliver's Travels* (Hallmark Home Entertainment, 1996). Made-for-TV movie with Ted Danson and Mary Steenburgen

On the Web:

http://www.phschool.com/atschool/literature
Go to the student edition of *The British Tradition.*
Proceed to Unit 3. Then, click Hot Links to
find Web sites featuring Jonathan Swift.

William Wordsworth In Depth

> "He is . . . the most original poet now living, and the one whose writings could the least be spared for they have no substitute elsewhere."
>
> —*William Hazlitt*

WILLIAM WORDSWORTH was one of England's greatest poets and the pioneer of the Romantic movement. His approach to poetry rejected the complex forms and subjects of his time period. Instead, Wordsworth placed his reliance on the imagination and simplicity of expression. He devoted much of his literature to the celebration of the "incidents and situations from common life."

Boyhood and Youth Wordsworth was born in 1770 in northwest England, near the Lake District. By the time he was a teenager, both his parents had died. At grammar school, the boy became a keen observer of nature, an avid reader, and a budding poet. At the age of seventeen, he entered St. John's College, Cambridge, and he graduated in 1791.

Love and Revolution In 1791–92, Wordsworth traveled to France, which was in revolutionary turmoil. He met and fell in love with Annette Vallon, but their plans to marry were frustrated by Wordsworth's lack of funds, and he returned to England. Soon afterwards, war between France and England broke out.

Crisis and Recovery Wordsworth was a strong supporter of the ideals of the French Revolution: liberty, equality, and universal brotherhood. However, these ideals soon crumbled amid the hatred and tyranny of the Reign of Terror in France (1793–94). Wordsworth's guilt over his affair with Annette Vallon and his political disillusionment brought him to the verge of an emotional collapse.

In 1795, together with his beloved sister Dorothy, Wordsworth settled in a cottage in Dorset, where he slowly recovered from his depression. It was during this period that Wordsworth first met the poet Samuel Taylor Coleridge, who was to have a great influence on Wordsworth's literary career. The two men met frequently, talked for hours about poetry, and composed at a startling rate. Their collaboration resulted in a small volume, anonymously published in 1798, called *Lyrical Ballads with a Few Other Poems.*

A Revolution in Poetry *Lyrical Ballads* was a landmark work. It represented a revolt against the artificial Neoclassicism of the previous generation. In 1800, Wordsworth published a second edition containing the famous "Preface," which served as an outline and defense of his poetic ideals. The heart of Wordsworth's theory was his doctrine that good poetry is the "spontaneous overflow of powerful feelings" that "takes its origin from emotion recollected in tranquillity."

The Final Years In 1799, Wordsworth and Dorothy settled at Grasmere in the Lake District, where he would spend the remainder of his life. In 1802, he married Mary Hutchinson. Over the next few decades, Wordsworth became increasingly prosperous and politically conservative. In 1843, Wordsworth was named Poet Laureate. He died in 1850, at the age of eighty, and was buried in Grasmere churchyard.

Poetry and Autobiography Critics generally agree that Wordsworth's long poem *The Prelude* is the greatest achievement of his career, although this work was unknown to the public until after the poet's death in 1850. *The Prelude* is an introspective account of Wordsworth's development as a poet.

◆ The French Revolution and Romanticism

The French Revolution erupted on July 14, 1789, with the storming of the Bastille, a fortress in Paris used as a prison. English liberals and radicals such as Wordsworth were strong supporters of the democratic aims of the Revolution's first phase. The widespread optimism of this period is reflected in two lines from Wordsworth's *The Prelude:*

> Bliss was it in that dawn
>   to be alive,
> But to be young was very heaven!

Although lofty expectations of political reform were dashed by the violent course the Revolution took in 1793–1794, the hope of a better future remained. The Romantic poets were unable to change the state of social affairs, but under the guidance of Wordsworth and Coleridge, they revolutionized the theory and practice of poetry.

◆ Literary Works

His Greatest Poetry Wordsworth aimed to write poetry "in a selection of language really used by men." This approach resulted in poems that combined clear language with familiar settings and simple expression. Much of Wordsworth's best poetry was written before 1815.

An Evening Walk and Descriptive Sketches (1793)

Lyrical Ballads (1798, second edition 1800), which included poems by Samuel Taylor Coleridge

Poems in Two Volumes (1807)

The Excursion (1814)

The Later Years After 1815, Wordsworth continued to compose poetry. He also revised his most famous work, *The Prelude,* which was not published until after his death.

Peter Bell and *The Waggoner* (1819)

Ecclesiastical Sketches (1822)

The Prelude (1850; completed 1805)

TIMELINE

Wordsworth's Life	World Events

Wordsworth's Life

1770 Born at Cockermouth, Cumberland, near the English Lake District

1771 Wordsworth's sister Dorothy born

1778 Death of Wordsworth's mother

1778–87 William Wordsworth attends Hawkshead Grammar School

1783 Death of Wordsworth's father

1787 Enters St. John's College, Cambridge

1790 Walking tours through France, Switzerland, Italy

1791 Departs for France

1792 Affair with Annette Vallon and birth of daughter, Caroline

1795 Settles with sister Dorothy at Racedown, Dorset; meets Coleridge

1797 Settles with Dorothy at Alfoxden to be near Coleridge

1798 *Lyrical Ballads* published

1799 Moves to Grasmere with Dorothy

1800 Second edition of *Lyrical Ballads* published with "Preface"

1802 Receives father's inheritance; visits Annette Vallon and Caroline in France, where he arranges an annual allowance for Caroline; marries Mary Hutchinson

1805 Death of brother John

1807 *Poems in Two Volumes* published

1814 *The Excursion* published

1815 First collected edition of poems published

1823–37 Various trips throughout Europe, including France and Switzerland

1843 Becomes Poet Laureate

1850 Dies; publication of *The Prelude*

World Events

1775 American Revolution begins; Jane Austen born

1789 French Revolution begins

1790 Edmund Burke attacks the revolution in his *Reflections on the Revolution in France*

1791 Thomas Paine supports the French Revolution in *The Rights of Man*

1793 England declares war on France; Reign of Terror under Robespierre begins

1794 William Blake's *Songs of Innocence and of Experience*

1804 Napoleon crowned emperor

1805 British victory at Battle of Trafalgar under Lord Nelson

1812 J. M. W. Turner paints *Snowstorm: Hannibal and His Army Crossing the Alps*

1814 George Stephenson constructs steam locomotive; Walter Scott publishes *Waverley*

1815 Napoleon defeated at Waterloo

1817 Coleridge publishes *Biographia Literaria*

1818 Mary Shelley's *Frankenstein* published; Byron begins *Don Juan*

1819 Percy Bysshe Shelley's "Ode to the West Wind"; Keats writes his great odes

1820 Accession of King George IV

1821 John Constable paints *The Hay-Wain*

1824 Beethoven composes *Symphony No. 9*; death of Byron

1833 Ralph Waldo Emerson visits England; meets Wordsworth and Coleridge

1834 Coleridge dies

1837 Accession of Queen Victoria; Nathaniel Hawthorne's *Twice-Told Tales* published

1850 Alfred, Lord Tennyson succeeds Wordsworth as Poet Laureate.

William Wordsworth

Strange Fits of Passion Have I Known

This poem and the three following pieces—"*She Dwelt Among the Untrodden Ways*," "*Three Years She Grew in Sun and Shower*," "*I Traveled Among Unknown Men*"— are part of a group, often labeled as the "*Lucy Poems.*"

Strange fits of passion have I known:
And I will dare to tell,
But in the Lover's ear alone,
What once to me befell.

5   When she I loved looked every day
Fresh as a rose in June,
I to her cottage bent my way,
Beneath an evening moon.

Upon the moon I fixed my eye,
10   All over the wide lea;[1]
With quickening pace my horse drew nigh[2]
Those paths so dear to me.

And now we reached the orchard-plot;
And, as we climbed the hill,
15   The sinking moon to Lucy's cot
Came near, and nearer still.

In one of those sweet dreams I slept,
Kind Nature's gentlest boon!
And all the while my eyes I kept
20   On the descending moon.

My horse moved on; hoof after hoof
He raised, and never stopped:
When down behind the cottage roof,
At once, the bright moon dropped.

25   What fond and wayward thoughts will slide
Into a Lover's head!
"O mercy!" to myself I cried,
"If Lucy should be dead!"

---

1. lea (lē) *n.:* Meadow; field.
2. nigh (nī) *adv.:* Near.

William Wordsworth

She Dwelt Among the Untrodden Ways

She dwelt among the untrodden ways
    Beside the springs of Dove,[1]
A maid whom there were none to praise
    And very few to love.

5   A violet by a mossy stone
    Half-hidden from the eye!
    —Fair, as a star when only one
    Is shining in the sky!
She lived unknown, and few could know
10   When Lucy ceased to be;
But she is in her grave, and Oh!
    The difference to me.

---

1. Dove: River in England near the Lake District.

Three Years She Grew in Sun and Shower

Three years she grew in sun and shower,
Then Nature said, "A lovelier flower
On earth was never sown;
This Child I to myself will take,
5   She shall be mine, and I will make
A Lady of my own.

"Myself will to my darling be
Both law and impulse, and with me
The Girl in rock and plain,
10   In earth and heaven, in glade and bower,
Shall feel an overseeing power
To kindle or restrain.

"She shall be sportive as the fawn
That wild with glee across the lawn
15   Or up the mountain springs,
And here shall be the breathing balm,[1]
And here the silence and the calm
Of mute insensate[2] things.

"The floating clouds their state shall lend
20   To her, for her the willow bend,
Nor shall she fail to see
Even in the motions of the storm
Grace that shall mould the Maiden's form
By silent sympathy.

25   "The stars of midnight shall be dear
To her, and she shall lean her ear
In many a secret place
Where rivulets[3] dance their wayward round,
And beauty born of murmuring sound
30   Shall pass into her face.

---

1. balm: Soothing ointment.
2. insensate: (in sən′ sāt) *adj.*: Without physical sensation.
3. rivulets: (riv′ yoo lits) *n.*: Small streams.

"And vital feelings of delight
Shall rear her form to stately height,
Her virgin bosom swell,
Such thoughts to Lucy I will give
35   While she and I together live
Here in this happy dell."[4]

Thus Nature spake — The work was done —
How soon my Lucy's race was run!
She died and left to me
40   This heath,[5] this calm and quiet scene,
The memory of what has been,
And never more will be.

---

4. dell: Small wooded valley.
5. heath: Area of flat land with low shrubs.

William Wordsworth

I Traveled Among Unknown Men

I traveled among unknown men,
   In lands beyond the sea;
Nor, England! did I know till then
   What love I bore to thee.

5   'Tis past, that melancholy dream!
   Nor will I quit thy shore
A second time; for still I seem
   To love thee more and more.

Among thy mountains did I feel
10   The joy of my desire;
And she I cherished turned her wheel
   Beside an English fire.

Thy mornings showed, thy nights concealed
   The bowers[1] where Lucy played;
15 And thine too is the last green field
   That Lucy's eyes surveyed.

---

1. **bowers:** Places enclosed by overhanging boughs of trees.

☑ Check Your Comprehension

1. (a) In "Strange Fits of Passion Have I Known," where is the speaker going?
(b) At what time of day does he travel?

2. In "She Dwelt Among the Untrodden Ways," where does the speaker say Lucy is now?

3. Who are the two speakers in "Three Years She Grew in Sun and Shower"?

4. What are three natural settings mentioned in "I Traveled Among Unknown Men"?

◆ Critical Thinking

1. What is the significance of the moon in "Strange Fits of Passion Have I Known"? Explain. **[Interpret]**

2. How is the title of "She Dwelt Among the Untrodden Ways" linked to the theme of the poem as a whole? **[Synthesize]**

3. What metaphor does the poet use in line 38 of "Three Years She Grew in Sun and Shower"? **[Analyze]**

4. What does the poem "I Traveled Among Unknown Men" reveal about the speaker's present condition? **[Infer]**

COMPARE LITERARY WORKS

5. These four poems all refer to the death of Lucy. In which one does the speaker express his grief most powerfully, in your opinion? Explain your choice.
[Make a Judgment]

William Wordsworth

Lucy Gray

This poem was written in 1799 while Wordsworth was staying in Germany, and was based on the true account of a young girl who lost her way in a snowstorm and drowned.

Oft I had heard of Lucy Gray
And when I crossed the Wild,
I chanced to see at break of day
The solitary Child.

5   No mate, no comrade Lucy knew;
She dwelt on a wild moor,
The sweetest Thing that ever grew
Beside a human door!

You yet may spy the fawn at play,
10   The hare upon the green;
But the sweet face of Lucy Gray
Will never more be seen.

"Tonight will be a stormy night,
You to the town must go,
15   And take a lantern, Child, to light
Your Mother through the snow."

That, Father! will I gladly do;
'Tis scarcely afternoon—
The minster clock[1] has just struck two,
20   And yonder is the moon.

At this the Father! raised his hook
And snapped a faggot-band;[2]
He plied his work, and Lucy took
The lantern in her hand.

25   Not blither[3] is the mountain roe,[4]
With many a wanton stroke
Her feet disperse the powd'ry snow

---

1. **minster-clock:** Church clock.
2. **faggot-band:** Cord binding a bundle of sticks to be used for fuel.
3: **blither** (blī thər) *adj.*: Happier, more cheerful.
4. **roe:** Small deer.

That rises up like smoke.

30 The storm came on before its time,
She wandered up and down,
And many a hill did Lucy climb
But never reached the town.

The wretched parents all that night
35 Went shouting far and wide;
But there was neither sound nor sight
To serve them for a guide.

At daybreak on a hill they stood
That overlooked the Moor
40 And thence they saw the bridge of wood
A furlong⁵ from their door.

And now they homeward turned, and cried
"In heaven we all shall meet!"
When in the snow the Mother spied
The print of Lucy's feet.

45 Then downward from the steep hill's edge
They tracked the footmarks small;
And through the broken hawthorn hedge,
And by the long stone wall;

And then an open field they crossed,
50 The marks were still the same;
They tracked them on, nor ever lost,
And to the bridge they came.

They followed from the snowy bank
The footmarks, one by one,
55 Into the middle of the plank,
And further there were none.

Yet some maintain that to this day
She is a living Child,
That you may see sweet Lucy Gray
60 Upon the lonesome wild.

O'er rough and smooth she trips along,
And never looks behind;

---

5. furlong (fʉr′ lȯŋ′): One eighth of a mile.

William Wordsworth

We Are Seven

A simple child, dear brother Jim,
That lightly draws its breath,
And feels its life in every limb,
What should it know of death?

5   I met a little cottage girl,
She was eight years old, she said;
Her hair was thick with many a curl
That clustered round her head.

She had a rustic, woodland air,
10   And she was wildly clad;
Her eyes were fair, and very fair,
—Her beauty made me glad.

"Sisters and brothers, little maid,
How many may you be?"
15   "How many? seven in all," she said,
And wondering looked at me.

"And where are they, I pray you tell?"
She answered, "Seven are we;
And two of us at Conway[1] dwell,
20   And two are gone to sea.

"Two of us in the churchyard lie,
My sister and my brother,
And in the churchyard cottage, I
Dwell near them with my mother."

20   "You say that two at Conway dwell,
And two are gone to sea,
Yet you are seven; I pray you tell
Sweet Maid, how this may be?"

---

1. **Conway:** A town in North Wales.

Then did the little Maid reply,
30   "Seven boys and girls are we;
"Two of us in the churchyard lie,
Beneath the churchyard tree."

"You run about, my little maid,
Your limbs they are alive;
35   If two are in the churchyard laid,
Then ye are only five."

"Their graves an green, they may be seen,"
The little Maid replied,
"Twelve steps or more from my mother's door,
40   And they are side by side.

"My stockings there I often knit,
My 'kerchief there I hem;
"And there upon the ground I sit—
I sit and sing to them.

45   "And often after sunset, Sir,
When it is light and fair,
I take my little porringer,
And eat my supper there.

"The first that died was little Jane;
50   In bed she moaning lay,
Till God released her of her pain,
And then she went away.

"So in the churchyard she was laid,
And all the summer dry,
55   Together round her grave we played,
My brother John and I.

"And when the ground was white with snow,
And I could run and slide,
My brother John was forced to go,
60   And he lies by her side."

"How many are you then," said I,
"If they two are in Heaven?"
The little Maiden did reply,
"O Master! we are seven."

65   "But they are dead; those two are dead!
Their spirits are in heaven!"
'Twas throwing words away; for still
The little Maid would have her will,
And said, "Nay, we are seven!"

☑ Check Your Comprehension

1. (a) What does Lucy Gray's father tell her to do? (b) What does Lucy's mother discover the following day?
2. According to the two final stanzas in "Lucy Gray," what do some people still maintain about the lost child?
3. Who are the two speakers in "We Are Seven"?
4. In "We Are Seven," what has happened to the cottage girl's sister Jane and her brother John?

◆ Critical Thinking

1. How does the poet use setting in "Lucy Gray" to contribute to the atmosphere or overall mood of the poem? **[Analyze]**
2. How does the first stanza of "We Are Seven" foreshadow the theme of the poem as a whole? **[Synthesize]**
3. The total effect in "We Are Seven" depends largely on a series of striking contrasts. What are some of these contrasts, and what tone do they produce? **[Analyze]**

COMPARE LITERARY WORKS

4. The Romantic poets often included supernatural elements in their poems. How does Wordsworth use the supernatural in "Lucy Gray" and "We Are Seven"? **[Connect]**

William Wordsworth

The Solitary Reaper

*This poem was inspired by a passage from
Thomas Willkinson's Tour of Scotland (1824):
"Passed a female who was reaping alone; she sung
in Erse (Scottish Gaelic) as she bended over her
sickle; the sweetest human voice I ever heard: her
strains were tenderly melancholy, and felt delicious
long after they were heard no more."*

Behold her, single in the field,
You solitary Highland lass!
Reaping and singing by herself;
Stop here, or gently pass!
5   Alone she cuts and binds the grain,
And sings a melancholy strain;
O listen! for the vale profound
Is overflowing with the sound.

No nightingale did ever chaunt
10   More welcome notes to weary bands
Of travelers in some shady haunt,
Among Arabian sands;
A voice so thrilling ne'er was heard
In springtime from the cuckoo-bird,
15   Breaking the silence of the seas
Among the farthest Hebrides.

Will no one tell me what she sings?
Perhaps the plaintive numbers flow
For old, unhappy, far-off things,
20   And battles long ago;
Or is it some more humble lay,
Familiar matter of today?
Some natural sorrow, loss, or pain,
That has been, and may be again?

25   Whate'er the theme, the maiden sang
As if her song could have no ending;
I saw her singing at her work,
And o'er the sickle bending;
I listened, motionless and still;
30   And, as I mounted up the hill,
The music in my heart I bore,
Long after it was heard no more.

William Wordsworth

It Is a Beauteous Evening, Calm and Free

It is a beauteous evening, calm and free,
The holy time is quiet as a Nun
Breathless with adoration; the broad sun
Is sinking down in its tranquility;
5   The gentleness of heaven broods o'er the Sea:
Listen! the mighty Being is awake,
And doth with his eternal motion make
A sound like thunder—everlastingly.
Dear Child! dear Girl! that walkest with me here,
10   If thou appear untouched by solemn thought,
Thy nature is not therefore less divine:
Thou liest in Abraham's bosom[1] all the year;
And worship'st at the Temple's inner shrine,
God being with thee when we know it not.

1. Abraham's bosom: Heaven (Luke:16:22).

Nutting

It seems a day,
(I speak of one from many singled out)
One of those heavenly days which cannot die,
When forth I sallied¹ from our cottage-door.
And with a wallet o'er my shoulder slung,
5   A nutting crook in hand, I turned my steps
Towards the distant woods, a Figure quaint,
Tricked out in proud disguise of Beggar's weeds
Put on for the occasion, by advice
And exhortation of my frugal Dame.
10   Motley accoutrement!² of power to smile
At thorns and brakes and brambles, and, in truth,
More ragged than need was. Among the woods
And o'er the pathless rocks, I foroed my way
Until at length, I came to one dear nook
15   Unvisited, where not a broken bough
Drooped with its withered leaves, ungracious sign
Of devastation, but the hazels rose
Tall and erect, with milk-white clusters hung,
A virgin scene!—A little while I stood,
20   Breathing with such suppression of the heart
As joy delights in; and with wise restraint
Voluptuous,³ fearless of a rival, eye,
The banquet, or beneath the trees I sate
Among the flowers, and with the flowers I played;
25   A temper known to those, who, after long
And weary expectation, have been blessed
With sudden happiness beyond all hope.
—Perhaps it was a bower beneath whose leaves
The violets of five seasons reappear
30   And fade, unseen by any human eye,

---

1. **sallied:** To set out on a trip or excursion.
2. **weeds . . . accoutrements** (ak͞oo trə mənts): "Weeds" and "motley accoutrements" (line 10) refer to the speaker's clothing, which appears to be ill-matched and beggarly.
3. **voluptuous:** full of delight or pleasure to the senses.

Where fairy water-breaks[4] do murmur on
For ever, and I saw the sparkling foam,
And with my cheek on one of those green stones
That fleeced with moss, beneath the shady trees,
35   Lay round me scattered like a flock of sheep,
I heard the murmur and the murmuring sound,
In that sweet mood when pleasure loves to pay
Tribute to ease, and, of its joy secure
The heart luxuriates[5] with indifferent things,
40   Wasting its kindliness on stocks and stones,[6]
And on the vacant air. Then up I rose.
And dragged to earth both branch and bough, with crash
And merciless ravage; and the shady nook
Of hazels, and the green and mossy bower
45   Deformed and sullied, patiently gave up
Their quiet being: and unless I now
Confound[7] my present feelings with the past,
Even then, when from the bower I turned away,
Exulting, rich beyond the wealth of kings
50   I felt a sense of pain when I beheld
The silent trees and the intruding sky.

Then, dearest Maiden ! move along these shades
In gentleness of heart with gentle hand
Touch,—for there is a Spirit in the woods.

---

4. water-breaks: Areas where the flow of a stream is blocked by rocks.
5. luxuriates (lug zhōōr ē āts)**:** Enjoys or relaxes in comfort.
6. stocks and stones: Inanimate objects.
7. Confound (kən found´) *v.*: Confuse.

☑ Check Your Comprehension

1. (a) In "The Solitary Reaper," to what does the speaker compare the woman's singing in the second stanza? (b) In the third stanza, what possible subjects of the woman's song does the speaker imagine?
2. What does the speaker in "The Solitary Reaper" bear in his heart as he continues his walk?
3. (a) Describe the setting in "It Is a Beauteous Evening." (b) Who is the poet's companion?
4. (a) What emotion does the speaker experience in lines 20–28 of "Nutting"? (b) Why does he feel pain in lines 51–52?

◆ Critical Thinking

1. In "The Solitary Reaper," what do the comparisons in the second stanza suggest about the woman's song? [Infer]
2. In what ways do you think the type of life portrayed in "The Solitary Reaper" would have contrasted with the type of life led by nineteenth-century factory workers? [Speculate]
3. (a) In "It Is a Beauteous Evening," how would you summarize the poet's ideas about the child? (b) his advice to the reader? [Apply]
4. What outlook toward nature does "Nutting" convey? [Synthesize]

COMPARE LITERARY WORKS

5. (a) Examine the rhyme scheme of each of these poems. Discuss similarities and differences. [Compare; Contrast]

William Wordsworth
Comparing and Connecting the Author's Works

◆ Literary Focus: Lyric Poetry

Many of Wordsworth's poems are lyric poems. **Lyric poems** usually express the observations and feelings of a single speaker. Types of lyric include the elegy, the ode, the hymn, and the sonnet.

Although the speaker in a poem may be a fictional person, in Wordsworth's lyrics the situation described by the speaker often corresponds to events from the poet's own life.

Main Features of a Lyric Poem

- Uses the first person
- Is usually brief
- Expresses observations and feelings about a single subject or experience

1. Review one of the following lyrics: "Strange Fits of Passion Have I Known," "I Traveled Among Unknown Men," "The Solitary Reaper," or "It Is a Beauteous Evening." Make a list of the ways in which the poem displays the leading traits of a lyric.
2. What are two or three events from Wordsworth's own life to which the events mentioned in these poems may refer?

◆ Drawing Conclusions About Wordsworth's Work

One way to evaluate Wordsworth's poetry is to compare his poems to his statements about the nature and function of poetry. In his "Preface" to the second edition of Lyrical Ballads, Wordsworth comments on his aims and methods as follows:

The principal object, then, which I proposed to myself in these poems was to choose incidents and situations from common life, and to relate or describe them, throughout, as far as was possible, in a selection of language really used by men; and, at the same time, to throw over them a certain coloring of imagination, whereby ordinary things should be presented to the mind in an unusual way.

The following chart shows how the poem "Strange Fits of Passion Have I Known" illustrates details from the "Preface." Create a similar chart in which you compare "The Solitary Reaper" or "It is a Beauteous Evening" to details in the "Preface." Write a summary of your findings, and determine whether the poem of your choice achieves Wordsworth's aims for poetry in general.

Details From the "Preface"	Examples From the Poem
"incidents and situations from a common life"	a man travels to visit his love
"selection of language really used by men"	"evening moon"; "we climbed the hill"
ordinary things made unusual	"strange fits of passion"

◆ Idea Bank

Writing

1. **News Article** Write an e-mail note to Wordsworth, explaining what you liked or disliked about one of his poems? Mention specific lines or stanzas in your message.
2. **Nature Poem** Write a poem about some aspect or force of nature. Use vivid imagery to capture one or more scenes from nature that stand out in your memory. You might also include personal reflections about the scene or scenes you describe. Your poem may or may not rhyme.
3. **Compare and Contrast** Write an essay exploring the similarities and

differences between two or more of Wordsworth's poems. Before you begin, make a Venn diagram like the one below to organize your thoughts. Write similarities—common images, settings, or forms—in the space where the circles overlap, and write differences in the outer regions of the circles.

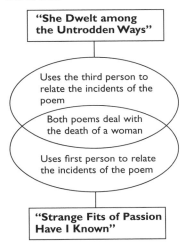

"She Dwelt among the Untrodden Ways"

Uses the third person to relate the incidents of the poem

Both poems deal with the death of a woman

Uses first person to relate the incidents of the poem

"Strange Fits of Passion Have I Known"

Speaking and Listening

4. **Poetry Reading** With a partner, take turns reading the poems "It Is a Beauteous Evening" and "I Traveled Among Unknown Men." As you read, emphasize the words and lines you feel are most important to the poem. After each reading, have your partner evaluate your oral interpretation. **[Performing Arts Link]**

5. **Debate** Debate Reread the poems "Three Years She Grew in Sun and Shower" and "Nutting." Form two groups and debate this question: What is Wordsworth's view of nature in these poems? One side should argue that Wordsworth views nature as being full of joy, and the other side should argue that he stresses sorrow in nature. **[Group Activity]**

Researching and Representing

6. **Compare and Contrast** William Wordsworth and the German composer Ludwig van Beethoven (1770–1827) were major figures of the Romantic period. Both artists glorified the dignity and value of the individual, though Beethoven's works mark only the very beginning of the Romantic period in music. Find and listen to a recording of Beethoven's *Symphony No. 5.* Reread Wordsworth's poetry, and then write a brief essay in which you (a) speculate on why Beethoven's symphony, especially the first movement, has become so famous; (b) compare its overall effect with that of one or more of Wordsworth's poems. **[Music Link]**

◆ Further Reading, Listening, and Viewing

- Stephen Gill: *William Wordsworth: A Life (1989).* Standard biography of the poet

- *Carl Woodring: Wordsworth* (1965) A useful introduction to the poetry.

- M. H. Abrams: *A Collection of Critical Essays* (1972)

- William Wordsworth: Poems (Highbridge Classics, 1998). Audiocassette featuring readings of poems from *Lyrical Ballads* and excerpts from *The Prelude*

- Graham Reynolds: *Turner* (1969) Illustrated biography of England's greatest Romantic painter.

On the Web:

http://www.phschool.com/atschool/literature
Go to the student edition of *The British Tradition.* Proceed to Unit 4. Then, click Hot Links to find Web sites featuring William Wordsworth

ohn Keats In Depth

"As to the poetical character itself . . . it is not itself, it has no self—it is everything and nothing . . . It enjoys light and shade; it lives in gusto, be it foul or fair, high or low, rich or poor, mean or elevated."
—*John Keats, Letter to Richard Woodhouse, 1818*

JOHN KEATS is a poet of rare genius —his astonishing development as a poet has few parallels in history. When Keats died in his mid-twenties, his poetic achievements far outstripped the accomplishments of Chaucer, Shakespeare, or Milton at the same age. During a brief career, he struggled against formidable obstacles to reach, as he told his friend Richard Woodhouse, "as high a summit in poetry as the nerve bestowed upon me will suffer."

Childhood and Adolescence The eldest son of a livery stable manager, Keats was born in 1795 in London. His father died in a riding accident when the boy was eight, and Keats's mother died six years later from tuberculosis, the disease that would eventually claim the poet's own life and that of his brother Tom. In 1810, Keats was apprenticed to an apothecary (pharmacist), and five years later he began medical studies, receiving his license in 1816. In that year, however, he decided to abandon medicine for poetry.

Early Poetry Keats's early poetry reveals the influence of Edmund Spenser, whose lyrical style and vivid imagery had a lasting impact on him. In 1817, Keats published his first collection of poems, which was well reviewed but sold few copies. In this year as well, Keats worked intensively on his first long poem, entitled *Endymion: A Poetic Romance*. Like many of his mature works, *Endymion* was inspired by ancient Greek mythology. In this period, Keats quickly became known

in London literary circles, largely thanks to introductions from his older friend, the poet Leigh Hunt.

The Miraculous Year From the start of his career, Keats had been strongly attracted to the sonnet, the hymn, and the ode. In 1819, he wrote most of his great odes, as well as *The Eve of St. Agnes,* "La Belle Dame Sans Merci," the first part of *Lamia,* and *The Fall of Hyperion.* Keats produced this steady stream of masterpieces despite the toll taken on him by bitter critical attacks on *Endymion* and by his brother Tom's illness and death in late 1818. During the winter of 1819, he fell passionately in love with Fanny Brawne, to whom he became engaged.

A Life Cut Short Even before his great burst of creative activity, Keats had been troubled by frequent sore throats. During 1820 his illness progressed, and he was emotionally torn by the poverty that seemed to rule out any marriage to Fanny. Together with a friend, Keats traveled to Italy in hopes of recovering his health. They settled in Rome, where Keats died in February 1821.

Keats's Style The following features are often singled out as typical of Keats's poetic style:
- slow-moving, expansive *rhythms*
- eloquent but concentrated *diction and phrasing*
- concreteness of *sensory imagery,* sometimes involving synesthesia, or an appeal to more than one sense in the same image

- a *tone of vibrant empathy,* which leads the poet to identify intensely with the world outside himself

◆ The Elgin Marbles

The mythology, literature, art, and sculpture of ancient Greece provided Keats with one of his principal sources of poetic inspiration. In 1816, the acquisition and display of the Elgin Marbles by the British Museum had a notable impact on the British public, and on Keats in particular. These sculptures and architectural ornaments had been removed from the Parthenon and other monuments in Athens and shipped to England by order of Thomas Bruce, Lord Elgin, who served as British ambassador to the Ottoman Empire from 1799 to 1803. Elgin claimed he acted out of fear that the priceless art works would be damaged if they were left in Greece, but many attacked him for dishonesty and vandalism. One of his most outspoken critics, in fact, was Lord Byron, another Romantic poet. Today the Elgin Marbles remain a sore point between Britain and Greece, which has frequently demanded their return.

The most famous of the monuments is the Parthenon frieze, a continuous band inside the temple's colonnade whose sculptures depict a solemn religious procession and a mythological battle. Many of the Parthenon sculptures are the work of the Athenian Phidias (born c. 490 B.C.), to whom Keats refers in line 10 of "Ode on Indolence."

◆ Literary Works

Sonnets and Other Short Poems: "On First Looking into Chapman's Homer," "When I Have Fears that I May Cease to Be," "Why Did I Laugh Tonight?," "La Belle Dame Sans Merci"

Odes: "Ode to a Nightingale," "Ode on a Grecian Urn," "Ode to Psyche," "Ode on Melancholy," "Ode on Indolence," "To Autumn"

Long Poems: Endymion: A Poetic Romance; Lamia; The Eve of St. Agnes; The Fall of Hyperion: A Dream

Letters

TIMELINE

Keats's Life		World Events	
1795	Keats born in London	1788	Birth of Byron
1803	Enters Clarke School at Enfield near London	1789	Beginning of French Revolution
		1792	Birth of Percy Bysshe Shelley
1804	Death of Keats's father in a riding accident	1798	Wordsworth and Coleridge publish *Lyrical Ballads*
1810	Death of Keats's mother from tuberculosis (consumption); Richard Abbey appointed guardian; Keats apprenticed to apothecary Thomas Hammond	1799	Decipherment of the Rosetta Stone in Egypt
		1801	Act of Union creates United Kingdom of Great Britain and Ireland
1815	Keats enters Guy's Hospital to study medicine	1803	Louisiana Purchase in United States
1816	Qualifies as apothecary-surgeon but decides to abandon medicine for poetry; meets Leigh Hunt, William Hazlitt, Charles Lamb; writes sonnet "On First Looking into Chapman's Homer"	1804	Beethoven writes *Symphony No. 3 (Eroica);* Napoleon crowns himself emperor
		1805	Battle of Trafalgar
		1807	Robert Fulton launches first steamboat
1817	First book of poems published	1808	Goethe's *Faust (Part 1)* published in Germany
1818	Publication of *Endymion;* summer walking tour; falls in love with Fanny Brawne; death of Keats's brother Tom	1809	American author Washington Irving writes "Rip Van Winkle"
		1812	Byron's *Childe Harold's Pilgrimage*
1819	"Miraculous year" of great odes, *The Eve of St. Agnes, Lamia;* is engaged to Fanny Brawne	1814	Sir Walter Scott's *Waverley*
		1815	Napoleon defeated at Waterloo
		1817	Coleridge's *Biographia Literaria*
1820	Keats moves to Italy to attempt recovery from tuberculosis	1818	Mary Shelley's *Frankenstein*
1821	Keats dies in Rome	1821	John Constable paints *The Hay-Wain;* Percy Bysshe Shelley writes his long poem *Adonais,* an elegy for Keats

John Keats

To Emma

O come, dearest Emma! the rose is full blown,
And the riches of Flora are lavishly strown,
The air is all softness, and crystal the streams,
And the West is resplendently clothèd in beams.

5   We will hasten, my fair, to the opening glades,
The quaintly[1] carved seats, and the freshening shades,
Where the fairies are chanting their evening hymns,
And in the last sunbeam the sylph[2] lightly swims.

And when thou art weary I'll find thee a bed
10   Of mosses and flowers to pillow thy head;
There, beauteous Emma, I'll sit at thy feet,
While my story of love I enraptured[3] repeat.

So fondly I'll breathe, and so softly I'll sigh,
Thou wilt think that some amorous Zephyr[4] is nigh—
15   Ah, no!—as I breathe, I will press thy fair knee,
And then thou wilt know that the sigh comes from me.

Then why, lovely girl, should we lose all these blisses?
That mortal's a fool who such happiness misses,
So smile acquiescence,[5] and give me thy hand,
20   With love-looking eyes, and with voice sweetly bland.

---

1. **quaintly** (kwānt lē) *adv*.: Cleverly or skillfully made.
2. **sylph** (silf) *n*.: A spirit that inhabits the air.
3. **enraptured** (in rap′ chərd) *adj*.: Filled with great pleasure or delight.
4. **Zephyr** (zef′ ər) *n*.: Soft gentle breeze.
5. **acquiescence** (ak′ wē es′ əns) *n*.: Agreement or consent without protest.

John Keats

On Seeing the Elgin Marbles[1]

My spirit is too weak—mortality
    Weighs heavily on me like unwilling sleep,
    And each imagined pinnacle and steep
Of godlike hardship, tells me I must die
5   Like a sick Eagle looking at the sky.
    Yet 'tis a gentle luxury to weep
    That I have not the cloudy winds to keep
Fresh for the opening of the morning's eye.
Such dim-conceivèd glories of the brain
10   Bring round the heart an undescribable feud;
So do these wonders a most dizzy pain,
    That mingles Grecian[2] grandeur with the rude
Wasting of old Time—with a billowy main—
    A sun—a shadow of a magnitude.[3]

---

1. Elgin Marbles: Marble sculptures that adorned the Parthenon in Athens, Greece, and which were brought to England by Lord Elgin in 1806.
2. Grecian (grē´ shən): Of Greece.
3. magnitude (mag´ nə to͞od´) *n.*: Greatness, of size, extent, or importance.

In Drear-Nighted December

I

In drear-nighted December,
   Too happy, happy tree,
Thy branches ne'er remember
   Their green felicity:[1]
5   The north cannot undo them,
With a sleety[2] whistle through them,
Nor frozen thawings glue them
   From budding at the prime.

II

In drear-nighted December,
10   Too happy, happy brook,
Thy bubblings ne'er remember
   Apollo's[3] summer look;
But with a sweet forgetting,
They stay their crystal fretting,
15   Never, never petting
   About the frozen time.

III

Ah! would 'twere so with many
   A gentle girl and boy!
But were there ever any
20   Writhed[4] not of passèd joy?
The feel of not to feel it,
When there is none to heal it,
Nor numbèd sense to steel it,
   Was never said in rhyme.

---

1. **felicity** (fə lis′ ə tē) *n*.: Happiness; bliss.
2. **sleety** (slēt′ ē) *adj*.: Of sleet, rain that freezes as it falls.
3. **Apollo's:** Apollo exemplifies manly youth and beauty.
4. **Writhed** (rīthd′) *v*.: Suffered great emotional stress.

John Keats

Bright Star, Would I Were Steadfast as Thou Art

Bright star, would I were steadfast as thou art—
    Not in lone splendor hung aloft the night
And watching. with eternal lids apart,
    Like nature's patient, sleepless Eremite,[1]
5   The moving waters at their priestlike task
    Of pure ablution[2] round earth's human shores,
Or gazing on the new soft-fallen mask
    Of snow upon the mountains and the moors—
No—yet still steadfast, still unchangeable,
10   Pillowed upon my fair love's ripening breast,
To feel forever its soft fall and swell,
    Awake forever in a sweet unrest,
Still, still to hear her tender-taken breath,
And so live ever—or else swoon to death.

---

1. **Eremite** (ēr′ mĭt) *n.*: Hermit.
2. **ablution:** (ab lōō′ shən) *n.*: Washing, as part of a religious ceremony.

☑ Check Your Comprehension

1. What is the setting in "To Emma"?

2. In "On Seeing the Elgin Marbles," how does the speaker react to the sight of these ancient Greek sculptures?

3. In the first stanza of "In Drear-Nighted December," why does the speaker call the tree happy?

4. In "Bright Star, Would I Were Steadfast as Thou Art," what two things does the speaker say the star watches from its position in the sky?

◆ Critical Thinking

1. The Latin expression *carpe diem* means "seize the day." How does this phrase sum up the speaker's theme in "To Emma"? **[Apply]**

2. Why do you think the speaker compares himself to "a sick eagle looking at the sky" in line 5 of "On Seeing the Elgin Marbles"? **[Infer]**

COMPARE LITERARY WORKS

3. Consider the speaker's thoughts about love, happiness, and the passage of time in "In Drear-Nighted December" and "Bright Star, Would I Were Steadfast as Thou Art." What do these poems have in common? Before writing, make a chart listing the similarities of the poems and use it to arrange your ideas and examine the relationships between them. **[Connect]**

Can Death Be Sleep, When Life Is but a Dream

I

Can death be sleep, when life is but a dream,
    And scenes of bliss pass as a phantom by?
The transient[1] pleasures as a vision seem,
    And yet we think the greatest pain's to die.

II

5   How strange it is that man on earth should roam,
        And lead a life of woe, but not forsake[2]
    His rugged path; nor dare he view alone
        His future doom which is but to awake.

---

1. transient (tran´shənt) *adj.*: Passing away with time; not permanent.
2. forsake (fôr sāk´) *v.*: Leave; abandon.

John Keats

To Sorrow

"To Sorrow" is a song taken from Keats's Endymion: A Poetic Romance. *The long four-book poem tells the story of Endymion, the shepherd prince, and the moon goddess, Cynthia, who falls in love with him.*

'O Sorrow,
Why dost borrow
The natural hue of health, from vermeil[1] lips?—
To give maiden blushes
5   To the white rose bushes?
Or is't thy dewy hand the daisy tips?

'O Sorrow
Why dost borrow
The lustrous[2] passion from a falcon-eye?—
10   To give the glow-worm light?
Or, on a moonless night,
To tinge, on siren[3] shores, the salt sea-spry?[4]

'O Sorrow,
Why dost borrow
15   The mellow ditties from a mourning tongue?—
To give at evening pale
Unto the nightingale,
That thou mayst listen the cold dews among?

---

1. **vermeil** (vur´ mil) *adj.*: Bright red or scarlet.
2. **lustrous** (lus´ trəs) *adj.*: Shining; bright; glorious.
3. **siren** (sī rən) *adj.*: Of a siren, a woman who uses her charms to allure men; dangerously seductive.
4. **spry**: Variant spelling of *spray*.

'O Sorrow,
20   Why dost borrow
Heart's lightness from the merriment of May?—
       A lover would not tread
       A cowslip[5] on the head,
Though he should dance from eve till peep of day—
25   Nor any drooping flower
       Held sacred for thy bower,[6]
Wherever he may sport himself and play.

'To Sorrow,
       I bade good-morrow,
30   And thought to leave her far away behind.
       But cheerly, cheerly,
       She loves me dearly;
She is so constant to me, and so kind:
       I would deceive her
35   And so leave her,
But ah! she is so constant and so kind.

---

5. **cowslip**: A plant with yellow or purple flowers.
6. **bower** (bou´ ər) *n.*: A place enclosed by overhanging trees.

John Keats

Ode on Melancholy

I

No, no, go not to Lethe,[1] neither twist
    Wolf's-bane,[2] tight-rooted, for its poisonous wine:
Nor suffer thy pale forehead to be kissed
    By nightshade, ruby grape of Proserpine;

5   Make not your rosary of yew-berries,[3]
       Nor let the beetle,[4] nor the death-moth be
          Your mournful Psyche,[5] nor the downy owl
    A partner in your sorrow's mysteries;[6]
       For shade to shade will come too drowsily,

10   And drown the wakeful anguish of the soul.

II

But when the melancholy fit shall fall
    Sudden from heaven like a weeping cloud,
That fosters the droop-headed flowers all,
    And hides the green hill in an April shroud;

15   Then glut[7] thy sorrow on a morning rose,
       Or on the rainbow of the salt sand-wave,
          Or on the wealth of globèd peonies;
    Or if thy mistress some rich anger shows,
       Emprison her soft hand, and let her rave,

20   And feed deep, deep upon her peerless eyes.

---

1. Lethe (lē´ thē): The river of forgetfulness flowing through Hades.
2. Wolf's-bane: A poisonous plant.
3. nightshade . . . yew-berries: "Proserpine" (prō sur´ pi nē´) is Queen of he under-
world. "Nightshade" is a poisonous plant with bright red berries ("ruby grape"). The yew-
tree also has small red berries which are poisonous.
4. beetle: To the ancient Egyptians the beetle was a symbol of resurrection.
5. Death-moth . . . Psyche: Psyche (sī´ kē), the soul, was sometimes represented
as a moth or butterfly.
6. sorrow's mysteries: Associated with religious ceremonies.
7. glut (glut) *v.*: To feed or fill to excess.

III

She dwells with Beauty—Beauty that must die;
    And Joy, whose hand is ever at his lips
Bidding adieu; and aching Pleasure nigh,
    Turning to poison while the bee-mouth sips:
25   Ay, in the very temple of Delight
        Veiled Melancholy has her sovran[8] shrine,
          Though seen of none save him whose strenuous tongue
      Can burst Joy's grape against his palate fine;
His soul shall taste the sadness of her might,
      And be among her cloudy trophies hung.[9]

---

8. sovran (säv´ rən) *adj.*: Variant form of sovereign, meaning, superior to all others.
9. cloudy trophies hung: Referring to the Greek and Roman practice of hanging trophies in the temples of the gods.

☑ Check Your Comprehension

1. What strikes the speaker as strange in "Can Death Be Sleep, When Life Is but a Dream"?

2. (a) In the final stanza of "To Sorrow," what does the speaker say he has wanted to do? (b) Why has he been unsuccessful?

3. (a) To what does the speaker compare the "melancholy fit" in lines 11–14 of "Ode on Melancholy"? (b) In the ode's third stanza, where is Melancholy said to dwell?

◆ Critical Thinking

INTERPRET

1. What can you conclude about the speaker's outlook on life and death in "Can Death Be Sleep, When Life Is but a Dream"? **[Infer]**

2. (a) What is the rhyme scheme in "To Sorrow"? (b) How do the rhyme scheme and the repeated use of questions affect the poem's tone? **[Analyze]**

3. (a) According to lines 27–28 of "Ode on Melancholy," who is the only person allowed to see the veiled goddess in her shrine? (b) How do these lines relate to the poem's overall theme? **[Interpret]**

COMPARE LITERARY WORKS

4. A **paradox** is a statement that seems to be contradictory but that actually presents a truth. How do all three poems in this group make use of paradox? **[Connect]**

John Keats

Ode on Indolence

They toil not, neither do they spin[1]

In a letter dated March 19, 1819, Keats describes himself as being in such a listless state that "pleasure has no show of enticement and pain no unbearable frown. Neither Poetry, nor Ambition, nor Love have any alertness of countenance as they pass by me: they seem rather like three figures on a Greek vase—a Man and two women—whom no one but myself could distinguish in their disguisement. This is the only happiness; and is a rare instance of advantage in the body overpowering the Mind." The ode was composed shortly after Keats had written this letter.

I

One morn before me were three figures seen,
 With bowèd necks, and joinèd hands, side-faced;
And one behind the other stepped serene,
 In placid sandals, and in white robes graced;
5 They passed, like figures on a marble urn,
  When shifted round to see the other side;
   They came again; as when the urn once more
Is shifted round, the first seen shades return;
 And they were strange to me, as may betide
10   With vases, to one deep in Phidian[2] lore.

II

How is it, Shadows! that I knew ye not?
 How came ye muffled in so hush a mask?
Was it a silent deep-disguisèd plot
 To steal sway, and leave without a task
15 My idle days? Ripe was the drowsy hour;
  The blissful cloud of summer-indolence
   Benumbed my eyes; my pulse grew less and less;
Pain had no sting, and pleasure's wreath no flower:
 0, why did ye not melt, and leave my sense
20   Unhaunted quite of all but—nothingness?

III

A third time passed they by, and, passing, turned
 Each one the face a moment whiles to me;

---

1. *They toil not, neither do they spin:* From the Bible, Matthew 6.28. "Consider the lilies of the field, how they grow; they toil not, neither do they spin."
2. Phidian (fid´ ē ən): Phidias was a Greek sculptor of the fifth century B.C.

Then faded, and to follow them I burned
 And ached for wings because I knew the three;
25 The first was a fair Maid, and Love her name;
  The second was Ambition, pale of cheek,
   And ever watchful with fatiguèd eye;
 The last, whom I love more, the more of blame
  Is heaped upon her, maiden most unmeek—
30   I know to be my demon Poesy.[3]

IV

They faded, and, forsooth![4] I wanted wings.
 O folly! What is love! and where is it?
And, for that poor Ambition—it springs
 From a man's little heart's short fever-fit.
35 For Poesy!—no, she him not a joy—
  At least for me—so sweet as drowsy noons,
   And evenings steeped in honeyed indolence.
 O, for an age so sheltered from annoy,[5]
  That I may never know how change the moons,
40   Or hear the voice of busy common-sense!

V

A third time came they by—alas! wherefore?
 My sleep had been embroidered with dim dreams;
My soul had been a lawn besprinkled o'er
 With flowers, and stirring shades, and baffled beams:
45 The morn was clouded, but no shower fell,
  Though in her lids hung the sweet tears of May;
   The open casement[6] pressed a new-leaved vine,
 Let in the budding warmth and throstle's[7] lay;
O Shadows! 'twas a time to bid farewell!
50   Upon your skirts had fallen no tears of mine.

VI

So, ye three Ghosts, adieu! Ye cannot raise
 My head cool-bedded in the flowery grass;
For I would not be dieted with praise,
 A pet-lamb in a sentimental farce!
55 Fade softly from my eyes, and be once more
  In mask-like figures on the dreamy urn.
   Farewell! I yet have visions for the night,
And for the day faint visions there is store.
   Vanish, ye Phantoms! from my idle sprite,[8]
60 Into the clouds, and never more return!

---

3. **Poesy** (pō′ ə sē′): Old-fashioned variation of poetry.
4. **forsooth** (fôr sooth′) *adv.*: Truly.
5. **annoy:** Here, pain; harm.
6. **casement:** A window frame that opens on hinges along the side.
7. **throstle's:** A throstle is a songbird.
8. **sprite:** Spirit.

John Keats

To Autumn

I

Season of mists and mellow fruitfulness,
 Close bosom-friend of the maturing sun;
Conspiring with him how to load and bless
 With fruit the vines that round the thatch-eves run;
5 To bend with apples the mossed cottage-trees,
  And fill all fruit with ripeness to the core;
   To swell the gourd, and plump the hazel shells
  With a sweet kernel; to set budding more,
And still more, later flowers for the bees,
10 Until they think warm days will never cease,
   For Summer has o'er-brimmed their clammy cells,

II

Who hath not seen thee oft amid thy store?
 Sometimes whoever seeks abroad may find
Thee sitting careless on a granary floor,
15 Thy hair soft-lifted by the winnowing[1] wind;
Or on a half-reaped furrow sound asleep,
 Drowsed with the fume of poppies, while thy hook[2]
  Spares the next swath and all its twined flowers:
And sometimes like a gleaner thou dost keep
20 Steady thy laden head across a brook;
 Or by a cider-press, with patient look,
  Thou watchest the last oozings hours by hours.

III

Where are the songs of Spring? Ay, where are they?
 Think not of them, thou hast thy music too —
25 While barred clouds bloom the soft-dying day,
 And touch the stubble–plains with rosy hue;
Then in a wailful choir the small gnats mourn
 Among the river sallows,[3] borne aloft
  Or sinking as the light wind lives or dies;
30 And full-grown lambs loud bleat from hilly bourn;[4]
  Hedge-crickets sing; and now with treble soft
  The red-breast whistles from a garden croft;[5]
   And gathering swallows twitter in the skies.

---

1. **winnowing:** Fanning; winnowing is a process in which the chaff is fanned from the gain.
2. **hook:** Scythe.
3. **sallows:** Willow trees.
4. **bourn:** Region.
5. **croft:** An enclosed plot of farm land.

☑ Check Your Comprehension

1. In "Ode on Indolence," who are the three mysterious figures that appear to the speaker?
2. In "Ode on Indolence," what metaphor does Keats use in lines 43–44?
3. What does the speaker wish for in lines 37–40?
4. (a) In stanza 1 of "To Autumn," what is the season described as doing? (b) With whom is the season "conspiring"?
5. In stanza 3, what are some of the songs of autumn?

◆ Critical Thinking

INTERPRET

1. What is the rhyme scheme in the first four stanzas of "Ode on Indolence"? **[Analyze]**

2. What positive side does Keats see in indolence? Consider his attitude toward the three ghostly figures, as well as the meaning of the biblical allusion that he uses as an epigraph for the ode. **[Interpret]**

3. In what way can Autumn be described as a "close bosom-friend of the maturing sun"? **[Analyze]**

4. (a) What activities frequently associated with the season are described in the second stanza? (b) What impression of Autumn is created by mentioning these activities? **[Interpret]**

5. Why do you think the speaker mentions the songs of Spring in line 23? **[Infer]**

$\mathcal{J}$ohn Keats

Comparing and Connecting the Author's Works

◆ Literary Focus: Imagery

Imagery is the descriptive language that poets and other writers use to recreate sensory experience. Keats was a master of vivid imagery that concretely appeals to the five senses: sight, hearing, smell, taste, and touch.

1. To what senses do these lines from "To Emma" appeal?

   So smile acquiescence, and give me thy hand,
   With love-looking eyes, and with voice sweetly bland.

2. Sometimes Keats blends appeals to two senses in the same image. Explain how the following lines from "Ode in Melancholy" illustrate **synesthesia,** or mingling of the senses:

   "Or if thy mistress some rich anger shows,
       Emprison her soft hand, and let her rave,
           And feed deep, deep upon her peerless eyes."

◆ Drawing Conclusions About Keats's Work

You can often draw important lessons about the creative process by comparing an earlier version of a writer's work with the finished product. Revisions not only affect the meaning of a particular passage, but also provide insight into a writer's themes and artistic values.

Read the following examples of Keats's revisions for two passages in "To Autumn," and compare each passage with the final version on page 158. Then answer the listed questions.

---

oft amid thy stores?
Who hath not seen thee? ~~for thy haunts~~
~~are many~~
                          abroad
Sometimes whoever seeks ~~for thee~~ may
    find
Thee sitting careless on a granary floor,
Thy hair soft-lifted by the winnowing
    wind.

(lines 12–15)

Where are the songs of Spring? Ay, where
    are they?
Think not of them, thou hast thy
    music too—
        barred   bloom
While ~~a gold~~ clouds ~~gilds~~ the soft-dying
    day,
And   with
~~And~~ touching the stubble-plains   ∧
    rosy hue.

(lines 23–26)

---

1. How do the revisions in lines 12–13 make the description of Autumn more specific?

2. What metaphor does Keats create through his revision of line 25?

◆ Idea Bank

Writing

1. **Paraphrase** Write a prose paraphrase of either "On Seeing the Elgin Marbles" or "Bright Star, Would I Were Steadfast as Thou Art." Be sure to include the speaker's main ideas in your paraphrase.

2. **Poetic Analysis** In a brief essay, analyze the poetic forms in "Ode on Melancholy," "Ode on Indolence," and "To Autumn." Compare and contrast

the elements of stanza form, rhyme scheme, and rhythm.

3. Ode in Free Verse Keats manages to see positive qualities in states or emotions that are usually regarded as negative: for example, melancholy and indolence. Write an ode in free verse in which you treat another such emotional state positively: for example, anger, forgetfulness, or stress.

Speaking and Listening

4. Oral Interpretation Choose your favorite poem in this group and prepare an oral interpretation (reading) of it. In your rehearsals, focus on elements such as pace, rhythm, pitch, and tone. Present your interpretation to a small audience of classmates or friends. **[Performing Arts Link]**

5. Music for Autumn Many of Keats's images in "To Autumn" suggest music. Find a piece of music that you feel would provide a suitable background for Keats's poem. Try reading the poem aloud as the music plays. Bring a recording of the music you select to class. **[Music Link]**

Researching and Representing

6. Illustrated Report Together with a small group, research the London neighborhood of Hampstead Heath, where Keats wrote much of his great poetry in 1819 and where many writers and artists live today. Try to find pictures of the Keats House, where the poet lived, and also investigate the memorable landscapes of this locale by the British Romantic painter John Constable (1776–1837). Together with your group members, present your results in an illustrated report to the class. **[Group Activity; Social Studies; Art Link]**

◆ Further Reading, Listening, and Viewing

- W. J. Bate: *John Keats* (1963). A landmark biography, with acute analysis of the poet's style
- Robert Gittings: *John Keats* (1968). Another excellent biography
- Helen Vendler: *The Odes of John Keats* (1986). A finely tuned, sensitive analysis of the great odes
- *The Poetry of Keats* (1996). Readings by Sir Ralph Richardson on audiocassette
- Michael Rosenthal: *Constable: The Painter and his Landscape* (1983). An introduction to the Romantic painter John Constable

On the Web:

http://www.phschool.com/atschool/literature Go to the student edition of *The British Tradition*. Proceed to Unit 4. Then, click Hot Links to find Web sites featuring John Keats.

Elizabeth Barrett Browning In Depth

> "How do I love thee? Let me count the ways."
> —*Elizabeth Barrett Browning*, **Sonnets from the Portuguese**

ELIZABETH BARRETT BROWNING was, during her lifetime, the most famous woman poet in England. When William Wordsworth died in 1850, Barrett Browning was considered one of the leading candidates to succeed him as Poet Laureate. (In the end, that honor went to Alfred, Lord Tennyson.) Browning's long narrative poem *Aurora Leigh* (1857) was so popular that it helped to support her and her husband Robert Browning, whose poetry was far less well-known than hers at the time.

Childhood and Youth Elizabeth Barrett was born in 1806 in the north of England. The eldest of twelve children, she was educated at home and quickly showed herself something of a literary prodigy. By the age of twelve, she had completed an epic in four books, set in ancient Greece.

In 1826, Barrett's first volume of poetry, entitled *An Essay on Mind,* was published anonymously and to little critical notice. It was not until 1838 that she won favorable reviews for another collection of verse, *The Seraphim and Other Poems.* This time the book was published under Barrett's own name. With the appearance in 1844 of her *Poems* in two volumes, her popularity was assured.

Barrett's personal development was limited, however, by her fragile health and by her tyrannically possessive father, who forbade any of his children to marry. By 1845, when the Barrett family had been living in London for ten years, Elizabeth seemed destined to live the rest of her days as a cloistered invalid.

Love and Marriage Enter Robert Browning, a little known poet six years her junior, whose impulsive fan letter to Barrett began one of the great romances of literary history. "I do as I say, love these books with all my heart—and I love you too," Browning wrote.

Despite the stern disapproval of Barrett's father, Browning continued his courtship. In September 1846, the couple secretly married and eloped to the Continent, settling in Florence, Italy. Their only child, a son nicknamed Pen, was born in 1849.

In Italy, Barrett Browning continued to write poetry. Her sequence of forty-four *Sonnets from the Portuguese* (1850), became some of the most popular love poems in English literature. The sonnets describe the development of her love for Browning; the title was intended to disguise the personal nature of the sonnets by implying that they were translated from another language.

Barrett Browning's second major work from this period is her long novel in verse, *Aurora Leigh* (1857). A portrait of the development of a woman poet, this is the first work in English by a woman writer in which the heroine is an author.

Barrett Browning died in Florence in 1861 in her husband's arms. Together with Pen, Browning moved back to London. Unable to bear revisiting the blissful setting of his life with Elizabeth, he never returned to Florence again.

◆ The Brownings' Italy

"Italy was my university," Robert Browning once remarked. His first visit there in 1838, when he traveled to Venice, may have inspired his early work *Sordello,* a long narrative poem set in the Middle Ages. In 1846, after the Brownings married and left England, they wintered in the Italian city of Pisa and then settled in Florence, which became their home for the rest of their married life.

This period was a time of great ferment in Italy, where nationalist sentiment led to the unification of Italy as an independent nation in 1861. Elizabeth Barrett Browning enthusiastically supported Italian liberation from Austria. Some literary critics have suggested that Barrett Browning's political activism was an expression of her inner struggle to find her own poetic identity. Robert Browning found inspiration for some of his best dramatic monologues in another aspect of Italian culture: the art of the Italian Renaissance, as exemplified in such fifteenth- and sixteenth-century painters as Andrea del Sarto and Fra Filippo Lippi.

◆ Literary Works

The Battle of Marathon (1820), an epic in four books, set in ancient Greece and published when the poet was thirteen years old

An Essay on Mind (1826), first collection of poems

Prometheus Bound (1833), translation of the ancient Greek tragedy by Aeschylus

The Seraphim and Other Poems (1838)

Poems (1844), a two-volume work for which Edgar Allan Poe wrote the introduction to the American edition

Sonnets from the Portuguese (1850), probably the poet's best-known work

Aurora Leigh (1857), a novel in verse featuring an aspiring poet as the heroine.

TIMELINE

Browning's Life

1806	Born at Coxhoe Hall, County Durham
1809	Family moves to Hope End, a country estate in Herefordshire
1818	Writes *The Battle of Marathon,* a narrative epic in four books
1825	First poem, "The Rose and Zephyr," published
1826	First volume of poetry, *An Essay on Mind* published
1832	Family moves to Sidmouth in Devon
1835	Family moves to London
1837	Illness caused by burst blood vessel
1838	*The Seraphim and Other Poems* published
1840	Death of favorite brother, Edward
1844	*Poems* published in two volumes
1845	Meets Robert Browning
1846	Secretly marries Robert in London; the couple leaves for the Continent and settles in Florence, Italy
1849	Birth of son Pen
1850	*Sonnets from the Portuguese* published
1857	*Aurora Leigh* published
1860	*Poems Before Congress* published
1861	Death in Florence

World Events

1808	Excavation of the ancient ruins at Pompeii begins in Italy
1812	Byron's *Childe Harold's Pilgrimage* published
1812	War between the United States and Britain
1813	Jane Austen's *Pride and Prejudice* published; Italian opera composer Giuseppe Verdi born
1815	Defeat of Napoleon at Waterloo
1816	Charlotte Brontë born
1819	Keats writes his great odes; novelist Marian Evans (George Eliot) born
1825	Bolshoi Ballet founded in Russia
1832	First Reform Act in England
1833	Slavery abolished in British Empire
1837	Accession of Queen Victoria
1842	Verdi's opera *Nabucco* performed
1843	John Ruskin publishes first volume of *Modern Painters*
1844	Samuel F. B. Morse patents telegraph
1845	Irish potato famine begins
1847	Charlotte Brontë's *Jane Eyre* and Emily Brontë's *Wuthering Heights* published
1848	Pre-Raphaelite Brotherhood—a group of British painters, artists, poets, and critics—founded in London
1854	Britain enters Crimean War
1857	Gustave Flaubert publishes *Madame Bovary* in France
1861	Civil War begins in United States

Elizabeth Barrett Browning

Man and Nature

A sad man on a summer day
Did look upon the earth and say—

"Purple cloud the hilltop binding;
Folded hills the valleys wind in;
5   Valleys with fresh streams among you;
Streams with bosky[1] trees along you;
Trees with many birds and blossoms;
Birds with music trembling bosoms;
Blossoms dropping dews that wreathe[2] you
10   To your fellow flowers beneath you;
Flowers that constellate[3] on earth;
Earth that shakest to the mirth
Of the merry Titan Ocean,[4]
All his shining hair in motion!
15   Why am I thus the only one
Who can be dark beneath the sun?

But when the summer day was past,
He looked to heaven and smiled at last,
Self answered so—

       "Because, O cloud,
20   Pressing with thy crumpled shroud
Heavily on mountain top,—
Hills that almost seem to drop
Stricken with a misty death
To the valleys underneath,—

---

1. bosky (bäs´ kē) adj.: Covered with trees or shrubs; wooded.
2. wreathe (rēth´) v.: Cover or envelop.
3. constellate (kän´ stə lāt´) v.: Unite in or as in a constellation; cluster.
4. Titan Ocean: Referring to Oceanus, the river supposed to encircle the plain of the Earth; also personified as one of the Titans of Greek mythology.

25   Valleys sighing with the torrent,—
        Waters streaked with branches horrent,[5]—
        Branchless trees that shake your head
        Wildly o'er your blossoms spread
        Where the common flowers are found,—
30   Flowers with foreheads to the ground,—
        Ground that shriekest while the sea
        With his iron smiteth[6] thee—
        I am, besides, the only one
        Who can be bright *without* the sun."

---

5. horrent (hôr´ ənt) *adj.*: (1) Standing up like bristles (2) Horrified, shuddering.
6. smiteth (smīt´ eth) *v.*: Struck; hit.

Elizabeth Barrett Browning

A Sea-Side Walk

I

We walked beside the sea
After a day which perished silently
Of its own glory—like the princess weird
Who, combating the Genius, scorched and seared,
5   Uttered with burning breath, 'Ho! victory!'
And sank adown, a heap of ashes pale:
    So runs the Arab tale.[1]

II

The sky above us showed
A universal and unmoving cloud
10   On which the cliffs permitted us to see
Only the outline of their majesty,
As masterminds when gazed at by the crowd:
And shining with a gloom, the water gray
    Swang in its moon taught way.

III

15   Nor moon, nor stars were out;
They did not dare to tread so soon about,
Through trembling, in the footsteps of the sun:
The light was neither night's nor day's, but one
Which, lifelike, had a beauty in its doubt,
20   And silence's impassioned breathings round
    Seemed wandering into sound.

IV

O solemn beating heart
Of nature! I have knowledge that thou art
Bound unto man's by cords he cannot sever;
25   And, what time they are slackened by him ever,
So to attest his own supernal[2] part,
Still runneth thy vibration fast and strong
    The slackened cord along:

---

1. princess weird. . . Arab tale: Referring to *The Thousand and One
Nights*, a collection of tales of Persian, Indian, and Arabian Origin.
2. supernal: (sə pɜrn′ əl) *adj.*: Celestial; heavenly; divine.

V

For though we never spoke

30 Of the gray water and the shaded rock
Dark wave and stone unconsciously were fused
Into the plaintive[3] speaking that we used
Of absent friends and memories unforsook;[4]
And, had we seen each other's face, we had
35 Seen haply[5] each was sad.

---

3. **plaintive** (hôr´ ənt) *adj.*: Expressing sorrow or melancholy.
4. **unforsook:** Unabandoned; unforgotten.
5. **haply:** By chance or by accident; perhaps.

Elizabeth Barrett Browning

Stanzas

I may sing; but minstrel's singing[1]
Ever ceaseth with his playing.
I may smile; but time is bringing
Thoughts for smiles to wear away in.
5   I may view thee, mutely loving;
But *shall* view thee so in dying!
I may sigh; but life's removing,
And with breathing endeth singing!
                  Be it so!

When no song of mine comes near thee,
10   Will its memory fail to soften?
When no smile of mine can cheer thee,
Will thy smile be used as often?
When my looks the darkness boundeth,
Will thine own be lighted after?
15   When my sigh no longer soundeth,
Wilt thou list[2] another's laughter?
                  Be it so!

---

1. minstrel's singing: A minstrel is an entertainer known for singing and reciting to musical accompaniment.
2. list: To wish; like; choose.

Elizabeth Barrett Browning

The Best Thing in the World

What's the best thing in the world?
June rose, by May dew impearled;[1]
Sweet south wind, that means no rain;
Truth, not cruel to a friend;
5   Pleasure, not in haste to end;
Beauty, not self decked and curled
Till its pride is over plain;
Light, that never makes you wink;
Memory, that gives no pain;
10 Love, when, *so*, you're loved again.
What's the best thing in the world?
—Something out of it, I think.

---

1. impearled (im purld´) *v.*: Formed into pearls or pearl-like drops.

☑ Check Your Comprehension

1. In "Man and Nature," what emotions does the principal speaker experience in the two halves of the poem?
2. What legend does the speaker refer to in the first stanza of "A Sea-Side Walk"?
3. (a) In "Stanzas," whom is the speaker addressing? (b) Which words function as a refrain in this poem?
4. What are four good things that the speaker mentions in "The Best Thing in the World"?

◆ Critical Thinking

INTERPRET
1. Why might the structure of "Man and Nature" be described as balanced or symmetrical? **[Analyze]**

2. How would you describe the atmosphere or overall mood in "A Sea-Side Walk"? **[Interpret]**

3. (a) In "Stanzas," what seems to be the speaker's attitude toward time and mortality? (b) How do you know? **[Infer]**

4. (a) How does the final answer to the question in lines 11–12 of "The Best Thing in the World" express the poem's theme? (b) Did this answer come as a surprise to you? **[Draw Conclusions]**

COMPARE LITERARY WORKS
5. Examine the similarities and differences in the poet's attitudes toward nature in "Man and Nature" and "A Sea-Side Walk." **[Compare and Contrast]**

Sonnet 6
from Sonnets from the Portuguese

The four following poems are taken from Browning's Sonnets
from the Portuguese, *a sequence of forty-four sonnets inspired by
her love for the poet Robert Browning.*

Go from me. Yet I feel that I shall stand
Henceforward in thy shadow. Nevermore
Alone upon the threshold of my door
Of individual life, I shall command
5 The use of my soul, nor lift my hand
Serenely in the sunshine as before,
Without the sense of that which I forbore[1]—
Thy touch upon the palm. The widest land
Doom[2] takes to part us, leave thy heart in mine
10 With pulses that beat double. What I do
And what I dream include thee, as the wine
Must taste of its own grapes. And when I sue[3]
God for myself, He hears that name of thine,
And sees within my eyes the tears of two.

1. **forbore:** Refrained from; avoided.
2. **Doom:** Ruin or death; Judgment Day.
3. **sue:** Appeal to; plead to.

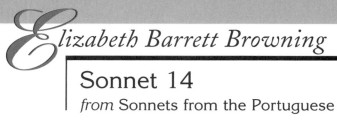

Elizabeth Barrett Browning

Sonnet 14

from Sonnets from the Portuguese

If thou must love me, let it be for nought[1]
Except for love's sake only. Do not say
"I love her for her smile—her look—her way
Of speaking gently,—for a trick of thought
5   That falls in well with mine, and certes[2] brought
A sense of pleasant ease on such a day"—
For these things in themselves, Belovèd, may
Be changed, or change for thee,—and love, so wrought,[3]
May be unwrought so. Neither love me for
10   Thine own dear pity's wiping my cheeks dry,—
A creature might forget to weep, who bore[4]
Thy comfort long, and lose thy love thereby!
But love me for love's sake, that evermore
Thou mayst love on, through love's eternity.

---

1. **nought:** Nothing.
2. **certes** (sʉr´ tēz´) *adv.*: Certainly; surely.
3. **wrought:** Formed; fashioned.
4. **bore:** Held; taken; possessed.

Sonnet 21

from Sonnets from the Portuguese

Say over again, and yet once over again,
That thou dost love me. Though the word repeated
Should seem "a cuckoo song,"[1] as thou dost treat it,
Remember, never to the hill or plain,
5   Valley and wood, without her cuckoo strain
Comes the fresh Spring in all her green completed.
Belovèd, I, amid the darkness greeted
By a doubtful spirit voice, in that doubt's pain
Cry, "Speak once more—thou lovest!" Who can fear
10   Too many stars, though each in heaven shall roll,
Too many flowers, though each shall crown the year?
Say thou dost love me, love me, love me—toll
The silver iterance![2]—only minding, Dear,
To love me also in silence with thy soul.

---

1. "a cuckoo song": The cuckoo bird repeats its call continually.
2. toll the silver iterance: Like the tolling of a bell, regularly repeat the words, "love me."

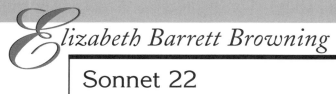

Elizabeth Barrett Browning

Sonnet 22
from Sonnets from the Portuguese

When our two souls stand up erect and strong,
Face to face, silent, drawing nigh and nigher,
Until the lengthening wings break into fire
At either curvèd point,—what bitter wrong
Can the earth do to us, that we should not long
5   Be here contented? Think. In mounting higher,
The angels would press on us and aspire
To drop some golden orb of perfect song
Into our deep, dear silence. Let us stay
10   Rather on earth, Belovèd,—where the unfit
Contrarious¹ moods of men recoil away
And isolate pure spirits, and permit
A place to stand and love in for a day,
With darkness and the death–hour rounding it.

---

1. **contrarious** (kən trer´ ē əs) *adj.*: Contrary to what is considered right; corrupt;
wicked.

☑ Check Your Comprehension

1. In line 1 of "Sonnet 6," what does the speaker request the beloved to do?
2. What does the speaker urge the beloved *not* to do in "Sonnet 14"?
3. According to the speaker in "Sonnet 21," what always accompanies the "fresh Spring"?
4. (a) In what posture does the speaker in "Sonnet 22" envision her own soul and that of her beloved? (b) Where does the speaker believe that she and her beloved will find happiness?

◆ Critical Thinking

1. What event in the relationship of the couple do you think might have provided the background for "Sonnet 6"? **[Speculate]**

2. Browning breaks up "Sonnet 14" in an unusual way by using **enjambment**, or the technique of continuing the sense from one line to the next without a rhythmic break. Find the lines that illustrate enjambment in the poem. **[Classify]**

3. (a) How does the poet use the idea of speech and sound in "Sonnet 21"? (b) How does she contrast speech with silence in the poem's concluding lines? **[Analyze]**

4. Explain the metaphor in lines 1–4 of "Sonnet 22." **[Analyze]**

COMPARE LITERARY WORKS

5. Which of these sonnets do you like most? Explain your choice. **[Make a Judgment]**

An Aspiring Poet

from Aurora Leigh

A novel in verse, Aurora Leigh *depicts the growth of a woman poet.* Aurora Leigh, *an orphan, has been sent to England to live with her conservative aunt, who is responsible for the girl's education. Aurora finds comfort from the oppressive conventionality of the aunt in nature and books, and aspires to become a poet. This excerpt from Book Two focuses on Aurora's aspirations in life and on a conversation with her cousin Romney about the role of women in a Victorian society.*

Times followed one another. Came a morn
I stood upon the brink of twenty years,
And looked before and after, as I stood
Woman and artist—either incomplete.
5   Both credulous[1] of completion. There I held
The whole creation in my little cup,
And smiled with thirsty lips before I drank
"Good health to you and me, sweet neighbor mine,
And all these peoples."

                I was glad, that day;
10   The June was in me, with its multitudes
Of nightingales all singing in the dark,
And Rosebuds reddening where the calyx[2] split.
I felt so young, so strong, so sure of God!
So glad, I could not choose be very wise!
15   And, old at twenty, was inclined to pull
My childhood backward in a childish jest
To see the face of't once more, and farewell!
In which fantastic mood I bounded forth
At early morning,—would not wait so long
20   As even to snatch my bonnet by the strings,
But, brushing a green trail across the lawn
With my gown in the dew, took will and away
Among the acacias[3] of the shrubberies,

---

1. credulous (krej′ ൦൦ ləs) *adj.*: Tending to believe to readily; easily convinced.
2. calyx (kal′ iks′) *n.*: The protective leaves of a flower.
3. acacias (ə kā shəs): Trees, shrubs, or other plants with clusters of yellow or white flowers.

To fly my fancies in the open air
25 And keep my birthday, till my aunt awoke
To stop good dreams. Meanwhile I murmured on
As honeyed bees keep humming to themselves,
"The worthiest poets have remained uncrowned
Till death has bleached their foreheads to the bone;
30 And so with me it must be unless I prove
Unworthy of the grand adversity,
And certainly I would not fail so much.
What, therefore, if I crown myself today
In sport, not pride, to learn the feel of it,
35 Before my brows be numbed as Dante's[4] own
To all the tender pricking of such leaves?
Such leaves! What leaves?"
                            I pulled the branches down
To choose from.
                   "Not the bay![5] I choose no bay
(The fates deny us if we are overbold),
40 Nor myrtle—which means chiefly love; and love
Is something awful which one dares not touch
So early o' mornings. This verbena[6] strains
The point of passionate fragrance; and hard by,
This guelder–rose,[7] at far too slight a beck
45 Of the wind; will toss about her flower–apples.
Ah—there's my choice,—that ivy on the wall,
That headlong ivy! not a leaf will grow
But thinking of a wreath. Large leaves, smooth leaves,
Serrated like my vines, and half as green.
50 I like such ivy, bold to leap a height
'Twas strong to climb; as good to grow on graves
As twist about a thyrsus;[8] pretty too
(And that's not ill) when twisted round a comb."
Thus speaking to myself, half singing it,
55 Because some thoughts are fashioned like a bell
To ring with once being touched, I drew a wreath
Drenched, blinding me with dew, across my brow,
And fastening it behind so, turning faced

---

4. **Dante's:** Dante (dän´ tā) Alighieri (1265–1321), Italian poet who wrote
The Divine Comedy.
5. **bay:** The leaves of a laurel tree; also symbolizing poetic achievement.
6. **verbena:** (vər bē´ nə): Plants with clusters of red, white, or purplish
flowers.
7. **guelder-rose:** Cranberry tree.
8. **thyrsus:** (thur´ səs): Staff tipped with a pine cone and entwined with ivy.

...My public!—cousin Romney—with a mouth
Twice graver than his eyes.

60   I stood there fixed,—
My arms up, like the caryatid,[9] sole
Of some abolished temple, helplessly
Persistent in a gesture which derides[10]
A former purpose. Yet my blush was flame,
As if from flax,[11] not stone.

65   "Aurora Leigh,
The earliest of Auroras!"[12]

                        Hand stretched out
I clasped, as shipwrecked men will clasp a hand,
Indifferent to the sort of palm. The tide
Had caught me at my pastime, writing down

70 My foolish name too near upon the sea
Which drowned me with a blush as foolish. "You,
My cousin!"

                The smile died out in his eyes
And dropped upon his lips, a cold dead weight,
For just a moment, "Here's a book I found!

75 No name writ on it—poems, by the form;
Some Greek upon the margin,—lady's Greek
Without the accents. Read it? Not a word.
I saw at once the thing had witchcraft in't,
Whereof the reading calls up dangerous spirits:
I rather bring it to the witch."

80   "My book.
You found it"...

             "In the hollow by the stream
That beech[13] leans down into—of which you said
The Oread in it has a Naiad's[14] heart
And pines for waters."

                  "Thank you."

                   "Thanks to *you*

85 My cousin! That I have seen you not too much
Witch, scholar, poet, dreamer, and the rest,

---

9. caryatid: (kar´ ē at´ id): Supporting column in the shape of a woman.
10. derides (di rīds) *v.*: Ridicules.
11. flax: A plant with delicate blue flowers: the fibers of the stem are spun
into linen thread; hence soft and delicate.
12. earliest of Auroras: Aurora is the Roman goddess of the dawn.
13. beech: Tree with smooth, gray bark, hard wood, and dark leaves.
14. Oread (ō´ rē ad´) **. . . Naiad's** (nī´ ads´): An oread is a mountain
nymph; naiads are water nymphs, minor nature goddesses known for their
youth and beauty.

To be a woman also."

                         With a glance
The smile rose in his eyes again and touched
The ivy on my forehead, light as air.
90   I answered gravely "Poets needs must be
Or men or women—more's the pity."

                                     "Ah,
But men, and still less women, happily,
Scarce need be poets. Keep to the green wreath,
Since even dreaming of the stone and bronze
95   Brings headaches, pretty cousin, and defiles
The clean white morning dresses."

                               "So you judge!
Because I love the beautiful I must
Love pleasure chiefly, and be overcharged
For ease and whiteness! well, you know the world,
100   And only miss your cousin, 'tis not much.
But learn this; I would rather take my part
With God's Dead, who afford to walk in white
Yet spread His glory, than keep quiet here
And gather up my feet from even a step
105   For fear to soil my gown in so much dust.
I choose to walk at all risks.—Here, if heads
That hold a rhythmic thought, much ache perforce,
For my part I choose headaches,—and today's
My birthday,"

                   "Dear Aurora, choose instead
To cure them. You have balsams."
110   "I perceive.
The headache is too noble for my sex.
You think the heartache would sound decenter,
Since that's the woman's special, proper ache,
And altogether tolerable, except
115   To a woman."

☑ Check Your Comprehension

1. (a) What is the setting for this excerpt? (b) Why does the narrator feel glad in the opening lines?

2. What plant does the narrator choose for her crown?

3. How is the narrator's cousin Romney described when he first appears?

4. What has Romney found?

5. What kind of life does the narrator say that she will choose, rather than "keep quiet"?

◆ Critical Thinking

1. (a) Why do you think it occurs to Aurora Leigh to crown herself? (b) How is this action symbolic? **[Interpret]**

2. Explain the similes at lines 55, 61, and 67. What is being compared with what in each simile? **[Analyze]**

3. What do Romney's reaction to Aurora's book (lines 74–80) and his advice to Aurora not to become a poet (lines 92–96) reveal about his character? **[Infer]**

4. (a) What does Aurora's name mean? (b) How is the meaning of her name linked to the setting and the overall theme of this excerpt? **[Analyze]**

Elizabeth Barrett Browning
Comparing and Connecting the Author's Works

◆ Literary Focus: Verse Forms

The **verse form** of a poem consists of the writer's choice of rhythm and meter, the poem's rhyme scheme, and the type of stanza used in the work. As is clear from the poems in this group, Elizabeth Barrett Browning boldly experimented with a number of verse forms. For example, her use in "Man and Nature" of rhyming, tetrameter (four-beat) couplets arranged in longer, symmetrical stanzas subtly reinforces the poem's theme by underlining the uniqueness of human feelings in nature's overall scheme.

1. (a) Describe the stanza structure and identify the rhyme scheme in "A Sea-Side Walk." (b) How do lines 1 and 7 in each stanza vary the predominant rhythm? (c) What is the effect of this rhythmical variation?

2. (a) What is the rhyme scheme in "Stanzas"? (b) How are the two stanzas balanced or symmetrical? (c) How would the total effect of the poem be different if the refrain were omitted?

3. (a) What is the verse form in *Aurora Leigh?* (b) What devices does Browning use to introduce rhythmic surprise and variety into the verse?

◆ Drawing Conclusions About Browning's Work

One way to analyze and evaluate a literary work is to consider it within the context of biographical or autobiographical materials. Read the following excerpt from a letter that Elizabeth Barrett Browning wrote to her sister shortly after the death of Robert Browning's mother and the couple's third wedding anniversary in 1849:

Since our marriage we have lost some precious things—he the earthly presence of an adorable affection; I some faith in attachments I had counted on for tenderness and duration. But you may thank God for us that we have lost none of our love, none of the belief in one another ... and that indeed we have consciously gained in both these things. There is more love between us two at this moment than there ever has been. He is surer of me. I am surer of him. I am closer to him, and he to me. Ours is a true marriage, and not a conventional match. We live heart to heart all day long, and every day the same.

In a brief essay, analyze and evaluate one of the following poems alongside Browning's letter and its context: "Stanzas," "A Sea-Side Walk," or the four sonnets from *Sonnets from the Portuguese.* You may find it helpful to use the chart below in order to organize your main ideas and supporting details or examples.

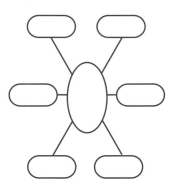

◆ Idea Bank

Writing

1. **Diary Entry** Assume that you are either Elizabeth Barrett Browning or

Robert Browning. Using the first-person point of view, write a diary entry about a real-life incident that you think might plausibly serve as the background for one of the *Sonnets from the Portuguese*.

2. **Sequel** Write a prose sequel to the excerpt from *Aurora Leigh* in which you recount how the relationship between Aurora and her cousin Romney turns out. When you have finished writing, exchange papers with a classmate and read each other's narratives.

3. **Essay** In a brief essay, compare and contrast the poet's outlook on nature in "Man and Nature" and "A Sea-Side and Walk." Be sure to support your main ideas with specific examples drawn from each work.

Speaking and Listening

4. **Reader's Theater** Together with a partner, organize a Reader's Theater presentation of the excerpt from *Aurora Leigh*. When you have polished your performance, present it to a small audience of classmates, friends, or family members. **[Performing Arts Link]**

5. **Soundtrack** Choose a piece of music that you think complements the mood of one of the poems in this group. Then read the poem aloud to a small audience and play your selection as background music. Ask members of the audience for their reactions. **[Music Link]**

Researching and Representing

6. **CD-ROM** In a small group develop a plan for a CD-ROM on "The Barretts of Wimpole Street." Research the play or the film of the same title. Also investigate three historical facts surrounding Elizabeth Barrett and her family, their London home, or Robert Browning's courtship of Elizabeth. Present your results to the class as a multimedia production. **[Group Activity; Media Link]**

◆ **Further Reading, Listening, and Viewing**

- Mermin: *Elizabeth Barrett Browning: The Origins of a New Poetry* (1989). The best critical biography.

- H. Cooper: *Elizabeth Barrett Browning, Woman and Artist* (1988). A provocative recent discussion of the poet.

- *Selected Poems of Elizabeth Barrett Browning.* (Blackstone Audio, 1995). Five audiocasettes, read by Nadia May. Audiocassette series

- *The Barretts of Wimpole Street* (1957). Film directed by Sidney Franklin, starring Jennifer Jones.

On the Web:

http://www.phschool.com/atschool/literature
Go to the student edition of *The British Tradition.* Proceed to Unit 5. Then, click Hot Links to find Web sites featuring Elizabeth Barrett Browning.

Charlotte and Emily Brontë In Depth

"The writer who possesses the creative gift owns something of which he is not always master—something that at times strangely wills and works for itself."

—Charlotte Brontë, Preface to the 1850 edition of Emily Brontë's **Wuthering Heights**

THE BRONTËS made landmark contributions to the development of the English novel. Published in the same year, 1847, Charlotte Brontë's *Jane Eyre* and Emily Brontë's *Wuthering Heights* are now familiar classics of English literature. In their day, however, these novels were boldly original, departing from established convention with regard to subject matter, characterization, point of view, and theme.

Childhood in Yorkshire Raised in a family of six children, Charlotte and Emily Brontë were the daughters of a Yorkshire clergyman. Charlotte, born in 1816, was two years Emily's senior. After their mother died in 1821, an aunt named Elizabeth Branwell helped to bring up the children. Two elder girls, Maria and Elizabeth, died prematurely, after a disastrous sojourn at a boarding school that ruined their health. Together with sister Anne and brother Branwell, Charlotte and Emily were educated mainly at home, in an atmosphere that nurtured their rich imaginations and fostered their artistic development. Charlotte and Emily created tales in imaginary kingdoms, and they immersed themselves in the works of the two Romantic writers they most admired— the poet Lord Byron and the novelist Sir Walter Scott.

Young Adulthood In 1835–1838, Charlotte Brontë was employed at a school that she had briefly attended as a student. In the three years that followed, she held two positions as governess. In 1842, Charlotte and Emily traveled to Brussels in Belgium, where they studied French and German. After an unsuccessful attempt to start their own school, the two Brontës—together with sister Anne—launched their literary careers with the publication of a volume of poetry in 1846. In keeping with the prevailing custom, the Brontës used pseudonyms to disguise their authorship; they became Currer, Ellis, and Acton Bell. The volume found few buyers and received scant critical attention.

First Novels and Early Deaths Remarkably, by 1847 Charlotte, Emily, and Anne had each completed a first novel. When Charlotte's *The Professor* was rejected for publication, she began to write *Jane Eyre,* which was published that same year and was an immediate success. Emily Brontë's *Wuthering Heights* encountered a more mixed reception, largely due to its atmosphere of dark, brooding intensity—an atmosphere Charlotte described as "a horror of great darkness." Anne Brontë's novel *Agnes Grey,* the story of a young governess, was also published in 1847. Once again, all three sisters used pseudonyms.

Any satisfaction that the sisters could take in their achievement, however, was short-lived. Their brother Branwell died in September 1848, followed by Emily three months later and Anne the following summer.

Charlotte's Final Years Seeking solace from her grief, Charlotte plunged again into her writing, completing the novels *Shirley* and *Villette* over the next five years. She also befriended the novelist Elizabeth Gaskell (1810–1865), who would become her biographer. In 1854, Brontë married a clergyman, A. B. Nicholls, who had served as her father's assistant. One year later, however, she died of toxemia during pregnancy. In 1857, her novel *The Professor* was published posthumously. Also published that year was Elizabeth Gaskell's biography of her life.

◆ The Governess in Victorian England

In 1850, there were 21,000 registered governesses in England. Both Jane Eyre and her creator Charlotte Brontë were governesses, and the ranks also included Becky Sharp, the heroine of Thackeray's *Vanity Fair*, and David Copperfield's mother in Dickens's famous novel.

The occupation of governess was one of the few socially acceptable alternatives for unmarried women who needed to support themselves. Governesses were expected to live in the homes of their employers, providing their children with academic instruction and moral guidance until they were sent off to school. A governess was in a unique position—expected to be "lady-like," she was nonetheless treated as one of the servants. The result was often painful isolation, although for some governesses—like the fictional Jane Eyre and Becky Sharp—the position led to marriage.

◆ Literary Works

Poems by Currer, Ellis, and Acton Bell (1846)

Charlotte Brontë
   Jane Eyre (1847)
   Shirley (1849)
   Villette (1853)
   The Professor (1857)

Emily Brontë
   Wuthering Heights (1847)

TIMELINE

The Brontës' Lives

1816	Charlotte born at Thornton, Yorkshire
1817	Branwell Brontë born
1818	Emily born
1820	Children's father, Patrick Brontë, becomes rector at Haworth, Yorkshire; family relocates; Anne Brontë born
1821	Children's mother dies; Elizabeth Branwell, children's aunt, moves in to help raise them
1824	Emily and Charlotte enroll at Clergy Daughters' School at Cowan Bridge, Lancashire, later to be protrayed as Lowood in Charlotte's *Jane Eyre*; the two elder Brontë girls, Maria and Elizabeth, die of tuberculosis
1825	Charlotte and Emily return home from school
1831	Charlotte attends Miss Wooler's School at Roe Head near Huddersfield
1835–38	Charlotte holds teaching post at Roe Head
1837	Emily works as governess
1839–41	Charlotte works as governess
1842	Charlotte and Emily travel to Brussels to study languages
1846	Charlotte, Emily, and Anne jointly publish volume of their poetry
1847	Charlotte Brontë's *Jane Eyre* published; Emily Brontë's *Wuthering Heights* published
1848	Branwell and Emily die
1849	Anne dies; Charlotte's novel *Shirley* is published
1850	Charlotte meets Elizabeth Gaskell
1853	Charlotte Brontë's *Villette* published
1854	Charlotte marries A. B. Nicholls, her father's curate
1855	Charlotte dies in pregnancy

World Events

1813	Robert Southey becomes Poet Laureate of England
1818	First steamship crosses Atlantic
1819	Shelley's "Ode to the West Wind" published
1821	Death of Keats
1822	Death of Shelley; Heinrich Heine's *Poems* published in Germany
1824	Death of Byron
1825	Horse-drawn buses appear on the streets of London
1827	Death of William Blake
1829	Robert Peel establishes Metropolitan Police in London
1831	Victor Hugo's *The Hunchback of Notre Dame* is published in France
1832	First Reform Act is passed into law
1833	Slavery abolished in the British Empire
1834	Death of Samuel Taylor Coleridge
1837	Accession of Queen Victoria; Dickens's *Oliver Twist* is published
1843	Death of Robert Southey
1844	J. M. W. Turner paints *Rain, Steam and Speed*
1845	Potato Famine begins in Ireland
1850	Death of Wordsworth; Tennyson's *In Memoriam, A.H.H.* is published
1850	Nathaniel Hawthorne's *The Scarlet Letter* is published
1851	Herman Melville's *Moby-Dick* is published
1854	Japan reopens trade with West; Britain enters Crimean War

Charlotte Brontë

from Jane Eyre

Charlotte Brontë's first published novel was Jane Eyre, *the fictionalized autobiography of the orphaned girl. It was an immediate success when it appeared in 1847. Despite long years of ill treatment, the heroine of the novel, Jane Eyre, remains unbroken in spirit and integrity. The following selection is the first chapter of the novel.*

Chapter I

There was no possibility of taking a walk that day. We had been wandering, indeed, in the leafless shrubbery an hour in the morning, but since dinner (Mrs. Reed, when there was no company, dined early) the cold winter wind had brought with it clouds so somber, and a rain so penetrating, that further outdoor exercise was now out of the question.

I was glad of it: I never liked long walks, especially on chilly afternoons: dreadful to me was the coming home in the raw twilight, with nipped fingers and toes, and a heart saddened by the chidings of Bessie, the nurse, and humbled by the consciousness of my physical inferiority to Eliza, John, and Georgiana Reed.

The said Eliza, John, and Georgiana were now clustered round their mama in the drawing room: she lay reclined on a sofa by the fireside, and with her darlings about her (for the time neither quarreling nor crying) looked perfectly happy. Me, she had dispensed from joining the group; saying. "She regretted to be under the necessity of keeping me at a distance; but that until she heard from Bessie, and could discover by her own observation that I was endeavoring in good earnest to acquire a more sociable and childlike disposition. a more attractive and sprightly[1] manner—something lighter, franker, more natural as it were—she really must exclude me from privileges intended only for contented, happy, little children."

"What does Bessie say I have done?" I asked.

"Jane, I don't like cavilers or questioners: besides, there is something truly forbidding in a child taking up her elders in that manner. Be seated somewhere; and until you can speak pleasantly, remain silent."

A small breakfast room adjoined the drawing room. I slipped

---

1. sprightly (sprīt′ lē) adj.: Lively.

in there. It contained a bookcase; I soon possessed myself of a volume, taking care that it should be one stored with pictures. I mounted into the window seat; gathering up my feet, I sat cross-legged, like a Turk; and, having drawn the red moreen[2] curtain nearly close. I was shrined in double retirement.

Folds of scarlet drapery shut in my view to the right hand; to the left were the clear panes of glass, protecting, but not separating me from the drear November day. At intervals, while turning over the leaves of my book, I studied the aspect of that winter afternoon. Afar, it offered a pale blank of mist and cloud; near, a scene of wet lawn and storm-beat shrub, with ceaseless rain sweeping away wildly before a long and lamentable blast.

I returned to my book, *Bewick's History of British Birds;*[3] the letterpress[4] thereof I cared little for, generally speaking; and yet there were certain introductory pages that, child as I was, I could not pass quite as a blank. They were those which treat of the haunts of seafowl: of "the solitary rocks and promontories" by them only inhabited; of the coast of Norway, studded with isles from its southern extremity, the Lindeness, or Naze, to the North Cape:

> *Where the Northern Ocean, in vast whirls,*
> *Boils round the naked, melancholy isles*
> *Of farthest Thule; and the Atlantic surge*
> *Pours in among the stormy Hebrides.*

Nor could I pass unnoticed the suggestion of the bleak shores of Lapland, Siberia, Spitzbergen, Nova Zembla, Iceland, Greenland, with "the vast sweep of the Arctic Zone, and those forlorn regions of dreary space—that reservoir of frost and snow, where firm fields of ice, the accumulation of centuries of winters, glazed in Alpine heights above heights, surround the pole, and concenter the multiplied rigors of extreme cold." Of these death-white realms I formed an idea of my own: shadowy, like all the half-comprehended notions that float dim through children's brains, but strangely impressive. The words in these introductory pages connected themselves with the succeeding vignettes,[5] and gave significance to the rock standing up alone in a sea of billow and spray; to the broken boat stranded on a desolate coast; to the cold and ghastly moon glancing through bars of cloud at a wreck just sinking.

---

2. **moreen** (mə rēn′) *v.*: Made from heavy woolen material.
3. *Bewick's History of British Birds:* A book published in 1804 by Thomas Bewick.
4. **letterpress:** Print.
5. **vignettes** (vin yets′) *n.*: Decorative designs or borderless pictures in a book.

I cannot tell what sentiment haunted the quiet solitary churchyard, with its inscribed headstone, its gate, its two trees, its low horizon, girdled by a broken wall, and its newly risen crescent, attesting the hour of eventide.

The two ships becalmed on a torpid sea, I believed to be marine phantoms.

The fiend pinning down the thief's pack behind him, I passed over quickly: it was an object of terror.

So was the black, horned thing seated aloof on a rock, surveying a distant crowd surrounding a gallows.

Each picture told a story; mysterious often to my undeveloped understanding and imperfect feelings, yet ever profoundly interesting—as interesting as the tales Bessie sometimes narrated on winter evenings, when she chanced to be in good humor; and when, having brought her ironing table to the nursery hearth, she allowed us to sit about it, and while she got up Mrs. Reed's lace frills, and crimped[6] her nightcap borders, fed our eager attention with passages of love and adventure taken from old fairy tales and older ballads, or (as at a later period I discovered) from the pages of *Pamela,* and *Henry, Earl of Moreland.*[7]

With Bewick on my knee, I was then happy: happy at least in my way. I feared nothing but interruption, and that came too soon. The breakfast room door opened.

"Boh! Madame Mope!" cried the voice of John Reed. Then he paused: he found the room apparently empty.

"Where the dickens is she?" he continued. "Lizzy! Georgy!" calling to his sisters. "Jane is not here. Tell mama she is run out into the rain—bad animal!"

"It is well I drew the curtain," thought I; and I wished fervently he might not discover my hiding place; nor would John Reed have found it out himself: he was not quick either of vision or conception; but Eliza just put her head in at the door, and said at once:

"She is in the window seat, to be sure, Jack."

And I came out immediately, for I trembled at the idea of being dragged forth by the said Jack.

"What do you want?" I asked, with awkward diffidence.[8]

"Say, 'What do you want, Master Reed?'" was the answer. "I want you to come here." and seating himself in an armchair, he intimated by a gesture that I was to approach and stand before him.

John Reed was a schoolboy of fourteen years old; four years

---

6. crimped (krimpd) *v.:* Shaped; creased.
7. Pamela . . . Moreland: *Pamela* (1740) is a novel by Samuel Richardson; *Henry, Earl of Moreland* (1781), by John Wesley.
8. diffidence (dif´ ə dəns) *n.:* Shyness; hesitation.

older than I, for I was but ten; large and stout for his age, with a dingy and unwholesome skin, thick lineaments in a spacious visage, heavy limbs and large extremities. He gorged himself habitually at table, which made him bilious[9], and gave him a dim and bleared eye and flabby cheeks. He ought now to have been at school; but his mama had taken him home for a month or two, "on account of his delicate health." Mr. Miles. the master, affirmed that he would do very well if he had fewer cakes and sweetmeats sent him from home; but the mother's heart turned from an opinion so harsh, and inclined rather to the more refined idea that John's sallowness was owing to overapplication and, perhaps, to pining after home.

John had not much affection for his mother and sisters, and an antipathy[10] to me. He bullied and punished me: not two or three times in the week, nor once or twice in the day, but continually; every nerve I had feared him, and every morsel of flesh on my bones shrank when he came near. There were moments when I was bewildered by the terror he inspired, because I had no appeal whatever against either his menaces or his inflictions: the servants did not like to offend their young master by taking my part against him, and Mrs. Reed was blind and deaf on the subject: she never saw him strike or heard him abuse me, though he did both now and then in her very presence; more frequently, however, behind her back.

Habitually obedient to John, I came up to his chair. He spent some three minutes in thrusting out his tongue at me as far as he could without damaging the roots. I knew he would soon strike, and while dreading the blow, I mused on the disgusting and ugly appearance of him who would presently deal it. I wonder if he read that notion in my face; for, all at once. without speaking, he struck suddenly and strongly. I tottered, and on regaining my equilibrium retired back a step or two from his chair.

"That is for your impudence[11] in answering mama awhile since," said he, "and for your sneaking way of getting behind curtains and for the look you had in your eyes two minutes since, you rat!"

Accustomed to John Reed's abuse, I never had an idea of replying to it; my care was how to endure the blow which would certainly follow the insult.

"What were you doing behind the curtain?" he asked.

"I was reading."

"Show the book."

---

9. **bilious** (bil´ yəs) *adj.*: Bad-tempered, resulting from an ailment of the liver.
10. **antipathy** (an tip ə thē) *n.*: Strong dislike.
11. **impudence** (im´ pyo͞o dəns) *n.*: Disrespectful in speech or conduct.

I returned to the window and fetched it thence.

"You have no business to take our books; you are a dependent, mama says; you have no money; your father left you none; you ought to beg, and not to live here with gentlemen's children like us, and eat the same meals we do, and wear clothes at our mama's expense. Now, I'll teach you to rummage[12] my bookshelves, for they *are* mine—all the house belongs to me, or will do in a few years. Go and stand by the door, out of the way of the mirror and the windows."

I did so, not at first aware what was his intention, but when I saw him lift and poise the book and stand in act to hurl it, I instinctively started aside with a cry of alarm; not soon enough, however: the volume was flung, it hit me, and I fell, striking my head against the door and cutting it. The cut bled, the pain was sharp, my terror had passed its climax, other feelings succeeded.

"Wicked and cruel boy!" I said. "You are like a murderer, you are like a slave driver, you are like the Roman emperors!"

I had read Goldsmith's *History of Rome,* and had formed my opinion of Nero, Caligula, etc. Also I had drawn parallels in silence, which I never thought thus to have declared aloud.

"What! what!" he cried. "Did you say that to me? Did you hear her, Eliza and Georgiana? Won't I tell mama? but first . . ."

He ran headlong at me. I felt him grasp my hair and my shoulder; he had closed with a desperate thing. I really saw in him a tyrant, a murderer. I felt a drop or two of blood from my head trickle down my neck, and was sensible of somewhat pungent sufferings. These sensations for the time predominated over fear, and I received him in frantic sort. I don't very well know what I did with my hands, but he called me "rat! rat!" and bellowed out aloud. Aid was near him: Eliza and Georgiana had run for Mrs. Reed, who was gone upstairs; she now came upon the scene, followed by Bessie and her maid Abbot. We were parted: I heard the words:

"Dear! dear! What a fury to fly at Master John!"

"Did ever anybody see such a picture of passion?"

Then Mrs. Reed subjoined:

"Take her away to the red room, and lock her in there." Four hands were immediately laid upon me, and I was borne upstairs.

---

12. rummage (rum′ ij) *v*: Search by thoroughly examining.

Charlotte Brontë
Letter to Robert Southey[1]

Charlotte Brontë had written to the author Robert Southey asking him for his opinion about her prospects as a writer. In his response, Southey told Charlotte Brontë that, although she did "evidently possess, and in no inconsiderable degree, what Wordsworth calls the 'faculty of verse,'" she must also remember her proper duties to life and avoid excessive daydreaming. Southey also urged Charlotte Brontë to "write poetry for its own sake; not in the spirit of emulation, and not with a view to celebrity"; this being "the surest means . . . of soothing the mind and elevating it." Following is Charlotte Brontë's response to Southey's letter.

March 16, 1837

Sir,

I cannot rest till I have answered your letter, even though by addressing you a second time I should appear a little intrusive; but I must thank you for the kind and wise advice you have condescended[2] to give me. I had not ventured to hope for such a reply; so considerate in its tone, so noble in its spirit. I must suppress what I feel, or you will think me foolishly enthusiastic.

At the first perusal of your letter I felt only shame and regret that I had ever ventured to trouble you with my crude rhapsody; I felt a painful heat rise to my face when I thought of the quires[3] of paper I had covered with what once gave me so much delight, but which now was only a source of confusion; but after I had thought a little, and read it again and again, the prospect seemed to clear. You do not forbid me to write; you do not say that what I write is utterly destitute of merit. You only warn me against the folly of neglecting real duties for the sake of imaginative pleasures; of writing for the love of fame; for the selfish excitement of emulation.[4] You kindly allow me to write poetry for its own sake, provided I leave undone nothing which I ought to do, in order to pursue that single, absorbing, exquisite gratification. I am afraid, sir, you think me very foolish. I know the first letter I wrote to you was all senseless trash from beginning to end; but I am not altogether the idle, dreaming being it would seem to denote.

---

1. **Robert Southey** (1774–1843), poet, historian, and biographer.
2. **condescended** (kän′ də send′ əd) *v.*: Agreed; assented.
3. **quires** (kwī′ ərs) *n.*: Notebooks.
4. **emulation** (em′ yə lā′ shən) *n.*: Ambitious rivalry.

My father is a clergyman of limited though competent income, and I am the eldest of his children. He expended quite as much in my education as he could afford in justice to the rest. I thought it therefore my duty, when I left school, to become a governess. In that capacity I find enough to occupy my thoughts all day long, and my head and hands too, without having a moment's time for one dream of the imagination. In the evenings, I confess, I do think, but I never trouble any one else with my thoughts. I carefully avoid any appearance of preoccupation and eccentricity, which might lead those I live amongst to suspect the nature of my pursuits. Following my father's advice—who from my childhood has counselled me, just in the wise and friendly tone of your letter—I have endeavoured not only attentively to observe all the duties a woman ought to fulfil, but to feel deeply interested in them. I don't always succeed, for sometimes when I'm teaching or sewing I would rather be reading or writing; but I try to deny myself; and my father's approbation amply rewarded me for the privation.[5] Once more allow me to thank you with sincere gratitude. I trust I shall never more feel ambitious to see my name in print; if the wish should rise, I'll look at Southey's letter, and suppress it. It is honour enough for me that I have written to him, and received an answer. That letter is consecrated;[6] no one shall ever see it but papa and my brother and sisters. Again I thank you. This incident, I suppose, will be renewed no more; if I live to be an old woman, I shall remember it thirty years hence as a bright dream. The signature which you suspected of being fictitious is my real name. Again, therefore, I must sign myself

C. Brontë

P.S.—Pray, sir, excuse me for writing to you a second time; I could not help writing, partly to tell you how thankful I am for your kindness, and partly to let you know that your advice shall not be wasted, however sorrowfully and reluctantly it may at first be followed.

C. B.

---

5. **privation** (prī vā′ shən) *n.*: An absence or deprivation of some quality or condition.
6. **consecrated** (kän′ sə krāt′ əd) *adj.*: Sacred.

☑ Check Your Comprehension

1. (a) Where are the Reed children at the beginning of the selection? (b) Why isn't Jane with them?
2. What does Jane do to entertain herself?
3. (a) How does the fight between John and Jane start? (b) What happens to Jane as a result of the fight?
4. What two reasons does Charlotte Brontë give for writing to Southey?

◆ Critical Thinking

1. How would you describe Jane's treatment by the Reed family? **[Interpret]**

2. What does Jane's reaction toward the Reed children—especially to John—reveal about her character? **[Infer]**
3. What kind of child might Aunt Reed have treated better than she did Jane? **[Evaluate]**
4. (a) What does this selection suggest about the era in which Jane lived? (b) How might things be different today for someone in Jane's position? **[Apply]**
5. How would you describe the tone of Charlotte Brontë's letter to Southey? **[Interpret]**

Emily Brontë

from Wuthering Heights

Emily Brontë's only novel, Wuthering Heights, *was published in 1847. The novel is regarded as a highly imaginative and passionate work of fiction that probes the darker aspects of human nature. Presented here is the first chapter of* Wuthering Heights, *in which the principal character of the novel, Heathcliff, is introduced.*

Chapter 1

1801—I have just returned from a visit to my landlord—the solitary neighbor that I shall be troubled with. This is certainly a beautiful country! In all England, I do not believe that I could have fixed on a situation so completely removed from the stir of society. A perfect misanthropist's[1] Heaven: and Mr. Heathcliff and I are such a suitable pair to divide the desolation between us. A capital fellow! He little imagined how my heart warmed towards him when I beheld his black eyes withdraw so suspiciously under their brows, as I rode up, and when his fingers sheltered themselves, with a jealous resolution, still further in his waistcoat, as I announced my name.

"Mr. Heathcliff?" I said.

A nod was the answer.

"Mr. Lockwood your new tenant, sir. I do myself the honor of calling as soon as possible after my arrival, to express the hope that I have not inconvenienced you by my perseverance in soliciting the occupation of Thrushcross Grange: I heard yesterday you had had some thoughts . . ."

"Thrushcross Grange is my own, sir," he interrupted, wincing. "I should not allow anyone to inconvenience me, if I could hinder it—walk in!"

The "walk in" was uttered with closed teeth and expressed the sentiment, "Go to the deuce";[2] even the gate over which he leaned manifested no sympathizing movement to the words; and I think that circumstance determined me to accept the invitation: I felt interested in a man who seemed more exaggeratedly reserved than myself.

When he saw my horse's breast fairly pushing the barrier, he did pull out his hand to unchain it, and then sullenly preceded

---

1. **misanthropist** (mis an´ thrə pist) *n*.: One who hates or mistrusts others.
2. **Go to the deuce:** An exclamation of annoyance.

me up the causeway, calling, as we entered the court, "Joseph, take Mr. Lockwood's horse, and bring up some wine."

"Here we have the whole establishment of domestics. I suppose," was the reflection, suggested by this compound order. "No wonder the grass grows up between the flags, and cattle are the only hedgecutters."

Joseph was an elderly, nay, an old man—very old, perhaps, though hale and sinewy. "The Lord help us!" he soliloquized[3] in an undertone of peevish displeasure, while relieving me of my horse; looking, meantime, in my face so sourly that I charitably conjectured he must have need of divine aid to digest his dinner, and his pious ejaculation had no reference to my unexpected advent.

Wuthering Heights is the name of Mr. Heathcliff's dwelling. "Wuthering" being a significant provincial adjective, descriptive of the atmospheric tumult to which its station is exposed in stormy weather. Pure, bracing ventilation they must have up there at all times, indeed: one may guess the power of the north wind blowing over the edge, by the excessive slant of a few stunted firs at the end of the house; and by a range of gaunt thorns all stretching their limbs one way, as if craving alms of the sun. Happily, the architect had foresight to build it strong: the narrow windows are deeply set in the wall, and the corners defended with large jutting stones.

Before passing the threshold, I paused to admire a quantity of grotesque carving lavished over the front, and especially about the principal door; above which, among a wilderness of crumbling griffins[4] and shameless little boys, I detected the date "1500" and the name "Hareton Earnshaw." I would have made a few comments, and requested a short history of the place from the surly owner; but his attitude at the door appeared to demand my speedy entrance, or complete departure, and I had no desire to aggravate his impatience previous to inspecting the penetralia.[5]

One step brought us into the family sitting room, without any introductory lobby or passage: they call it here "the house" preeminently. It includes kitchen and parlor, generally; but I believe at Wuthering Heights the kitchen is forced to retreat altogether into another quarter: at least I distinguished a chatter of tongues, and a clatter of culinary utensils, deep within; and I

---

3. **soliloquized** (sə lil′ ə kwīzd′) v.: Talked to oneself.
4. **griffins:** Mythological animals with the body and hind legs of a lion and the head and wings of an eagle.
5. **penetralia** (pen′ ə trā′ lē ə) n.: The innermost parts of a building.

observed no signs of roasting, boiling, or baking, about the huge fireplace; nor any glitter of copper saucepans and tin colanders on the walls. One end, indeed, reflected splendidly both light and heat from ranks of immense pewter dishes, interspersed with silver jugs and tankards, towering row after row, on a vast oak dresser, to the very roof. The latter had never been underdrawn:[6] its entire anatomy lay bare to an inquiring eye, except where a frame of wood laden with oatcakes and clusters of legs of beef, mutton, and ham, concealed it. Above the chimney were sundry villainous old guns, and a couple of horse-pistols; and, by way of ornament, three gaudily painted canisters disposed along its ledge. The floor was of smooth, white stone: the chairs, high-backed, primitive structures, painted green; one or two heavy black ones lurking in the shade. In an arch under the dresser, reposed a huge, liver-colored pointer, surrounded by a swarm of squealing puppies; and other dogs haunted other recesses.

The apartment and furniture would have been nothing extraordinary as belonging to a homely, northern farmer, with a stubborn countenance, and stalwart limbs set out to advantage in knee breeches and gaiters.[7] Such an individual seated in his armchair, his mug of ale frothing on the round table before him, is to be seen in any circuit of five or six miles among these hills, if you go at the right time after dinner. But Mr. Heathcliff forms a singular contrast to his abode and style of living. He is a dark-skinned gypsy in aspect, in dress and manners a gentleman: that is, as much a gentleman as many a country squire: rather slovenly, perhaps, yet not looking amiss with his negligence, because he has an erect and handsome figure, and rather morose. Possibly, some people might suspect him of a degree of underbred pride; I have a sympathetic chord within that tells me it is nothing of the sort: I know, by instinct, his reserve springs from an aversion to showy displays of feeling—to manifestations of mutual kindliness. He'll love and hate equally under cover, and esteem it a species of impertinence[8] to be loved or hated again. No, I'm running on too fast: I bestow my own attributes over liberally on him. Mr. Heathcliff may have entirely dissimilar reasons for keeping his hand out of the way when he meets a would-be acquaintance, to those which actuate me. Let me hope my constitution is almost peculiar: my dear mother used to say I

---

6. **underdrawn:** Covered with boards or plaster.
7. **gaiters** (gāt´ ərs) *n.*: Cloth coverings for the instep and lower leg.
8. **impertinence** (im pʉr´ tən əns) *n.*: Rudeness.

should never have a comfortable home; and only last summer I proved myself perfectly unworthy of one.

While enjoying a month of fine weather at the seacoast, I was thrown into the company of a most fascinating creature: a real goddess in my eyes, as long as she took no notice of me. I "never told my love" vocally; still, if looks have language, the merest idiot might have guessed I was over head and ears: she understood me at last, and looked a return—the sweetest of all imaginable looks. And what did I do? I confess it with shame—shrunk icily into myself, like a snail; at every glance retired colder and farther; till finally the poor innocent was led to doubt her own senses, and, overwhelmed with confusion at her supposed mistake, persuaded her mamma to decamp.[9] By this curious turn of disposition I have gained the reputation of deliberate heartlessness; how undeserved, I alone can appreciate.

I took a seat at the end of the hearthstone opposite that towards which my landlord advanced, and filled up an interval of silence by attempting to caress the canine mother, who had left her nursery, and was sneaking wolfishly to the back of my legs, her lip curled up, and her white teeth watering for a snatch. My caress provoked a long, guttural gnarl.

"You'd better let the dog alone," growled Mr. Heathcliff in unison, checking fiercer demonstrations with a punch of his foot. "She's not accustomed to be spoiled—not kept for a pet." Then, striding to a side door, he shouted again, "Joseph!"

Joseph mumbled indistinctly in the depths of the cellar, but gave no intimation of ascending; so his master dived down to him, leaving me vis-à-vis[10] the ruffianly dog and a pair of grim shaggy sheepdogs, who shared with her a jealous guardianship over all my movements. Not anxious to come in contact with their fangs, I sat still; but, imagining they would scarcely understand tacit insults, I unfortunately indulged in winking and making faces at the trio, and some turn of my physiognomy[11] so irritated madam, that she suddenly broke into a fury, and leapt on my knees. I flung her back, and hastened to interpose the table between us. This proceeding roused the whole hive. Half a dozen four-footed fiends, of various sizes and ages, issued from hidden dens to the common center. I felt my heels and coat laps peculiar subjects of assault; and, parrying off the larger combatants as effectually as I could with the poker. I was constrained to

---

9. **decamp:** Leave suddenly.
10. **vis-à-vis** (vē′ zə vē′): Face to face with.
11. **physiognomy** (fiz′ ē äg′ nə mē) *n*.: Facial features thought to reveal one's character.

demand, aloud, assistance from some of the household in reestablishing peace.

Mr. Heathcliff and his man climbed the cellar steps with vexatious phlegm.[12] I don't think they moved one second faster than usual, though the hearth was an absolute tempest of worrying and yelping. Happily, an inhabitant of the kitchen made more dispatch: a lusty dame, with tucked-up gown, bare arms, and fire-flushed cheeks, rushed into the midst of us flourishing a frying pan; and used that weapon, and her tongue, to such purpose, that the storm subsided magically, and she only remained, heaving like a sea after a high wind, when her master entered on the scene.

"What the devil is the matter?" he asked, eyeing me in a manner I could ill endure after this inhospitable treatment.

"What the devil, indeed!" I muttered. "The herd of possessed swine could have had no worse spirits in them than those animals of yours, sir. You might as well leave a stranger with a brood of tigers!"

"They won't meddle with persons who touch nothing," he remarked, putting the bottle before me, and restoring the displaced table. "The dogs do right to be vigilant. Take a glass of wine?"

"No thank you."

"Not bitten, are you?"'

"If I had been, I would have set my signet[13] on the biter."

Heathcliff's countenance relaxed into a grin.

"Come, come," he said, "you are flurried, Mr. Lockwood. Here, take a little wine. Guests are so exceedingly rare in this house that I and my dogs, I am willing to own, hardly know how to receive them. Your health, sir!"

I bowed and returned the pledge; beginning to perceive that it would be foolish to sit sulking for the misbehavior of a pack of curs;[14] besides, I felt loath to yield the fellow further amusement at my expense; since his humor took that turn. He—probably swayed by prudential considerations of the folly of offending a good tenant—relaxed a little in the laconic style of chipping off his pronouns and auxiliary verbs, and introduced what he supposed would be a subject of interest to me—a discourse on the advantages and disadvantages of my present place of retirement. I found him very intelligent on the topics we touched; and before

12. **phlegm** (flem) *n.*: Sluggishness.
13. **signet:** Seal.
14. **curs:** Dogs of mixed breed.

I went home. I was encouraged so far as to volunteer another visit tomorrow. He evidently wished no repetition of my intrusion. I shall go, notwithstanding. It is astonishing how sociable I feel myself compared with him.

☑ Check Your Comprehension

1. Who is the narrator of the story, and what is his relationship to Heathcliff?
2. Why is Heathcliff's home named "Wuthering Heights"?
3. Why does the narrator resist the temptation to ask Heathcliff for a history of the house?
4. According to the narrator, how has he gained a reputation for heartlessness?
5. How is the narrator rescued from the dogs?

◆ Critical Thinking

1. What does Heathcliff's appearance and speech suggest about his personality? [Interpret]

2. How is the narrator's personality revealed by (a) his comments about Heathcliff? (b) the narrator's conduct with the dogs? [Interpret]

3. Considering the encounter between Heathcliff and the narrator, what would you say about the narrator's willingness to return to Wuthering Heights? [Infer]

COMPARE LITERARY WORKS

4. Compare and contrast the settings in the opening chapters of *Jane Eyre* and *Wuthering Heights*. How does setting help to create a mood or atmosphere in each selection? [Connect]

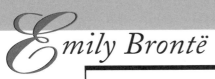
Emily Brontë

The Night-Wind

In summer's mellow midnight
A cloudless moon shone through
Our open parlor window
And rosetrees wet with dew

5   I sat in silent musing—
The soft wind waved my hair
It told me Heaven was glorious
And sleeping Earth was fair—

I needed not its breathing
10   To bring such thoughts to me.
But still it whispered lowly
"How dark the woods will be!—

"The thick leaves in my murmur
Are rustling like a dream,
15   And all their myriad[1] voices
Instinct with spirit seem"

I said, "Go gentle singer;
Thy wooing[2] voice is kind
But do not think its music
20   Has power to reach my mind—

"Play with the scented flower,
The young tree's supple bough—
And leave my human feelings
In their own course to flow"

25   The Wanderer would not leave me
Its kiss grew warmer still—
"O come," it sighed so sweetly
"I'll win thee 'gainst thy will—

"Have we not been from childhood friends?
30   Have I not loved thee long?
As long as thou hast loved the night
Whose silence wakes my song?

"And when thy heart is laid at rest,
Beneath the church-yard stone
35   I shall have time enough to mourn
And thou to be alone—"

---

1. **myriad** (mir′ ē ed) *adj.*: Countless; innumerable.
2. **wooing** (wōō′ iŋ) *adj.*: Coaxing; urging.

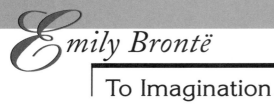

To Imagination

When weary with the long day's care,
   And earthly change from pain to pain,
And lost and ready to despair,
   Thy kind voice calls me back again:
5   Oh, my true friend! I am not lone,
While thou canst speak with such a tone!

So hopeless is the world without;
   The world within I doubly prize;
Thy world, where guile,[1] and hate, and doubt,
10   And cold suspicion never rise;
Where thou, and I, and Liberty,
Have undisputed sovereignty.[2]

What matters it, that, all around,
   Danger, and guilt, and darkness lie,
15   If but within our bosom's bound
   We hold a bright, untroubled sky,
Warm with ten thousand mingled rays
Of suns that know no winter days?

Reason, indeed, may oft complain
20   For Nature's sad reality,
And tell the suffering heart how vain
   Its cherished dreams must always be;
And Truth may rudely trample down
The flowers of Fancy, newly-blown:

25   But, thou art ever there, to bring
   The hovering vision back, and breathe
New glories o'er the blighted[3] spring,
   And call a lovelier Life from Death,
And whisper, with a voice divine,
30   Of real worlds, as bright as thine.

---

1. **guile** (gīl) *n.*: Deceit.
2. **sovereignty** (säv′ rən tē) *n.*: Supreme power or authority; independence.
3. **blighted** (blīt′ əd) *adj.*: Withered.

I trust not to thy phantom bliss,
    Yet, still, in evening's quiet hour,
With never-failing thankfulness,
    I welcome thee, Benignant[4] Power;
35   Sure solacer of human cares,
    And sweeter hope, when hope despairs!

---

4. Benignant (bi nig′ nənt) *adj.*: Kindly or gracious, sometimes in a patronizing way.

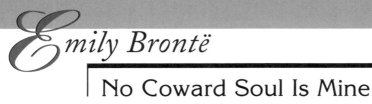

No Coward Soul Is Mine

No coward soul is mine
No trembler in the world's storm-troubled sphere
I see Heaven's glories shine
And Faith shines equal arming me from Fear

5   O God within my breast
Almighty ever-present Deity
Life, that in me hast rest
As I Undying Life, have power in thee

Vain are the thousand creeds
10   That move men's hearts, unutterably vain,
Worthless as withered weeds
Or idlest froth[1] amid the boundless main

To waken doubt in one
Holding so fast by thy infinity
15   So surely anchored on
The steadfast rock of Immortality

With wide-embracing love
Thy spirit animates eternal years
Pervades and broods[2] above,
20   Changes, sustains, dissolves, creates and rears[3]

Though Earth and moon were gone
And suns and universes ceased to be
And thou wert left alone
Every Existence would exist in thee

25   There is not room for Death
Nor atom that his might could render void
Since thou art Being and Breath
And what thou art may never be destroyed

---

1. **froth** (frôth) *n.*: (1) Foam; (2) Worthless talk or ideas.
2. **broods** (bro͞ods) *v.*: Hovers over and protects.
3. **rears** (rirs) *v.*: Educates; nourishes.

☑ Check Your Comprehension

1. (a) What is the setting of "The Night Wind"? (b) Who are the two main speakers in the poem?
2. (a) In lines 7–10 of "To Imagination," why does the speaker "doubly prize" the inner world? (b) In this poem's final stanza, how does the speaker welcome imagination in "evening's quiet hour"?
3. In line 4 of "No Coward Soul Is Mine," what arms the speaker against fear?

◆ Critical Thinking

1. In view of the final stanza of "The Night Wind," what do you think the wind symbolizes? **[Interpret]**
2. In "To Imagination," what do the lines about "the world without" and "the world within," tell us about the speaker's personality? **[Infer]**
3. (a) What rhyme scheme and rhythmical pattern does Brontë use in "No Coward Soul Is Mine"? (b) How effectively do you think these formal features of the poem contribute to the overall effect and theme? **[Evaluate]**

COMPARE LITERARY WORKS

4. Acccording to her sister Charlotte, "No Coward Soul Is Mine" was Emily's last poem. An epitaph is an inscription written on a tomb or burial place that memorializes the person who died. In what ways might this poem be a fitting epitaph for its author? **[Apply]**

Charlotte and Emily Brontë

Comparing and Connecting the Authors' Works

◆ Literary Focus: First-Person Point of View

The **point of view**, or perspective, of a first-person narrator can vary widely. In *Jane Eyre,* for example, Charlotte Brontë uses **first-person participant** point of view: Jane, the narrator, is an integral part of the story and has the power to affect the outcome and the fate of the other characters. As seen through the eyes of a participating first-person narrator, the events in a novel take on an immediacy that is otherwise not possible. Jane permits the reader to glimpse her own inner struggles, while also offering her views of the events and characters that figure in her life. In the opening chapter of *Wuthering Heights,* Emily Brontë uses **first-person observer** point of view. Lockwood is a witness to events, but he is not at the center of the action. It is important to recognize, however, that even when a first-person narrator speaks purely as an observer, his or her comments and interpretations are *subjective,* that is, colored by his or her own perceptions and values.

1. For each of the following portions of the narrative in *Jane Eyre,* describe what you believe young Jane was feeling:
   (a) curling up in the window seat
   (b) being struck with the book
   (c) being taken to the red room
2. In *Wuthering Heights,* to what extent do you think Lockwood is responsible for the attack by the dogs?

◆ Drawing Conclusions About the Brontës' Work

One way to evaluate a literary work is to respond to a critical opinion. Read the following comment by W. A. Craik:

The shape of Jane Eyre *is very much represented by the places where the action occurs, which Charlotte Brontë makes an essential part of the structure, as well as the atmosphere, of her stories. Places have indeed as much character as people, and serve many of the same purposes, a use which* Jane Eyre *shares with* Wuthering Heights.

In a brief essay, explore how the setting affects the three elements shown in the diagram below in either *Jane Eyre* or *Wuthering Heights.*

Setting → Atmosphere
Setting → Plot
Setting → Characters

◆ Idea Bank

Writing

1. **Diary Notes** Imagine that you are Bessie or Abbot the maid in the Reed household. Make some diary notes about your reactions to events on the day Jane Eyre fought with John Reed and was locked in the red room.
2. **Sequel** Continue Jane Eyre's first-person account of her life by writing Chapter 2. Begin with what happens to Jane after she is taken to the red room. You may be as creative as you like and introduce new characters,

but try to maintain the tone and atmosphere that Charlotte Brontë has created up to this point. Be sure to relate events in chronological order.

Speaking and Listening

3. **Oral Interpretation** Prepare an oral interpretation of either an excerpt from the novels or one of the poems by Emily Brontë. In your rehearsals, focus on elements such as tone, pace, volume, and emphasis. Present your reading to an audience of classmates, friends, or family members. **[Performing Arts Link]**

4. **Dramatized Dialogue** Together with a partner, create and perform an imaginary dialogue between Charlotte and Emily Brontë, in which they discuss the progress of their novels. You might have the sisters exchange ideas, for example, on the strategies they are planning to use in the opening chapters in order to hook the attention of their readers. When you have rehearsed your dialogue, perform it for a live audience. **[Media Link]**

Researching and Representing

5. **Historical Research** Just as the Brontës were considered literary rebels, the age in which they lived was one of widespread revolutionary sentiment, especially on the European continent. Together with a small group, research the causes and effects of the revolutions of 1848 in France, Germany, and Italy. In what ways does the social protest involved in these rebellions parallel what you know about the social criticism of such English novelists as Charles Dickens and Charlotte Brontë? Present your results in an illustrated report to the class as a whole. **[Group Activity; Social Studies Link]**

◆ Further Reading, Listening, and Viewing

- Elizabeth Gaskell: *The Life of Charlotte Brontë* (1857, reprinted 1960). A landmark biography by a fellow novelist whom Brontë befriended.

- Edward Chitham: *A Life of Emily Brontë* (1988)

- Harold Bloom, ed.: Charlotte Brontë's *Jane Eyre* (1987) and Emily Brontë's *Wuthering Heights* (1987). Collections of insightful critical essays

- *Jane Eyre* [unabridged] (1994). Read by Juliet Stevenson on audiocassette

- *Wuthering Heights* [unabridged] (1998).

- *Jane Eyre* (1971): film directed by Delbert Mann

- *Wuthering Heights* (1970). Film directed by Robert Fuest

- *Megan Aldrich: Gothic Revival* (1997). Covers architecture and decorative arts

On the Web:

http://www.phschool.com/atschool/literature
Go to the student edition of *The British Tradition*. Proceed to Unit 5. Then, click Hot Links to find Web sites featuring Charlotte and Emily Brontë.

William Butler Yeats In Depth

"O sages standing in God's holy fire
As in the gold mosaic of a wall,
Come from the holy fire, perne in a gyre,
And be the singing-masters of my soul.
Consume my heart away: sick with desire
And fastened to a dying animal
It knows not what it is: and gather me
Into the artifice of eternity."

—*W. B. Yeats, "Sailing to Byzantium"*

WILLIAM **B**UTLER **Y**EATS'S life can be seen as a quest. During his long career, Yeats immersed himself in his people's struggle for freedom, and he became an Irish national hero. On a personal level, Yeats constantly sought a system of belief that could replace the traditional Christian orthodoxy that he abandoned as a youth. In his poetry, Yeats was never satisfied with one style: like the modernist painter Pablo Picasso, Yeats was constantly evolving.

Painting, Politics, and Young Love

William Butler Yeats was born in Dublin in 1865. Both his father and his brother were painters, and young William attended art school for three years. At the age of twenty-one, however, he abandoned painting for literature and nationalist politics.

In 1889, Yeats published his first collection of poems, *The Wanderings of Oisin.* The same year, he met and fell passionately in love with Maude Gonne, a beautiful young revolutionary whose refusals to marry Yeats deeply anguished the poet. In many of his works over the following decade, Yeats alludes to this unhappy relationship.

From Poetry to Plays

In 1896, Yeats met Lady Augusta Gregory, a wealthy and talented widow who became one of the major figures in the revival of Irish culture. Together with Lady Gregory, Yeats helped to found the Abbey Theater in Dublin, which opened in 1904. Yeats, who wrote dramas as well as poetry throughout his career, drew on native legends and folklore for many of his plays, including *The Countess Cathleen* (1892) and *Deirdre* (1907).

The Middle Years

In the decade prior to World War I, Yeats published several collections of poetry that marked a shift in his style from Romanticism to a more colloquial idiom. Although he had become disillusioned with Irish nationalism, the Easter Rebellion of 1916 reignited Yeats's nationalist sympathies. In 1917, the poet's marriage to Georgie Hyde-Lees, a devotee of spiritualism, initiated a new phase in Yeats's career. His interest in elaborating a personal system of symbols culminated in *A Vision* (1925), a major work in which Yeats elaborated his complex, philosophical theories of history and human personality.

The Final Years

In the last phase of his career, Yeats produced much of his greatest poetry, including the collections entitled *The Tower* (1928) and *The Winding Stair* (1933). Towers, spirals, and whirling motion are important symbols in this body of work; Yeats used these symbols to suggest that the human journey through life involves both repetition and progression. Yeats died in southern France in 1939, less than a year before the outbreak of World War II. In 1948, his body was returned to Ireland and interred in County Sligo, a region where he had passed much of his childhood.

◆ Dublin's Abbey Theater

The Abbey Theater in Dublin opened in 1904 with three one-act plays, two of which were written by William Butler Yeats. The third play was the work of Yeats's close friend, Lady Augusta Gregory. As the permanent home of the Irish National Theater Society, the Abbey soon became a focus for nationalist sentiment. For nearly a century, the Abbey has been one of Dublin's best-known cultural landmarks.

The early history of the institution was marked by controversy: for example, the production of John Millington Synge's The Playboy of the Western World (1907) caused a riot, and the authorities threatened to censor an early play by George Bernard Shaw. Yeats and Lady Gregory became leading shareholders of the Abbey in 1910, but Yeats soon gave up his active role in the theater's management.

During the 1920's, the Abbey was a showcase for the early dramas of Sean O'Casey (1880-1964), which dealt realistically with the themes of Irish patriotism and the life of the urban poor. In 1925, the Abbey received a grant from the Irish government, thus becoming the first state-subsidized theater in the English-speaking world. Beginning in the 1930's, the Abbey staged a number of plays in Gaelic. In 1951, the original building burned down; the new Abbey Theater opened in 1966.

◆ Literary Works

Early Verse

The Wanderings of Oisin and Other Poems (1889)

The Land of Heart's Desire (1894)

The Secret Rose (1897)

Mature Poetry

In the Seven Woods (1903)

The Green Helmet and Other Poems (1910)

The Wild Swans at Coole (1917)

The Tower (1928)

The Winding Stair (1929)

Plays

The Countess Cathleen (1892)

On Baile's Strand (1904)

Deirdre (1907)

Prose

A Vision (1925)

T I M E L I N E

Yeat's Life		World Events	
1865	Born in Sandymount, Dublin	1865	American Civil War ends; Leo Tolstoy's *War and Peace* is published
1884	Enters art school		
1885	Publishes first poems		
1887	Moves with family to London	1869	Debtors' prisons abolished in England; Suez Canal completed in Egypt
1889	Meets and falls in love with Maude Gonne; publishes *The Wanderings of Oisin and Other Poems*		
		1876	Alexander Graham Bell patents the telephone
1891	Helps found Irish Literary Society of London	1882	James Joyce born in Dublin
1892	Writes *The Countess Cathleen*	1884	First edition of the *Oxford English Dictionary*
1895	Publishes *Poems,* a collected edition of his writings		
		1887	Sir Arthur Conan Doyle's first Sherlock Holmes' tale is published
1896	Meets Lady Augusta Gregory		
1897	*The Secret Rose* is published	1888	T. S. Eliot born in St. Louis
1903	*In the Seven Woods* is published	1895	Oscar Wilde's *The Importance of Being Earnest* is published
1904	Produces two plays for the opening of the Abbey Theater		
		1901	Death of Queen Victoria; accession of Edward VII
1912	Meets American poet Ezra Pound		
1916	Easter Rebellion in Ireland	1904	Russo-Japanese War begins
1917	Buys castle at Ballylee; marries Georgie Hyde-Lees; publishes *The Wild Swans at Coole*	1905	Albert Einstein proposes theory of relativity
		1907	W. H. Auden born in Birmingham, England
1922	Irish Free State formed; Yeats appointed a senator	1910	George V becomes king of England
1923	Receives Nobel Prize for Literature	1914	Outbreak of World War I
1925	*A Vision* is published	1916	James Joyce's *A Portrait of the Artist as a Young Man* is published
1928	*The Tower* is published		
1933	*The Winding Stair and Other Poems* is published	1918	End of World War I
		1922	T. S. Eliot's *The Waste Land* is published; James Joyce's *Ulysses* is published
1939	Dies in southern France		
1948	Returned to County Sligo for burial in Ireland	1925	Franz Kafka's *The Trial* is published in Czechoslovakia
		1927	Charles Lindbergh flies solo over the Atlantic
		1929	Stock market crash triggers the Great Depression
		1933	Adolf Hitler comes to power in Germany
		1936	Spanish Civil War begins
		1939	World War II begins in Europe

William Butler Yeats

A Dream of Death

I dreamed that one had died in a strange place
Near no accustomed hand;
And they had nailed the boards above her face,
The peasants of that land,
5   Wondering to lay her in that solitude,

And raised above her mound
A cross they had made out of two bits of wood,
And planted cypress¹ round;
And, left her to the indifferent stars above
10   Until I carved these words:
She was more beautiful than thy first love,
But now lies under boards.

---

1. cypress: Tree with hard wood and dark foliage; regarded as a symbol of mourning.

William Butler Yeats

The Song of Wandering Aengus[1]

I went out to the hazel wood,[2]
Because a fire was in my head,
And cut and peeled a hazel wand,
And hooked a berry to a thread,

5 And when white moths were on the wing,
And moth-like stars were flickering out,
I dropped the berry in a stream
And caught a little silver trout.

When I had laid it on the floor

10 I went to blow the fire aflame,
But something rustled on the floor,
And some one called me by my name:
It had become a glimmering girl
With apple blossom in her hair

15 Who called me by my name and ran
And faded through the brightening air.

Though I am old with wandering
Through hollow lands and hilly lands,
I will find out where she has gone,

20 And kiss her lips and take her hands;
And walk among long dappled[3] grass,
And pluck till time and times are done
The silver apples of the moon,
The golden apples of the sun.

---

1. Aengus: Aengus was described by Yeats as "the god of youth, beauty, and poetry. He reigned in Tir-Nan-Oge, the country of the young."

2. hazel wood: Yeats commented that "The hazel tree was the Irish tree of Life or of Knowledge, and in Ireland it was doubtless, as elsewhere of the heavens."

3. dappled (dap´ əld): *adj.*: Marked with spots of color or shade.

Never Give All the Heart

Never give all the heart, for love
Will hardly seem worth thinking of
To passionate women if it seem
Certain, and they never dream
5   That it fades out from kiss to kiss;
For everything that's lovely is
But a brief, dreamy, kind delight.
O never give the heart outright,
For they, for all smooth lips can say,
10   Have given their hearts up to the play.
And who could play it well enough
If deaf and dumb and blind with love?
He that made this knows all the cost,
For he gave all his heart and lost.

☑ Check Your Comprehension

1. In "A Dream of Death," what do the peasants do after the death of the speaker's beloved?

2. (a) Who is Aengus in the poem that bears his name? (b) Why has Aengus gone out to the hazel wood?

3. (a) In "The Song of Wandering Aengus," what happens to the trout caught by the speaker? (b) In the last stanza, what does the speaker say he will do?

4. How would you paraphrase lines 1–7 of "Never Give All the Heart"?

◆ Critical Thinking

1. In line 9 of "A Dream of Death," why do you think the speaker calls the stars "indifferent"? **[Interpret]**

2. (a) In "A Dream of Death," who is meant by "thy" in line 11? (b) How do the words the speaker carves (lines 11–12) affect the tone of the poem as a whole? **[Interpret]**

3. (a) In "The Song of Wandering Aengus," how does the description of the setting in the first stanza prepare you for the magical transformation that follows? (b) What do you think the speaker's journeying, as described in the third stanza, may symbolize? **[Interpret]**

4. From the last two lines in "Never Give All the Heart," what can you infer about the speaker? **[Infer]**

COMPARING LITERARY WORKS

5. These three poems share a dream-like atmosphere as well as specific references to dreams. Compare and contrast the poems with respect to the role that dreaming plays in them. **[Connect]**

William Butler Yeats

Adam's Curse

The Bible tells us that Adam was expelled from the gar-
den of Eden because of disobedience; after the fall he
was cursed with pain and labor (Genesis 3.17–19).

We sat together at one summer's end,
That beautiful mild woman, your close friend,
And you and I, and talked of poetry.
I said, 'A line will take us hours maybe;
5   Yet if it does not seem a moment's thought,
Our stitching and unstitching has been naught.
Better go down upon your marrow-bones
And scrub a kitchen pavement, or break stones
Like an old pauper, in all kinds of weather;
10   For to articulate sweet sounds together
Is to work harder than all these, and yet
Be thought an idler by the noisy set
Of bankers, schoolmasters, and clergymen
The martyrs call the world.'
15   And thereupon
That beautiful mild woman for whose sake
There's many a one shall find out all heartache
On finding that her voice is sweet and low
Replied, 'To be born woman is to know—
20   Although they do not talk of it at school—
That we must labour to be beautiful.'

I said, 'It's certain there is no fine thing
Since Adam's fall but needs much labouring.
There have been lovers who thought love should be
25   So much compounded¹ of high courtesy
That they would sigh and quote with learned looks
Precedents out of beautiful old books;
Yet now it seems an idle trade enough.'

We sat grown quiet at the name of love;
30   We saw the last embers of daylight die,
And in the trembling blue-green of the sky
A moon, worn as if it had been a shell
Washed by time's waters as they rose and fell
About the stars and broke in days and years.

35   I had a thought for no one's but your ears:
That you were beautiful, and that I strove
To love you in the old high way of love;
That it had all seemed happy, and yet we'd grown
As weary-hearted as that hollow moon.

---

1. **compounded** (käm pound´ əd): *v.*: Mixed or combined.

On a Political Prisoner

She that but little patience knew,
From childhood on, had now so much
A grey gull¹ lost its fear and flew
Down to her cell and there alit,
5   And there endured her fingers' touch
And from her fingers ate its bit.

Did she in touching that tone wing
Recall the years before her mind
Become a bitter, an abstract thing,
10   Her thought some popular enmity:²
Blind and leader of the blind
Drinking the foul ditch where they lie?

When long ago I saw her ride
Under Ben Bulben³ to the meet,
15   The beauty of her country-side
With all youth's lonely wildness stirred,
She seemed to have grown clean and sweet
Like any rock-bred, sea-borne bird:

Sea-borne, or balanced on the air
20   When first it sprang out of the nest
Upon some lofty rock to stare
Upon the cloudy canopy,
While under its storm-beaten breast
Cried out the hollows of the sea.

---

1. **gull:** Web-footed sea bird, usually with white plumage.
2. **enmity** (en´ mə tē): n.: Hostility; antagonism.
3. **Ben Bulben:** Mountain in County Sligo, Ireland.

William Butler Yeats

No Second Troy

In Homer's Iliad, *the city Troy was destroyed during the Trojan War, a ten-year war fought over the abduction of Helen by Paris.*

Why should I blame her that she filled my days
With misery, or that she would of late
Have taught to ignorant men most violent ways,
Or hurled the little streets upon the great,
5   Had they but courage equal to desire?
What could have made her peaceful with a mind
That nobleness made simple as a fire,
With beauty like a tightened bow, a kind
That is not natural in an age like this,
10   Being high and solitary and most stern?
Why, what could she have done, being what she is?
Was there another Troy for her to burn?

The Mask

'Put off that mask of burning gold
With emerald eyes.'
'O no, my dear, you make so bold
To find if hearts be wild and wise,
5   And yet not cold.'

'I would but find what's there to find,
Love or deceit.'
'It was the mask engaged your mind,
And after set your heart to beat,
10   Not what's behind.'

'But lest you are my enemy,
I must enquire.'
'O no, my dear, let all that be;
What matter, so there is but fire
15   In you, in me?'

☑ Check Your Comprehension

1. (a) In "Adam's Curse," what do the three people talk about at summer's end? (b) According to line 28, why do the speakers grow quiet?

2. (a) How does the political prisoner demonstrate her newly found patience in "On a Political Prisoner"? (b) What scene does the speaker recall in the flashback in the third stanza?

3. According to lines 1–2 of "No Second Troy," how has the woman treated the speaker?

4. (a) What does the first speaker in "The Mask" want to know at lines 6–7 and 11–12 of the poem? (b) How does the second speaker respond at lines 13–15?

◆ Critical Thinking

1. (a) What philosophy of poetry does the speaker set forth in lines 4–14 of "Adam's Curse"? (b) How does the speaker refer to the alienation of the artist in these lines? **[Interpret]**

2. Explain Yeats's use of figurative language in lines 30–33 of "Adam's Curse." How does the poet combine a simile with a metaphor in these lines? **[Analyze]**

3. (a) Explain the allusion in the title of "No Second Troy." (b) How would you describe the personality of the woman who is the subject of the poem? **[Interpret]**

4. How would you state the poet's theme in "The Mask"? **[Synthesize]**

COMPARING LITERARY WORKS

5. Compare and contrast the speaker's attitudes toward love in "Adam's Curse," "No Second Troy," and "The Mask." **[Connect]**

William Butler Yeats

An Irish Airman Foresees His Death

Major Robert Gregory, a young Irish artist who was the son of Yeat's friend Lady Augusta Gregory, was killed during World War I while flying over Italy as a member of England's Royal Flying Corps. Gregory's death inspired Yeats to write this poem.

I know that I shall meet my fate
Somewhere among the clouds above;
Those that I fight I do not hate,
Those that I guard I do not love;[1]
5   My country is Kiltartan[2] Cross,
My countrymen Kiltartan's poor.
No likely end could bring them loss
Or leave them happier than before.
Nor law, nor duty bade me fight,
10   Nor public men, nor cheering crowds,
A lonely impulse of delight
Drove to this tumult in the clouds;
I balanced all. brought all to mind,
The years to come seemed waste of breath,
15   A waste of breath the years behind
In balance with this life. this death.'

---

1. Those . . . love: Because Ireland was under English rule during World War I, many Irish fought as members of the English forces during the war. However, because of their desire for independence many of the Irish felt a great deal of resentment toward the English.
2. Kiltartan: A village near Lady Gregory's estate.

After Long Silence

Speech after long silence; it is right,
All other lovers being estranged or dead,
Unfriendly lamplight hid under its shade,
The curtains drawn upon unfriendly night,
5   That we descant[1] and yet again descant
Upon the supreme theme of Art and Song:
Bodily decrepitude is wisdom; young
We loved each other and were ignorant.

---

1. descant (des kant´) v.: Discourse; discuss ideas.

Easter, 1916

On Easter Monday of 1916, Irish Nationalists claimed independence and unsuccessfully revolted against the British government. The names alluded to in the poem were leaders of the Rebellion who were court-martialed and executed by the English.

I have met them at close of day
Coming with vivid faces
From counter or desk among grey
Eighteenth-century houses.
5   I have passed with a nod of the head
Or polite meaningless words,
Or have lingered awhile and said
Polite meaningless words,
And thought before I had done
10   Of a mocking tale or a gibe[1]
To please a companion
Around the fire at the club,
Being certain that they and I
But lived where motley[2] is worn:
15   All changed, changed utterly:
A terrible beauty is born.

That woman's days were spent
In ignorant good-will,
Her nights in argument
20   Until her voice grew shrill.
What voice more sweet than hers
When, young and beautiful,
She rode to harriers?
This man had kept a school[3],
25   And rode our wingèd horse;
This other his helper and friend
Was coming into his force;
He might have won fame in the end,
So sensitive his nature seemed,
30   So daring and sweet his thought.

---

1. **gibe:** Jeering or taunting remark.
2. **motley** (mät´ lē): *n.:* A garment of various colors, worn by a clown or jester.
3. **wingèd horse:** Pegasus, connected with poetry in Greek mythology.

This other man I had dreamed
A drunken, vainglorious lout.[4]
He had done most bitter wrong
To some who are near my heart,
35   Yet I number him in the song;
He, too, has resigned his part
In the casual comedy;
He, too, has been changed in his turn,
Transformed utterly:
40   A terrible beauty is born.

Hearts with one purpose alone
Through summer. and winter seem
Enchanted to a stone
To trouble the living stream.
45   The horse that comes from the road,
The rider, the birds that range
From cloud to tumbling cloud,
Minute by minute they change;
A shadow of cloud on the stream
50   Changes minute by minute;
A horse-hoof slides on the brim,
And a horse plashes within it;
The long-legged moor-hens dive,
And hens to moor-cocks call;
55   Minute by minute they live:
The stone's in the midst of all.

Too long a sacrifice
Can make a stone of the heart.
0 when may it suffice?
60   That is Heaven's part, our part
To murmur name upon name,
As a mother names her child
When sleep at last has come
On limbs that had run wild.
65   What is it but nightfall?
No, no, not night but death;
Was it needless death after all?
For England may keep faith

---

4. vainglorious (vān´ glôr´ ē əs) **lout:** An extremely vain and ill-mannered person.

For all that is done and said.
70 We know their dream; enough
    To know they dreamed and are dead;
    And what if excess of love
    Bewildered them till they died?
    I write it out in a verse—
75 MacDonagh and MacBride
    And Connolly and Pearse⁵
    Now and in time to be,
    Wherever green is worn,
    Are changed, changed utterly:
80 A terrible beauty is born.

---

5. MacDonagh . . . Pearse: Thomas MacDonagh, Major John MacBride, James Connolly, and Patrick Pearse were four of the fifteen leaders of the Easter Rebellion who were executed in 1916.

☑ Check Your Comprehension

1. (a) What does the Irish airman believe will happen to him? (b) How does he feel about those he is fighting against?

2. How does the airman view (a) his past? (b) his future?

3. (a) In "After Long Silence," what two things does the speaker describe as unfriendly? (b) Why does the speaker believe that the old have more reason than the young to "descant and yet again descant"?

4. (a) According to lines 57–58 of "Easter, 1916," what can result from "too long a sacrifice"? (b) In lines 74–80, what prediction does the speaker make about the rebels?

◆ Critical Thinking

1. The Irish airman does not love those he guards—the English. (a) Do you think his lack of love includes those he calls his countrymen? (b) What lines in the poem support your answer? **[Interpret]**

2. Suppose the Irish airman were to survive the war. What do you think he might do with the rest of his life? Explain your answer. **[Speculate]**

3. The speaker in "After Long Silence" seems to have mixed feelings about old age. How would you describe his feelings? **[Interpret]**

4. (a) What verse occurs as a refrain at lines 16, 40, and 80 of "Easter, 1916"? (b) What does this refrain reveal about Yeats's attitude toward the uprising and the rebels? **[Interpret]**

5. (a) In "After Long Silence," what relationship exists between the people who are being urged to speak? (b) How can you tell? **[Analyze]**

William Butler Yeats
Comparing and Connecting the Author's Works

◆ Literary Focus: Symbolism

A **symbol** in literature is a word, character, object, or action that stands both for itself and for something beyond itself. A symbol may possess more than one level of meaning. For example, in "The Song of Wandering Aengus," the mythological god Aengus symbolizes youth, beauty, and poetry.

The use of symbols allows writers to achieve intensity and complexity in their work. Yeats embraced symbolism in his early poems and then abandoned the technique for a while. He returned to symbolism with enthusiasm in his later work, however, and invented an elaborate symbolic system of his own. In his best poetry, an appreciation of the symbolism does not require expertise in Yeats's system, but only the practiced eye of a careful reader.

1. In "The Song of Wandering Aengus," what do you think the "glimmering girl" (line 13) may symbolize?
2. What might the word *play*—as both a noun and a verb—symbolize in "Never Give All the Heart"?
3. The gull plays a prominent part in Yeats's imagery in "On a Political Prisoner." Reread the poem, and then explain what you think this sea-borne bird may symbolize.

Early Draft	Comparison Points	Final Version
	Rhythm	
	Rhyme	
	Word Choice	
	Theme	

◆ Drawing Conclusions About Yeats's Work

Yeats continually revised his poetry. By examining earlier versions of his poems, readers can often draw important lessons about the creative process. Besides affecting the meaning of a particular passage, revisions provide insight into a writer's themes and artistic values.

Read the following early draft of "After Long Silence":

> Once more I have kissed your hand & it
>   is right—
> All other lovers being estranged or dead
> The heavy curtain drawn—the candle light
> Waging a doubtful battle with the shade
> We call our wisdom up upon our wisdom &
>   descant
> Upon the supreme theme of art & song—
> Decrepitude increases wisdom—young
> We loved each other & were ignorant

In an essay, compare and contrast the early draft of "After Long Silence" with the final version. You might use some or all of the following points of comparison: rhythm, rhyme scheme, word choice, figurative language, and theme. Why do you think Yeats made the revisions he did? You might use a graphic organizer such as the one shown below in order to organize your main ideas and supporting points.

◆ Idea Bank

Writing

1. **Personal Choice** These poems exemplify a wide variety of verse forms and touch on a broad range of themes. Which poem in this group is your personal favorite? In a paragraph or two, identify and explain your choice.

2. **Dialogue** In "Adam's Curse" and "No Second Troy," Yeats refers to his passionate love for Maude Gonne, the beautiful Irish nationalist who refused to marry him. Write a dialogue between Maude Gonne and W. B. Yeats on a subject of your choice: for example, politics, art, nature, love, or youth and old age. When you have finished your work, exchange papers with a classmate and comment on each other's writing.

3. **Yeats the Playwright** Research some of Yeats's plays, such as The Land of Heart's Desire, The Countess Cathleen, On Baile's Strand, or Purgatory. You might also investigate the influence on Yeats of ritualistic, symbolic dramas such as the Japanese Noh plays. Summarize your results in a research report.

Speaking and Listening

4. **Choral Reading** Together with a small group, prepare a choral reading of "Easter, 1916." Focus on oral elements such as pace, rhythm, pitch, volume, and emphasis. When you are satisfied with your interpretation, present your reading to an audience of classmates or friends. **[Performing Arts Link]**

5. **TV Review** Locate the film version (1957) of Yeats's translation of Sophocles' classic Greek tragedy, Oedipus Rex. This film, directed by Tyrone Guthrie, was based on a Canadian production of the play in Stratford, Ontario. Watch the film, and then write and present a television review of it. Read your review to an audience of classmates. **[Media Link]**

Researching and Representing

6. **Folklore Anthology** With a small group of classmates, develop an illustrated anthology of Irish folklore. Depending on the interests of group members, research Gaelic mythology, folk art, language, music, tales, clothing, holidays, and crafts. When you have finished work, display your anthology to the class as a whole. **[Group Activity; Social Studies Link]**

◆ Further Reading, Listening, and Viewing

- Richard Ellman: *Yeats: The Man and the Masks* (second edition, 1978). The best critical biography.

- Balachandra Rajan: *W. B. Yeats: A Critical Introduction* (second edition, 1969). A short introductory study.

- The Poetry of William Butler Yeats. Dove Audio (1996). Audiocassette.

- Benedict Kiely: *Yeats' Ireland* (1989). An illustrated companion.

On the Web:

http://www.phschool.com/atschool/literature
Go to the student edition of The British Tradition. Proceed to Unit 6. Then, click Hot Links to find Web sites featuring William Butler Yeats.

James Joyce In Depth

> "Welcome, O life! I go to encounter for the millionth time the reality of experi-
> ence and to forge in the smithy of my soul the uncreated conscience of my race."
> —*James Joyce,* **A Portrait of the Artist as a Young Man**

JAMES JOYCE is considered by many to be the most innovative, and also one of the most challenging writers of the twentieth-century. Joyce's brilliant use of myth and his radical experiments with language and stream-of-consciousness narrative technique produced a body of work that greatly influenced the course of Western literature.

Youth and Education James Joyce was born in Rathgar, a suburb of Dublin, the capital city of Ireland. He was educated in Catholic institutions run by the Jesuit order of priests: first at Clongowes Wood College, then at Belvedere, and finally at University College, Dublin, where Joyce studied modern languages.

The period of Joyce's youth was dominated by intense political debates on the subject of Irish nationalism. While still a teenager, Joyce began to rebel against what he perceived to be the narrowness of Irish nationalist fervor. He also had disdain for the bigotry he saw in Irish Catholicism, as well as for the cultural poverty of Dublin. By 1902, when he left the university, Joyce had decided on a career as a writer—a vocation he believed would lead to a life of rebellion and exile.

Young Adulthood Joyce left Dublin for Paris in 1902, but returned home the following year to care for his fatally-ill mother. In 1904 he met and fell in love with Nora Barnacle, a simple, relatively uneducated woman whose temperament could not have been more unlike that of her intense, cerebral husband. (She is said once to have asked Joyce, "Why don't you write sensible books that people can understand?") The couple moved to the Italian city of Trieste, where Joyce became a teacher of English. Joyce's literary career developed slowly for several reasons, including the demands of earning a living and the inaccessibility of his work to the literary community. His first major book was *Dubliners* (1914), a volume of carefully crafted short stories. These realistic sketches of Dublin life were enthusiastically reviewed by the American poet Ezra Pound, who then arranged to publish Joyce's next work, *A Portrait of the Artist as a Young Man,* in serial form in *The Egoist*, an influential avante-garde literary magazine.

In the semi-autobiographical *Portrait of the Artist,* Joyce tells the story of Stephen Dedalus, a young boy whose feelings of rootlessness and alienation parallel his own at that age. The name Dedalus is an allusion to the Greek mythological character Daedalus, known for his artistic gifts. In *Portrait of the Artist* Joyce explores the relationship between the artist and society.

Mature Career Although Joyce was much troubled by health problems during the second half of his life, he produced two more novels whose innovative features have few parallels in the history of English literature. The first was *Ulysses* (1922), an account of one day in the life of the city of Dublin. Every episode in the novel corresponds to an event in Homer's *Odyssey*—a structure that developed from Joyce's belief that Odysseus (Ulysses) was the most "complete" or universal man in all of world literature.

Joyce's use of stream-of-consciousness narration in *Ulysses* helped to revolutionize the twentieth-century novel. Attacked as obscene for some of its more explicit passages, *Ulysses* was at first banned in both Britain and the United States; however, a landmark court decision in late 1933 reversed the ban in the United States.

Even more challenging than *Ulysses* is the author's final work, *Finnegans Wake* (1939). Filled with puns in multiple languages, abounding in esoteric allusions and complex symbolism, and sprinkled with bawdy jokes, this novel completely abandons the narrative as a literary model.

Joyce died in Zurich, Switzerland, in 1941.

◆ Charles Stewart Parnell and Irish Nationalism

Although James Joyce spent most of his adult life in exile from his native Ireland, his work is very much about Dublin. Dublin, for Joyce, was a microcosm of human experience.

For much of Joyce's childhood and early adulthood, Ireland was in the throes of a long, wrenching struggle for independence from Britain. One of the most important Irish nationalist leaders was Charles Stewart Parnell (1846–1891), mentioned several times in the excerpt from Joyce's *A Portrait of the Artist as a*

Young Man. A member of the British Parliament, Parnell was imprisoned briefly in 1881 for his activism. By the time of Joyce's birth he was known as "the uncrowned king of Ireland." A Protestant by birth, Parnell had lost the support of the Catholics in 1889 when he was implicated in a scandalous divorce suit. In *A Portrait of the Artist,* Joyce alludes to the controversy swirling around Parnell by portraying Stephen Daedalus' father as a supporter of Parnell and Aunt Dante as a vigorous opponent. Ireland did not achieve home rule until 1922.

◆ Literary Works

Chamber Music (1907): early poems

Dubliners (1914): a carefully crafted volume of short stories, including "Eveline"

Exiles (1916): a play about an Irish writer alienated from his society

A Portrait of the Artist as a Young Man (serialized in 1914–1915, published in book form in 1916): a semi-autobiographical novel

Ulysses (1922): Joyce's epic narrative of a single day in the life of the city of Dublin; in the opinion of many, the writer's masterpiece

Finnegans Wake (1939): the story of an Irishman's cosmic dream; in this novel, Joyce abandoned realism altogether

TIMELINE

Joyce's Life		World Events	
1882	Joyce born in Rathgar, a suburb of Dublin	1882	Britain conquers Egypt
1884	Brother Stanislaus born	1883	Robert Louis Stevenson's *Treasure Island* published
1888	Enters Clongowes, a Jesuit boarding school	1884	Mark Twain's *The Adventures of Huckleberry Finn* published
1893	Attends Belvedere College	1891	Death of Charles Stewart Parnell, Irish nationalist
1898	Enters University College Dublin		
1902	Leaves Dublin for Paris	1896	A. E. Housman's *A Shropshire Lad* published; first modern Olympics takes place in Athens, Greece
1903	Returns to Dublin; death of Joyce's mother		
1904	Starts autobiographical novel *Stephen Hero,* which will turn out to be a first draft of *A Portrait of the Artist;* meets and falls in love with Nora Barnacle	1898	Discovery of radium by French scientists Marie and Pierre Curie
		1900	Sigmund Freud's *The Interpretation of Dreams* published
		1901	Death of Queen Victoria; accession of King Edward VII
1905	Moves with Nora to Trieste, Italy; works as an English teacher; son Giorgio born	1902	Joseph Conrad's *Heart of Darkness* published
1907	Publishes *Chamber Music;* daughter Lucia born	1903	Wright brothers build first successful airplane
1914	Publication of *Dubliners;* Ezra Pound runs serial installments of *A Portrait of the Artist* in *The Egoist*	1913	D. H. Lawrence's *Sons and Lovers* published; Igor Stravinsky's ballet *The Rites of Spring* first produced
1915	Moves to Zurich, Switzerland	1914	World War I breaks out in Europe
1916	Publication of *A Portrait of the Artist* in book form	1916	Easter Rebellion in Ireland
		1917	Russian Revolution begins
1917	Drafts first three episodes of *Ulysses*	1918	End of World War I
1920	Moves to Paris	1922	Irish Free State founded; T. S. Eliot's *The Waste Land* published
1922	*Ulysses* published in Paris		
1923	Begins work on *Finnegans Wake*	1927	Charles Lindbergh flies across the Atlantic
1931	Joyce's father dies		
1932	Daughter Lucia suffers nervous breakdown	1936	First BBC television broadcast; Spanish Civil War begins
1933	Court ruling allows *Ulysses* to be published in United States	1939	Outbreak of World War II in Europe
1939	*Finnegans Wake* published		
1941	Death of Joyce in Zurich		

James Joyce

Eveline

She sat at the window watching the evening invade the avenue. Her head was leaned against the window curtains and in her nostrils was the odor of dusty cretonne.[1] She was tired.

Few people passed. The man out of the last house passed on his way home; she heard his footsteps clacking along the concrete pavement and afterwards crunching on the cinder path before the new red houses. One time there used to be a field there in which they used to play every evening with other people's children. Then a man from Belfast bought the field and built houses in it—not like their little brown houses but bright brick houses with shining roofs. The children of the avenue used to play together in that field—the Devines, the Waters, the Dunns, little Keogh the cripple, she and her brothers and sisters. Ernest, however, never played: he was too grown up. Her father used often to hunt them in out of the field with his blackthorn stick but usually little Keogh used to keep nix[2] and call out when he saw her father coming. Still they seemed to have been rather happy then. Her father was not so bad then, and besides her mother was alive. That was a long time ago; she and her brothers and sisters were all grown up; her mother was dead. Tizzie Dunn was dead, too, and the Waters had gone back to England. Everything changes. Now she was going to go away like the others, to leave her home.

Home! She looked round the room reviewing all its familiar objects which she had dusted once a week for so many years, wondering where on earth all the dust came from. Perhaps she would never see again those familiar objects from which she had never dreamed of being divided. And yet during all those years she had never found out the name of the priest whose yellowing photograph hung on the wall above the broken harmonium beside the colored print of the promises made to Blessed Margaret Mary Alacoque.[3] He had been a school friend of her father's. Whenever he showed the photograph to a visitor her father used to pass it with a casual word:

1. **cretonne** (krē tän′) *n.*: A heavy, unglazed, printed cotton or linen cloth, used for curtains.
2. **keep nix:** Keep watch.
3. **Blessed Margaret Mary Alacoque:** Seventeenth-century French nun who was said to have experienced divine visitations from Christ.

He is in Melbourne now.

She had consented to go away, to leave her home. Was that wise? She tried to weigh each side of the question. In her home anyway she had shelter and food; she had those whom she had known all her life about her. Of course she had to work hard both in the house and at business. What would they say of her in the stores when they found out that she had run away with a fellow? Say she was a fool, perhaps; and her place would be filled up by advertisement. Miss Gavan would be glad. She had always had an edge on her, especially whenever there were people listening.

—Miss Hill, don't you see these ladies are waiting?

—Look lively, Miss Hill, please.

She would not cry many tears at leaving the stores

But in her new home, in a distant unknown country, it would not be like that. Then she would be married–she, Eveline. People would treat her with respect then. She would not be treated as her mother had been. Even now, though she was over nineteen, she sometimes felt herself in danger of her father's violence. She knew it was that that had given her the palpitations[4]. When they were growing up he had never gone for her, like he used to go for Harry and Ernest, because she was a girl; but latterly he had begun to threaten her and say what he would do to her only for her dead mother's sake. And now she had nobody to protect her. Ernest was dead and Harry, who was in the church decorating business, was nearly always down somewhere in the country. Besides, the invariable squabble for money on Saturday nights had begun to weary her unspeakably. She always gave her entire wages-seven shillings –and Harry always sent up what he could but the trouble was to get any money from her father. He said she used to squander the money, that she had no head, that he wasn't going to give her his hard earned money to throw about the streets and much more for he was usually fairly bad of a Saturday night. In the end he would give her the money and ask her had she any intention of buying Sunday's dinner. Then she had to rush out as quickly as she could and do her marketing, holding her black leather purse tightly in her hand as she elbowed her way through the crowds and returning home late under her load of provisions. She had hard work to keep the house together and to see that the two young children who had been left to her charge went to school regularly and got their meals regularly. It was hard work —a hard life—but now that she was about to leave it she did not find it a wholly undesirable life.

She was about to explore another life with Frank. Frank was

---

4. palpitations (pal′ pə tā′ shəns) *n.*: Rapid beatings of the heart, esp. that one is conscious of.

very kind, manly, openhearted. She was to go away with him by the night boat to be his wife and to live with him in Buenos Aires[5] where he had a home waiting for her. How well she remembered the first time she had seen him; he was lodging in a house on the main road where she used to visit. It seemed a few weeks ago. He was standing at the gate, his peaked cap pushed back on his head and his hair tumbled forward over a face of bronze. Then they had come to know each other. He used to meet her outside the stores every evening and see her home. He took her to see the *Bohemian Girl* and she felt elated as she sit in an unaccustomed part of the theatre with him. He was awfully fond of music and sang a little. People knew that they were courting and when he sang about the lass that loves a sailor she always felt pleasantly confused. He used to call her Poppens out of fun. First of all it had been an excitement for her to have a fellow and then she had begun to like him. He had tales of distant countries. He had started as a deck boy at a pound a month on a ship of the Allan line going out to Canada. He told her the names of the ships he had been on and the names of the different services. He had sailed through the Straits of Magellan and he told her stories of the terrible Patagonians. He had fallen on his feet in Buenos Aires, he said, and had come over to the old country just for a holiday. Of course, her father had found out the affair and had forbidden her to have anything to say to him:

—I know these sailor chaps, he said.

One day he had quarrelled with Frank and after that she had to meet her lover secretly.

The evening deepened in the avenue. The white of two letters in her lap grew indistinct. One was to Harry, the other was to her father. Ernest had been her favorite but she liked Harry too. Her father was becoming old lately, she noticed; he would miss her. Sometimes he could be very nice. Not long before, when she had been laid up for a day, he had read her out a ghost story and made toast for her at the fire. Another day, when their mother was alive, they had all gone for a picnic to the Hill of Howth. She remembered her father putting on her mother's bonnet to make the children laugh.

Her time was running out but she continued to sit by the window, leaning her head against the window curtain, inhaling the odor of dusty cretonne. Down far in the avenue she could hear a street organ playing. She knew the air. Strange that it should come that very night to remind her of the promise to her mother, her promise to keep the home together as long as she could. She

---

5. Buenos Aires (bwā´ nəs er´ ēz): Capital of Argentina.

remembered the last night of her mother's illness; she was again in the close dark room at the other side of the hall and outside she heard a melancholy air of Italy. The organ player had been ordered to go away and given sixpence. She remembered her father strutting back into the sickroom. saying:

—Damned Italians! coming over here!

As she mused the pitiful vision of her mother's life laid its spell on the very quick of her being-that life of commonplace sacrifices closing in final craziness. She trembled as she heard again her mother's voice saying constantly with foolish insistence:

—Derevaun Seraun! —Derevaun Seraun!

She stood up in a sudden impulse of terror. Escape! She must escape! Frank would save her. He would give her life, perhaps love too. But she wanted to live. Why should she be unhappy? She had a right to happiness. Frank would take her in his arms, fold her in his arms. He would save her.

She stood among the swaying crowd in the station at the North Wall. He held her hand and she knew that he was speaking to her, saying something about the passage over and over again. The station was full of soldiers with brown baggages. Through the wide doors of the sheds she caught a glimpse of the black mass of the boat lying in beside the quay wall, with illumined portholes. She answered nothing. She felt her cheek pale and cold and out of a maze of distress she prayed to God to direct her, to show her what was her duty. The boat blew a long mournful whistle into the mist. If she went, tomorrow she would be on the sea with Frank, steaming towards Buenos Aires. Their passage had been booked. Could she still draw back after all he had done for her? Her distress awoke a nausea in her body and she kept moving her lips in silent fervent prayer.

A bell clanged upon her heart. She felt him seize her hand:
—Come

All the seas of the world tumbled about her heart. He was drawing her into them: he would drown her. She gripped with both hands at the iron railing.
—Come!

No! No! No! It was impossible. Her hands clutched the iron in frenzy. Amid the seas she sent a cry of anguish.
—Eveline! Evvy!

He rushed beyond the barrier and called to her to follow. He was shouted at to go on but he still called to her. She set her white face to him, passive, like a helpless animal. Her eyes gave him no sign of love or farewell or recognition.

☑ Check Your Comprehension

1. (a) How old is Eveline? (b) As the story opens, what important step is she about to take?

2. What was the result of the quarrel between Eveline's father and Frank?

3. To whom has Eveline written letters?

4. What did Eveline promise her mother before she died?

5. (a) Where does the last scene of the story take place? (b) What is Eveline's dilemma in this scene?

6. In the end, what does Eveline decide to do?

◆ Critical Thinking

1. In the story's opening paragraphs, what atmosphere or mood is created by the setting? **[Interpret]**

2. How would you describe Eveline's relationship with her father? **[Interpret]**

3. (a) What qualities in Frank's personality appeal to Eveline? (b) Why do you think Eveline's father dislikes Frank? **[Infer]**

4. How does Joyce quicken the pace and sharpen the suspense in the second half of the story? **[Interpret]**

5. Do you think the main issues in this story are still relevant to young people today? Explain your answer. **[Apply]**

James Joyce

from A Portrait of the Artist as a Young Man

The protagonist of the story is Stephen Dedalus, the child who will become the artist. This excerpt, taken from the first chapter of the novel, recounts Stephen's childhood at Clongowes, a Catholic boarding school in Ireland. The excerpt depicts Stephen's artistic sensibilities and his trouble fitting in with the other boys at school. The story is told in a continuous flow that combines the memory and the imaginative insights of Stephen, as well as external narrative devoted to descriptions and actions of other characters.

It was the hour for sums. Father Arnall wrote a hard sum on the board and then he said:

—Now then, who will win? Go ahead, York! Go ahead, Lancaster[1].

Stephen tried his best but the sum was too hard and he felt confused. The little silk badge with the white rose on it that was pinned on the breast of his jacket began to flutter. He was no good at sums but he tried his best so that York might not lose. Father Arnall's face looked very black but he was not in a wax:[2] he was laughing. Then Jack Lawton cracked his fingers and Father Arnall looked at his copybook and said:

—Right. Bravo Lancaster! The red rose wins. Come on now, York! Forge ahead!

Jack Lawton looked over from his side. The little silk badge with the red rose on it looked very rich because he had a blue sailor top on. Stephen felt his own face red too, thinking of all the bets about who would get first place in elements,[3] Jack Lawton or he. Some weeks Jack Lawton got the card for first and some weeks he got the card for first. His white silk badge fluttered and fluttered as he worked at the next sum and heard Father Arnall's voice. Then all his eagerness passed away and he felt his face quite cool. He thought his face must be white because it felt so cool. He could not get out the answer for the sum but it did not matter. White roses and red roses: those were beautiful colors to think of. And the cards for first place and second place and third place were beautiful colors too: pink and

---

1. **York . . . Lancaster:** In the fifteenth-century, England was engaged in a number of civil wars known as the Wars of the Roses, the red rose being the emblem of the house of Lancaster; the white, of York.
2. **wax:** A fit of anger or temper; a rage.
3. **elements:** Mathematical problems.

cream and lavender. Lavender and cream and pink roses were beautiful to think of. Perhaps a wild rose might be like those colors: and he remembered the song about the wild rose blossoms on the little green place. But you could not have a green rose. But perhaps somewhere in the world you could.

The bell rang and then the classes began to file out of the rooms and along the corridors towards the refectory. He sat looking at the two prints of butter on his plate but could not eat the damp bread. The tablecloth was damp and limp. But he drank off the hot weak tea which the clumsy scullion,[4] girt with a white apron, poured into his cup. He wondered whether the scullion's apron was damp too or whether all white things were cold and damp. Nasty Roche and Saurin drank cocoa that their people sent them in tins. They said they could not drink the tea; that it was hogwash. Their fathers were magistrates, the fellows said.

All the boys seemed to him very strange. They had all fathers and mothers and different clothes and voices. He longed to be at home and lay his head on his mother's lap. But he could not: and so he longed for the play and study and prayers to be over and to be in bed.

He drank another cup of hot tea and Fleming said:

—What's up? Have you a pain or what's up with you?

—I don't know, Stephen said.

—Sick in your breadbasket, Fleming said, because your face looks white. It will go away.

—O yes, Stephen said.

But he was not sick there. He thought that he was sick in his heart if you could be sick in that place. Fleming was very decent to ask him. He wanted to cry. He leaned his elbows on the table and shut and opened the flaps of his ears. Then he heard the noise of the refectory[5] every time he opened the flaps of his ears. It made a roar like a train at night. And when he closed the flaps the roar was shut off like a train going into a tunnel. That night at Dalkey the train had roared like that and then, when it went into the tunnel, the roar stopped. He closed his eyes and the train went on, roaring and then stopping; roaring again, stopping. It was nice to hear it roar and stop and then roar out of the tunnel again and then stop.

Then the higher line fellows began to come down along the matting in the middle of the refectory, Paddy Rath and Jimmy Magee and the Spaniard who was allowed to smoke cigars and the little Portuguese who wore the woolly cap. And then the lower line tables and the tables of the third line. And every single fellow

4. **scullion** (skul´ yən) n.: A kitchen servant.
5. **refectory** (ri fek´ tər ē) n.: A dining hall in a monastery, college, etc.

had a different way of walking.

He sat in a corner of the playroom pretending to watch a game of dominos and once or twice he was able to hear for an instant the little song of the gas. The prefect[6] was at the door with some boys and Simon Moonan was knotting his false sleeves. He was telling them something about Tullabeg.

Then he went away from the door and Wells came over to Stephen and said:

—Tell us, Dedalus, do you kiss your mother every night before you go to bed?

Stephen answered:

—I do.

Wells turned to the other fellows and said:

—O, I say, here's a fellow says he kisses his mother every night before he goes to bed.

The other fellows stopped their game and turned round, laughing. Stephen blushed under their eyes and said:

—I do not.

Wells said:

—O, I say, here's a fellow says he doesn't kiss his mother before he goes to bed.

They all laughed again. Stephen tried to laugh with them. He felt his whole body hot and confused in a moment. What was the right answer to the question? He had given two and still Wells laughed. But Wells must know the right answer for he was in third of grammar. He tried to think of Wells's mother but he did not dare to raise his eyes to Wells's face. He did not like Wells's face. It was Wells who had shouldered him into the square ditch the day before because he would not swop his little snuffbox for Wells's seasoned hacking chestnut, the conqueror of forty. It was a mean thing to do; all the fellows said it was. And how cold and slimy the water had been! And a fellow had once seen a big rat jump plop into the scum.

The cold slime of the ditch covered his whole body; and, when the bell rang for study and the lines filed out of the playrooms, he felt the cold air of the corridor and staircase inside his clothes. He still tried to think what was the right answer. Was it right to kiss his mother or wrong to kiss his mother? What did that mean, to kiss? You put your face up like that to say good-night and then his mother put her face down. That was to kiss. His mother put her lips on his cheek; her lips were soft and they wetted his cheek; and they made a tiny little noise: kiss. Why did people do that with their two faces?

Sitting in the studyhall he opened the lid of his desk and

---

6. prefect (prē´ fekt´) *n.*: An older student with disciplinary authority.

changed the number pasted up inside from seventy-seven to seventy-six. But the Christmas vacation was very far away: but one time it would come because the earth moved round always. There was a picture of the earth on the first page of his geography: a big ball in the middle of clouds. Fleming had a box of crayons and one night during free study he had colored the earth green and the clouds maroon. That was like the two brushes in Dante's press, the brush with the green velvet back for Parnell and the brush with the maroon velvet back for Michael Davitt.[7] But he had not told Fleming to color them those colors. Fleming had done it himself.

He opened the geography to study the lesson; but he could not learn the names of places in America. Still they were all different places that had those different names. They were all in different countries and the countries were in continents and the continents were in the world and the world was in the universe.

He turned to the flyleaf of the geography and read what he had written there: himself, his name and where he was.

Stephen Dedalus
Class of Elements
Clongowes Wood College
Sallins
County Kildare
Ireland
Europe
The World
The Universe

That was in his writing: and Fleming one night for a cod[8] had written on the opposite page:

Stephen Dedalus is my name,
Ireland is my nation.
Clongowes is my dwellingplace
And heaven my expectation.

He read the verses backwards but then they were not poetry. Then he read the flyleaf from the bottom to the top till he came to his own name. That was he: and he read down the page again. What was after the universe? Nothing. But was there anything round the universe to show where it stopped before the nothing place began? It could not be a wall but there could be a thin thin line there all round everything. It was very big to think about

---

7. **Parnell . . . Davitt:** Charles Stewart Parnell (1846–1891), Irish nationalist leader; Michael Davitt (1846–1906), Irish journalist and political activist.
8. **cod:** Hoax or trick.

everything and everywhere. Only God could do that. He tried to think what a big thought that must be but he could think only of God. God was God's name just as his name was Stephen. *Dieu* was the French for God and that was God's name too; and when anyone prayed to God and said Dieu then God knew at once that it was a French person that was praying. But though there were different names for God in all the different languages in the world and God understood what all the people who prayed said in their different languages still God remained always the same God and God's real name was God.

It made him very tired to think that way. It made him feel his head very big. He turned over the flyleaf and looked wearily at the green round earth in the middle of the maroon clouds. He wondered which was right, to be for the green or for the maroon, because Dante had ripped the green velvet back off the brush that was for Parnell one day with her scissors and had told him that Parnell was a bad man. He wondered if they were arguing at home about that. That was called politics. There were two sides in it: Dante was on one side and his father and Mr Casey were on the other side but his mother and uncle Charles were on no side. Every day there was something in the paper about it.

It pained him that he did not know well what politics meant and that he did not know where the universe ended. He felt small and weak. When would he be like the fellows in poetry rhetoric? They had big voices and big boots and they studied trigonometry. That was very far away. First came the vacation and then the next term and then vacation again and then again another term and then again the vacation. It was like a train going in and out of tunnels and that was like the noise of the boys eating in the refectory when you opened and closed the flaps of the ears. Term, vacation; tunnel, out; noise, stop. How far away it was! It was better to go to bed to sleep. Only prayers in the chapel and then bed. He shivered and yawned. It would be lovely in bed after the sheets got a bit hot. First they were so cold to get into. He shivered to think how cold they were first. But then they got hot and then he could sleep. It was lovely to be tired. He yawned again. Night prayers and then bed: he shivered and wanted to yawn. It would be lovely in a few minutes. He felt a warm glow creeping up from the cold shivering sheets, warmer and warmer till he felt warm all over, ever so warm; ever so warm and yet he shivered a little and still wanted to yawn.

The bell rang for night prayers and he filed out of the studyhall after the others and down the staircase and along the corridors to the chapel. The corridors were darkly lit and the chapel was

---

9. **Dieu** (dyö).

darkly lit. Soon all would be dark and sleeping. There was cold night air in the chapel and the marbles were the color the sea was at night. The sea was cold day and night: but it was colder at night. It was cold and dark under the seawall beside his father's house. But the kettle would be on the hob[10] to make punch.

The prefect of the chapel prayed above his head and his memory knew the responses:

> O Lord, open our lips
> And our mouth shall announce Thy praise.
> Incline unto our aid, O God!
> O Lord, make haste to help us!

There was a cold night smell in the chapel. But it was a holy smell. It was not like the smell of the old peasants who knelt at the back of the chapel at Sunday mass. That was a smell of air and rain and turf and corduroy. But they were very holy peasants. They breathed behind him on his neck and sighed as they prayed. They lived in Clane, a fellow said: there were little cottages there and he had seen a woman standing at the halfdoor of a cottage with a child in her arms as the cars had come past from Sallins. It would be lovely to sleep for one night in that cottage before the fire of smoking turf, in the dark lit by the fire, in the warm dark, breathing the smell of the peasants, air and rain and turf and corduroy. But, O, the road there between the trees was dark! You would be lost in the dark. It made him afraid to think of how it was.

He heard the voice of the prefect of the chapel saying the last prayer. He prayed it too against the dark outside under the trees.

> Visit, we beseech Thee, O Lord, this habitation
> and drive away from it all the snares of the enemy. May
> Thy holy angels dwell herein to preserve us in peace
> and may Thy blessing be always upon us through
> Christ, Our Lord. Amen.

His fingers trembled as he undressed himself in the dormitory. He told his fingers to hurry up. He had to undress and then kneel and say his own prayers and be in bed before the gas was lowered so that he might not go to hell when he died. He rolled his stockings off and put on his nightshirt quickly and knelt trembling at his bedside and repeated his prayers quickly quickly fearing that the gas would go down. He felt his shoulders shaking as he murmured:

> God bless my father and my mother and spare them to
> me!

---

10. hob: A projecting ledge at the back or side of a fireplace, used for keeping a kettle warm.

> *God bless my little brothers and sisters and spare them
> to me!*
> *God bless Dante and uncle Charles and spare them to
> me!*

He blessed himself and climbed quickly into bed and, tucking
the end of the nightshirt under his feet, curled himself together
under the cold white sheets, shaking and trembling. But he
would not go to hell when he died; and the shaking would stop. A
voice bade the boys in the dormitory goodnight. He peered out for
an instant over the coverlet and saw the yellow curtains round
and before his bed that shut him off on all sides. The light was
lowered quietly.

The prefect's shoes went away. Where? Down the staircase
and along the corridors or to his room at the end? He saw the
dark. Was it true about the black dog that walked there at night
with eyes as big as carriagelamps? They said it was the ghost of a
murderer. A long shiver of fear flowed over his body. He saw the
dark entrance hall of the castle. Old servants in old dress were in
the ironingroom above the staircase. It was long ago. The old servants were quiet. There was a fire there but the hall was still
dark. A figure came up the staircase from the hall. He wore the
white cloak of a marshal;[11] his face was pale and strange; he held
his hand pressed to his side. He looked out of strange eyes at the
old servants. They looked at him and saw their master's face and
cloak and knew that he had received his deathwound But only
the dark was where they looked: only dark silent air. Their master had received his deathwound on the battlefield of Prague[12]far
away over the sea. He was standing on the field; his hand was
pressed to his side; his face was pale and strange and he wore
the white cloak of a marshal.

O how cold and strange it was to think of that! All the dark
was cold and strange. There were pale strange faces there, great
eyes like carriagelamps. They were the ghosts of murderers, the
figures of marshals who had received, their deathwound on bat-
tlefields far away over the sea. What did they wish to say that
their faces were so strange?

> *Visit, we beseech Thee, O Lord, this habitation and drive
> away from it all ....*

Going home for the holidays! That would be lovely: the fellows
had told him. Getting up on the cars in the early wintry morning
outside the door of the castle. The cars were rolling on the gravel.
Cheers for the rector![13]

---

11. marshal: A high official of a royal household or court, in charge of military
affairs or ceremonies.
12. Prague (präg): Capital of the Czech Republic.
13. rector: A priest leading the members of a ministry; the headmasters of a
school.

Hurray! Hurray! Hurray!

The cars drove past the chapel and all caps were raised. They drove merrily along the country roads. The drivers pointed with their whips to Bodenstown. The fellows cheered. They passed the farmhouse of the Jolly Farmer. Cheer after cheer after cheer. Through Clane they drove, cheering and cheered. The peasant women stood at the halfdoors, the men stood here and there. The lovely smell there was in the wintry air: the smell of Clane: rain and wintry air and turf smouldering and corduroy.

The train was full of fellows: a long long chocolate train with cream facings. The guards went to and fro opening, closing, locking, unlocking the doors. They were men in dark blue and silver; they had silvery whistles and their keys made a quick music: click, click: click, click.

And the train raced on over the flat lands and past the Hill of Allen. The telegraphpoles were passing, passing. The train went on and on. It knew. There were colored lanterns in the hall of his father's house and ropes of green branches. There were holly and ivy round the pierglass[14] and holly and ivy, green and red, twined round the chandeliers. There were red holly and green ivy round the old portraits on the walls. Holly and ivy for him and for Christmas.

Lovely ......

All the people. Welcome home, Stephen! Noises of welcome. His mother kissed him. Was that right? His father was a marshal now: higher than a magistrate.[15] Welcome home, Stephen!

Noises .....

There was a noise of curtainrings running back along the rods, of water being splashed in the basins. There was a noise of rising and dressing and washing in the dormitory: a noise of clapping of hands as the prefect went up and down telling the fellows to look sharp. A pale sunlight showed the yellow curtains drawn back, the tossed beds. His bed was very hot and his face and body were very hot.

He got up and sat on the side of his bed. He was weak. He tried to pull on his stocking. It had a horrid rough feel. The sunlight was queer and cold.

Fleming said:

—Are you not well?

He did not know; and Fleming said:

—Get back into bed. I'll tell McGlade you're not well.

—He's sick.

—Who is?

—Tell McGlade.

---

14. **pierglass:** A tall mirror set in the wall section between windows.
15. **magistrate** (maj′ is trāt′) *n.:* A minor official with limited judicial powers.

—Get back into bed.

—Is he sick?

A fellow held his arms while he loosened the stocking clinging to his foot and climbed back into the hot bed.

He crouched down between the sheets, glad of their tepid glow. He heard the fellows talk among themselves about him as they dressed for mass. It was a mean thing to do, to shoulder him into the square ditch, they were saying.

Then their voices ceased; they had gone. A voice at his bed said:

—Dedalus, don't spy on us, sure you won't?

Wells's face was there. He looked at it and saw that Wells was afraid.

—I didn't mean to. Sure you won't?

His father had told him, whatever he did, never to peach[16] on a fellow. He shook his head and answered no and felt glad. Wells said:

—I didn't mean to, honor bright. It was only for cod. I'm sorry.

The face and the voice went away. Sorry because he was afraid. Afraid that it was some disease. Canker was a disease of plants and cancer one of animals: or another different. That was a long time ago then out on the playgrounds in the evening light, creeping from point to point on the fringe of his line, a heavy bird flying low through the grey light. Leicester Abbey lit up. Wolsey died there. The abbots buried him themselves.

It was not Wells's face, it was the prefect's. He was not foxing. No, no: he was sick really. He was not foxing.[17] And he felt the prefect's hand on his forehead; and he felt his forehead warm and damp against the prefect's cold damp hand. That was the way a rat felt, slimy and damp and cold. Every rat had two eyes to look out of. Sleek slimy coats, little little feet tucked up to jump, black shiny eyes to look out of. They could understand how to jump. But the minds of rats could not understand trigonometry. When they were dead they lay on their sides. Their coats dried then. They were only dead things.

The prefect was there again and it was his voice that was saying that he was to get up, that Father Minister had said he was to get up and dress and go to the infirmary. And while he was dressing himself as quickly as he could the prefect said:

—We must pack off to Brother Michael because we have the collywobbles.[18] Terrible thing to have the collywobbles! How we wobble when we have the collywobbles!

He was very decent to say that. That was all to make him

---

16. **peach:** To give evidence against another; turn informer.
17. **foxing:** Tricking or deceiving.
18. **the collywobbles:** Pain in the abdomen; bellyache.

laugh. But he could not laugh because his cheeks and lips were all shivery: and then the prefect had to laugh by himself.

The prefect cried:

—Quick march! Hayfoot! Strawfoot!

They went together down the staircase and along the corridor and past the bath. As he passed the door he remembered with a vague fear the warm turfcolored bogwater, the warm moist air, the noise of plunges, the smell of the towels, like medicine.

Brother Michael was standing at the door of the infirmary and from the door of the dark cabinet on his right came a smell like medicine. That came from the bottles on the shelves. The prefect spoke to Brother Michael and Brother Michael answered and called the prefect sir. He had reddish hair mixed with grey and a queer look. It was queer that he would always be a brother. It was queer too that you could not call him sir because he was a brother and had a different kind of look. Was he not holy enough or why could he not catch up on the others?

There were two beds in the room and in one bed there was a fellow: and when they went in he called out:

—Hello! It's young Dedalus! What's up?

—The sky is up, Brother Michael said.

He was a fellow out of third of grammar and, while Stephen was undressing, he asked Brother Michael to bring him a round of buttered toast.

—Ah, do! he said.

—Butter you up! said Brother Michael. You'll get your walking papers in the morning when the doctor comes.

—Will I? the fellow said. I'm not well yet.

Brother Michael repeated:

—You'll get your walking papers, I tell you.

He bent down to rake the fire. He had a long back like the long back of a tramhorse He shook the poker gravely and nodded his head at the fellow out of third of grammar.

Then Brother Michael went away and after a while the fellow out of third of grammar turned in towards the wall and fell asleep.

That was the infirmary. He was sick then. Had they written home to tell his mother and father? But it would be quicker for one of the priests to go himself to tell them. Or he would write a letter for the priest to bring.

Dear Mother

I am sick. I want to go home. Please come and take me home. I am in the infirmary.

Your fond son,
Stephen

How far away they were! There was cold sunlight outside the window. He wondered if he would die. You could die just the same on a sunny day. He might die before his mother came. Then he would have a dead mass in the chapel like the way the fellows had told him it was when Little had died. All the fellows would be at the mass, dressed in black, all with sad faces. Wells too would be there but no fellow would look at him. The rector would be there in a cope[19] of black and gold and there would be tall yellow candles on the altar and round the catafalque.[20] And they would carry the coffin out of the chapel slowly and he would be buried in the little graveyard of the community off the main avenue of limes. And Wells would be sorry then for what he had done. And the bell would toll slowly.

He could hear the tolling. He said over to himself the song that Brigid had taught him.

> *Dingdong! The castle bell!*
> *Farewell, my mother!*
> *Bury me in the old churchyard*
> *Beside my eldest brother.*
> *My coffin shall be black,*
> *Six angels at my back,*
> *Two to sing and two to pray*
> *And two to carry my soul away.*

How beautiful and sad that was! How beautiful the words were where they said *Bury me in the old churchyard!* A tremor passed over his body. How sad and how beautiful! He wanted to cry quietly but not for himself: for the words, so beautiful and sad, like music. The bell! The bell! Farewell! O farewell!

The cold sunlight was weaker and Brother Michael was standing at his bedside with a bowl of beeftea. He was glad for his mouth was hot and dry. He could hear them playing on the playgrounds. It was after lunchtime. And the day was going on in the college just as if he were there.

Then Brother Michael was going away and the fellow out of third of grammar told him to be sure and come back and tell him all the news in the paper. He told Stephen that his name was Athy and that his father kept a lot of racehorses that were spiffing jumpers and that his father would give a good tip to Brother Michael any time he wanted it because Brother Michael was very decent and always told him the news out of the paper they got every day up in the castle. There was every kind of news in the paper: accidents, shipwrecks, sports and politics.

---

19. cope: A large capelike robe or gown worn by priests.
20. catafalque (kat´ ə falk´) *n.*: A wooden framework, usually draped, on which the body in a coffin lies during an elaborate funeral.

—Now it is all about politics in the paper, he said. Do your people talk about that too?

—Yes, Stephen said.

—Mine too, he said.

Then he thought for a moment and said:

—You have a queer name, Dedalus, and I have a queer name too, Athy. My name is the name of a town. Your name is like Latin.

Then he asked:

—Are you good at riddles?

Stephen answered:

—Not very good.

Then he said:

—Can you answer me this one? Why is the county Kildare like the leg of a fellow's breeches?

Stephen thought what could be the answer and then said:

—I give it up.

—Because there is a thigh in it, he said. Do you see the joke? Athy is the town in the county Kildare and a thigh is the other thigh.

—O, I see, Stephen said.

—That's an old riddle, he said.

After a moment he said:

—I say!

—What? asked Stephen.

—You know, he said, you can ask that riddle another way?

—Can you? said Stephen.

—The same riddle, he said. Do you know the other way to ask it?

—No, said Stephen.

—Can you not think of the other way? he said.

He looked at Stephen over the bedclothes as he spoke. Then he lay back on the pillow and said:

—There is another way but I won't tell you what it is.

Why did he not tell it? His father, who kept the racehorses, must be a magistrate too like Saurin's father and Nasty Roche's father. He thought of his own father, of how he sang songs while his mother played and of how he always gave him a shilling when he asked for sixpence[21] and he felt sorry for him that he was not a magistrate like the other boys' fathers. Then why was he sent to that place with them? But his father had told him that he would be no stranger there because his granduncle had presented an address to the liberator there fifty years before. You could know the people of that time by their old dress. It seemed to him a solemn time: and he wondered if that was the time when the fellows in Clongowes wore blue coats with brass buttons and yellow

---

21. shilling . . . sixpence: A shilling is a former monetary unit of the United Kingdom, and was worth 12 pence.

waistcoats and caps of rabbitskin and drank beer like grownup people and kept greyhounds of their own to course the hares with.

He looked at the window and saw that the daylight had grown weaker. There would be cloudy grey light over the playgrounds. There was no noise on the playgrounds. The class must be doing the themes or perhaps Father Arnall was reading a legend out of the book.

It was queer that they had not given him any medicine. Perhaps Brother Michael would bring it back when he came. They said you got stinking stuff to drink when you were in the infirmary. But he felt better now than before. It would be nice getting better slowly. You could get a book then. There was a book in the library about Holland. There were lovely foreign names in it and pictures of strangelooking cities and ships. It made you feel so happy.

How pale the light was at the window! But that was nice. The fire rose and fell on the wall. It was like waves. Someone had put coal on and he heard voices. They were talking. It was the noise of the waves. Or the waves were talking among themselves as they rose and fell.

He saw the sea of waves, long dark waves rising and falling, dark under the moonless night. A tiny light twinkled at the pierhead where the ship was entering: and he saw a multitude of people gathered by the waters' edge to see the ship that was entering their harbor A tall man stood on the deck, looking out towards the flat dark land: and by the light at the pierhead he saw his face, the sorrowful face of Brother Michael.

He saw him lift his hand towards the people and heard him say in a loud voice of sorrow over the waters:

—He is dead. We saw him lying upon the catafalque.

A wail of sorrow went up from the people.

—Parnell! Parnell! He is dead!

They fell upon their knees, moaning in sorrow.

And he saw Dante in a maroon velvet dress and with a green velvet mantle hanging from her shoulders walking proudly and silently past the people who knelt by the waters' edge.

☑ Check Your Comprehension

1. What is the setting for these episodes?
2. (a) How does Wells tease Stephen in the playroom? (b) What mean thing had Wells done to Stephen the day before?
3. (a) How does Stephen feel after he climbs into bed? (b) Describe the dream he has and its effect on him.
4. (a) Who is Brother Michael? (b) Who is Athy?

◆ Critical Thinking

1. What point of view is reflected in *A Portrait of the Artist?* **[Interpret]**

2. What details in the narrative imply that the main character is beginning to define his own identity? **[Interpret]**

3. Do you think Stephen's sensory impressions, fears, and anxieties are typical or unusual for a child his age? Explain your answer. **[Evaluate]**

4. In ancient Greek mythology, Daedalus was an outstanding artist who used his skills to escape from bondage. How do you think this myth relates to Stephen's story? **[Draw Conclusions]**

James Joyce
Comparing and Connecting the Author's Works

◆ Literary Focus: Internal Monologue

Internal monologue is a style of prose or verse narrative that zooms in on the unspoken thoughts of a single character. A heightened form of internal monologue occurs in **stream-of-consciousness**, when the reader is privy to the half-conscious meanderings and free-floating mental associations that run through a given character's mind, reported moment-to-moment as if there were no ordering or intervention whatever by the writer.

In *A Portrait of the Artist as a Young Man*, James Joyce employs the technique of internal monologue; with his later novel *Ulysses*, Joyce became one of the pioneers of stream-of-consciousness narration. Among other modernist practitioners of this technique were Virginia Woolf, the French novelist Marcel Proust, and the American writer William Faulkner.

1. Stephen Dedalus' interior monologues in *A Portrait of the Artist* often link internal associations and memories together with the story's plot. Analyze the paragraph on page 231 beginning, "But he was not sick there." How does Joyce use Stephen's associations and memories in this paragraph?

2. This excerpt from Joyce's novel includes three passages that report Stephen's dreams. In the first passage, Stephen imagines going home for the holidays; in the second, he imagines his own funeral; in the third, he dreams about Brother Michael and the death of Charles Stewart Parnell. Reread the description of one of these dreams, and identify the transitions that link the dream to the rest of the narrative. Then comment on the effect of this dream on the narrative as a whole.

◆ Drawing Conclusions About Joyce's Work

One way to evaluate literature is to compare and contrast two characters, settings, styles, moods—either within the same selection or as features of different selections. A comparison of "Eveline" and *A Portrait of the Artist as a Young Man* illustrates Joyce's development as a writer. In a brief essay, compare and contrast these selections with respect to one or more of the following elements: setting, characterization, imagery, tone, theme, and narrative structure. Use a graphic organizer such as the one shown below to organize your ideas.

Criteria	Eveline	Portrait of the Artist
Setting		
Characterization		
Imagery		
Tone		
Theme		
Narrative structure		

◆ Idea Bank

Writing

1. **Letter** The excerpt from *A Portrait of the Artist as a Young Man* contains a short letter that Stephen imagines writing to his mother. Write a longer letter that Stephen might have written home about one of his experiences at school. You can invent the incident

you report, but try to remain faithful to Joyce's setting and characterization.

2. **Prequel** In "Eveline," Joyce includes a number of brief flashbacks that fill in the background for Eveline's present state of mind. Using one of these flashbacks as a springboard, write a prequel or introductory episode in which you recount one of Eveline's experiences prior to the start of Joyce's narrative.

3. **Interior Monologue** Choose or invent a character with a point of view very different from your own, and imagine a specific setting for this character. Then write an interior monologue in which you present the character's moment-to-moment internal thoughts, feelings, memories, and associations. When you have finished writing, read your monologue aloud to a small group of classmates.

Speaking and Listening

4. **Oral Report** Using Internet or library resources, investigate the athletic programs of British and Irish schools in order to identify popular sports or physical activities for young people. Describe the rules for one of these sports, soccer, rugby or cricket? Sum up your findings in an oral report and present it to the class. **[Physical Education Link]**

5. **Oral Interpretation** Choose a passage from the excerpt of *A Portrait of the Artist* that features one of the following settings: the classroom, the refectory, the playroom, the study hall, the chapel, the dormitory, or the infirmary. Rehearse a reading of the passage you select, and present your reading to the class. **[Performing Arts Link]**

Researching and Representing

6. **Multimedia Report** Using travel guides, encyclopedias, atlases, song anthologies, collections of photographs, cookbooks, or other reference works, work together with a small group to develop a multimedia report on contemporary Dublin. Have the group present its report to the class, each group member taking part in the presentation. **[Social Studies Link; Group Activity]**

◆ Further Reading, Listening, and Viewing

- Richard Ellman: *James Joyce* (second edition, 1982). The standard biography

- A. Walton Litz: *James Joyce* (revised edition, 1972). A clearly written, accessible appraisal of Joyce's achievement in fiction

- James Joyce, *Dubliners.* Audiocassette series (Highbridge Audio)

- J. W. Jackson and B. McGinley, ed.: *James Joyce's Dubliners: An Illustrated Edition* (1993)

- Frank Delaney: James Joyce's *Odyssey: A Guide to the Dublin of Ulysses* (1981). A pictorial companion

- *A Portrait of the Artist as a Young Man* (1979). Film directed by Joseph Strick and starring Bosco Hogan as Stephen Dedalus

On the Web:

http://www.phschool.com/atschool/literature
Go to the student edition of *The British Tradition.* Proceed to Unit 6. Then, click Hot Links to find Web sites featuring James Joyce.

Photo Credits

Cover photos clockwise from upper left:
Emily Brontë: The Granger Collection, New York; Charlotte Brontë:
The Granger Collection, New York; John Donne: The Granger
Collection, New York; Geoffrey Chaucer: Image Select/Art Resource,
NY; William Wordsworth: The Granger Collection, New York; Edmund
Spenser: The Granger Collection, New York; James Joyce: The
Granger Collection, New York; John Keats: The Granger Collection,
New York; Jonathan Swift: The Granger Collection, New York; William
Butler Yeats: The Granger Collection, New York.

• • • •